BAD BOYS

2

MORE LEGENDS OF HOCKEY'S TOUGHEST, MEANEST, MOST-FEARED PLAYERS!

STAN FISCHLER

McGraw-Hill Ryerson
Toronto   Montreal

Bad Boys 2

First published in 1994 by
McGraw-Hill Ryerson Limited
300 Water Street
Whitby, Ontario
L1N 9B6

1 2 3 4 5 6 7 8 9 0   M P 3 2 1 0 9 8 7 6 5 4

Canadian Cataloguing in Publication Data

Fischler, Stan, 1932–
   Bad boys 2 : more legends of hockey's toughest, meanest, most-feared players

ISBN 0-07-551637-3

1. Hockey — Biography.   2. Violence in sports.
3. National Hockey League — Biography.   I. Title.

GV848.5.A1F4 1993   796.962′092′2   C93-095378-9

Editorial services provided by Word Guild, Toronto.

Cover design: Dave Hader/Studio Conceptions

Photographs by Bruce Bennett Studios, Hicksville, NY 11801 reproduced by permission.

Printed and bound in Canada

CONTENTS

ABOUT THE AUTHOR

Stan Fischler is regarded as the dean of North American hockey writers. The prize-winning author has written more than 60 books on hockey. One of them, *The Hockey Encyclopedia* which was co-authored by his wife, Shirley, is regarded as the bible of the sport. Fischler also writes a weekly column, *Inside Sports,* which has been carried for the past 20 years by the *Toronto Star* Syndicate. Among other publications which have carried his byline are *The New York Times, Sports Illustrated, Newsweek* and *The Village Voice.*

The versatile Fischler is also a prominent hockey broadcaster, having done TV analysis for 20 years. Stan has taught journalism at Columbia University, Fordham University, and Queens College.

A native of Brooklyn, Fischler lives in Manhattan with his wife and two children.

DEDICATION

To Heather Somerville, one of a kind, who was not only a good friend and an inspiration but also one of the best Public Relations people in the business.

ACKNOWLEDGMENTS

The job of a hockey enforcer is not an easy one; nor was the task of chronicling their stories. Since the subjects of this book were located throughout the continent — and in some cases not easily available — we counted on several correspondents for help — and they came through in novel fashion.

Unbound gratitude is therefore due to Joel Bergman and Scott Sandell (Los Angeles); Sandra MacPherson (Vancouver); Brian McDonough (Boston); Keith Drabik (Buffalo); Keven Friedman (Chicago); Jim Ramsey (Detroit); Dan Carle (Edmonton); Kevin Allenspach (Minnesota); Richard Middleton (Ottawa); Diane Gerace (Philadelphia); Al Goldfarb (San Jose); Randy Hu (St. Louis); Thomas Losier (Tampa Bay); Chris Lemon (Toronto); Mary McCarthy (Washington); and John Plozary and Reg Jenkins (Winnipeg).

Eric Servetah, the project's coordinator, proved an invaluable asset as an interviewer and evaluator of genuine toughness. It would not be an overstatement to say that the book would never have reached the printer without him.

Our gratitude, as usual, to the folks at McGraw-Hill Ryerson — who supported and encouraged the idea.

In addition, several others delivered vital support work in fact-checking, research and advice. I therefore thank Harris Kuhr, Michael Smyth, David Margalit, Matt Messina, James Robinson, Michael Lieberman, Lewis Hamilton and Dan Hurwitz for their considerable efforts.

INTRODUCTION

In its infinite wisdom, the National Hockey League has, over the past few years, chosen to regulate (that is, minimize) fighting as an integral aspect of the game's fabric.

Whether this sanitizing campaign is good or bad remains a moot point and no doubt will be debated as long as there are high sticks, butt ends, and elbows to the ears.

But this much is certain: no matter how energetic the crackdown, hockey by its very physical nature will always be a violent sport. It cannot be any other way when two players, each moving at 25-plus miles per hour, and wielding sticks, collide at speeds of over 50 mph on a hard, ice-slick surface.

Played with a blend of passion and intensity that exceeds any of its rival professional sports, hockey in a perfectly natural way has lent itself to intimidation. This, in turn, has inspired teams to protect their stars; hence the policeman, enforcer, ice cop or any euphemism you like. As a result every NHL club can lay claim to at least two, if not more, tough, rugged players, known in the trade as "Bad Boys."

Some, such as defenseman Ulf Samuelsson of the two-time champion Pittsburgh Penguins, have been described in such august publications as Sports Illustrated as downright dirty. Others, like Washington Capitals defenseman Al Iafrate, are less violent but no less vigorous in their pursuit of the puck.

In point of fact, there are several categories of punishing puck-chasers but they all display one comforting characteristic — to a man, the Bad Boys are Good Guys. Even after NHL commissioner Gary Bettman handed down a 21-game suspension to Washington's Dale Hunter for clobbering Pierre Turgeon from behind, Bettman casually noted that off-the-ice Hunter "seemed like a nice guy."

Likewise, a relentlessly mean hitter such as New York Rangers forward Adam Graves emerges in person as a warm, sensitive son of a Toronto cop who will go out of his way to make an interviewer comfortable.

Rick Tocchet, the two-fisted Penguins sharpshooter, may have an endless list of fights on his resume but the sinewy slugger is polite, charming and wonderfully ingenuous during a one-on-one interview.

Hard-hitting heavyweights Tony Twist and Todd Ewen have been in more than their share of fights throughout the years, but happen to be devoted family men and extremely articulate fellows.

The aim of Bad Boys 2 *is twofold. In the original volume, I detailed the growth of hockey's vigorous roots and painted word portraits of its swashbuckling sluggers of yesteryear as well as some oral histories of a few contemporary characters.*

Happily, the reaction to the original Bad Boys *was enthusiastic, especially when it came to the first-person segments dealing with the likes of Joe Kocur and Tie Domi. Readers wanted more of the contemporaries and less of the oldtimers.*

With that in mind, I decided that Bad Boys 2 *would primarily focus on today's rugged individuals, allowing them to explain in their own words how they view their often difficult roles, how they got to be where they are, and their perception (not to mention feelings) about the view critics take of them.*

Many interviews were conducted in the New York Metropolitan Area (Madison Square Garden, Nassau Coliseum and Byrne Meadowlands Arena) by reporter-research editor Eric Servetah, as well as a network of reporters in cities through the NHL. Taped in various cities across the continent, the words of hockey's hitters were transcribed to print form after which they were edited to book form while retaining the essence of their thinking. In some cases the precise question-and-answer technique was employed for the sake of variety.

I am fully aware that some critics will suggest that this work is an attempt to glorify the seamy side of hockey and paint the enforcers in a roseate hue. Far from it.

Bad Boys 2 *is neither an attempt to deify, defend nor deplore the behavior of hockey's hard guys. Rather it is one NHL historian's attempt to allow these individuals to personally detail how they see themselves, the game, and explain why they are what they are — major players on hockey's ever-exciting stage.*

Stan Fischler
New York, NY
July 1993

I

TOUGH GUYS WITH SKILL

Chapter 1

THE STRONG, SILENT TYPE: OWEN NOLAN

"The key is not whether you win or lose the fight — it's whether you have the balls to show up. That means more to me than winning or losing."

A top draft choice who appeared to be a flop in his first NHL year, Owen Nolan has burst to the top of the NHL charts in no time at all.

The formidable 6-foot-1, 200-pound Quebec Nordique right wing is a marvel with or without the puck. Nolan, who hails from Belfast, Ireland, is a hard-hitting player with an assortment of skills.

Interestingly, Nolan likes to compare himself to Cam Neely and Rick Tocchet, both skilled thumpers. In Neely's first three campaigns — played at the same age as Nolan's first three — Cam finished with 31, 39 and 34 points respectively and 57, 137 and 126 penalty minutes. Owen had only 13 points in his rookie season but tallied 73 and 77 points in the next two, along with 109, 183 and 185 penalty minutes. Not until Neely's sixth season did he put up big numbers.

Tocchet, who began his NHL career at the age of 20 — not 18 as Neely and Nolan did — didn't hit the 70-point level until his fifth season. He had more penalty minutes than Nolan, but Rick's skill level wasn't there at the start.

One can only conclude that Nolan is en route to superstardom. At the start of the 1993-94 campaign, Nolan was only 21 — several years away from his prime.

*On the ice Nolan possesses speed, tenacity, meanness
and a cannon shot. He can be a goalie's worst nightmare
and the bane of a sleeping defenseman.*

*It had been mentioned that Owen's "moodiness" would
make for a difficult interview. However, he quickly
dispelled those reports with a free-wheeling, pleasant
look into his hockey career. While recuperating from an
injury, Nolan made himself available to Eric Servetah
between periods of a game with the New Jersey Devils at
the Meadowlands Arena in New Jersey. Among other
subjects, Nolan discussed early hockey life, his role with
the Nordiques and his love for physical play.*

I started playing hockey when I was nine. Until that point I never
really paid much attention to the game. Instead I played a lot of
soccer and baseball. One day I saw a couple of my friends out on
the pond skating, so I bought a pair of skates and off I went to the
ice. It was a little rough at first, but I picked the game up pretty
quickly.

I grew up in a small town, just outside of Belfast in Northern
Ireland. I have two younger brothers, Gavin and Murray, who are
into hockey and football respectively. But I don't think Gavin is
going to become an NHLer because he's out there to have fun and
that's the main thing for him. I was probably the typical older
brother with the two of them. I would rough them up a bit and I
think I was good for their growing-up process. They got to learn at
a young age that no one should push them around.

My toughness came from going to school and having to deal with
my classmates. I had a lot of fights when I was in school, so I guess
that's where I got my toughness. The fights I had were regular street
fights, and at that age you could see that I was pretty good at
handling myself.

My dad, Owen, grew up in Ireland and played a lot of soccer. That
was the big sport over there and he didn't really know much about
hockey until he came overseas. So I wasn't given much advice on
how to play the game, but he and my mom, Ellen, were both very
supportive of me.

My mom wasn't too nervous about me playing the game until I
started in Junior hockey. When you are younger, fighting is forbid-
den in the leagues and we wore full face masks. In Juniors I would
get stitches here and there, and that's when my mom started to
worry.

When I was growing up, we won a couple of championships with
my pee wee and bantam teams. From bantam I went to Junior A at
Cornwall as a 15-year-old and I was fortunate to play on an excellent

team. We gave Peterborough a good run for the Memorial Cup, but they ended up beating us.

I played with a lot of good players, like Rick Tabaracci and Mathieu Schneider. They really helped tip me off as to who were the best fighters and goal scorers on the other teams.

Orval Tessier was my coach at Cornwall and the first coach to help me out. In a sense, he was like all Junior coaches, testing you to see how much you're going to put out on the ice to determine the depth of your real talents. I was about 6 feet and 187 pounds at that time, and I had most of the skills then that I have now. But I definitely developed them more by playing in the NHL with higher-caliber players. Plus I've grown an inch and added 13 pounds since then and that helped a lot.

In Junior, I played an aggressive game. I was a good skater, had a good shot and hit a lot. Those were my strong points back then, as they are now in the NHL. I do remember back then that I liked the hitting more than I did the scoring. I liked the rough style of play and I admired anybody who fought.

My first Junior hockey fights took place in a couple of exhibition games. I had been watching all of the big heavyweights on our team fight and I wanted to do it, too. Those guys were 19 or 20 years old and I was only 15, so I was a little iffy about it. But I said, "Why not? Let's go."

Naturally, I wound up getting into a couple of fights. My teammates showed me what to do and I held my own against a lot of the older players. I watched, listened and learned a lot of different techniques that eventually helped me out.

Back then, my style of fighting was to grab on to the center of the shirt and start throwing away as fast and as hard as I could. It's a lot different in the NHL, because if you're not grabbing on to the guy's strong arm, he could hurt you. I think in Junior, winning was a lot more a function of how hard you could throw a punch and how quick you could get them away. In the NHL, there's a lot more technique involved in a fight.

Not that I was fighting all the time in Juniors. In my first year, I had 34 goals and 213 penalty minutes. I also received Rookie of the Year honors, so I couldn't complain at all.

By far the toughest guy that I fought back then was huge Shawn Antoski. He was probably 19 at the time and I was 15 or 16 when I went up against him. Everyone told me to keep away from him, but I got my nose dirty and went right in to fight him. Generally, when people tell me not to do something, I like to try to prove them wrong and prove that I can do it. In the case of fighting Antoski, I was not favored to win anyway. So if I won, it was a bonus for myself.

Going into my second season, I knew that it was my draft year and people started to take notice of me. Mike Ricci was the guy who was supposed to go first overall, but some people started putting my name in the same category as Mike's. I scored 51 goals that year and took 240 penalty minutes. Quebec drafted me, because they liked my all-around stats and the way I played.

When I was younger I always said I was going to play in the NHL, but I never took it seriously until after my first year of Junior. After that year I thought to myself, hey, maybe I've got a chance. But as far as being drafted first overall, that certainly was not my expectation.

I realized during my second year of Juniors that it was tough to know when and how to separate my skill game from playing it tough. If the team was winning by a lot, and I was looking to go after someone, the time was good. But if the team was losing, I had to pick my spots and then try and get the team a little motivated from a fight or a hard hit. If the score was tied, I couldn't go out and play my hard game. I realized that sometimes I had to bite the bullet rather than fight somebody.

I really enjoyed fighting and having the odd tussle, so it wasn't a problem to have to do it. In my second year of Juniors I fought mostly every tough guy in the league once. Antoski was the only player I fought a couple of times. He stands out in my mind more than anybody else that I've fought because he was so big. I remember once he hit me and his hand almost covered my face, but I hung in there.

Fighting in the NHL is a lot different than in Juniors because the players are smarter. Guys know how to pick their spots — like fighting you at the end of your shift. In Junior, guys would be half-tired and never think about these things. I would be angry and want to fight and I didn't think twice about a strategy. But now it requires a lot of technique and smart stuff up here. The guys who do the fighting are smart and good at what they do.

My first year in the NHL was really frustrating because I didn't get a lot of ice time, whereas in Junior hockey I was one of the better players on the team and got plenty of ice. Then I came to Quebec and I didn't get much at all. It also didn't help that the Nordiques weren't a good team at the time. I finished my rookie NHL season with only three goals and 10 assists, and it seemed like every time I was on the ice, I missed an opportunity to score. After a while I had all of this anger built up inside me, which helps explain why I fought a lot more my first year. I figured I wasn't scoring, so I might as well get some penalty minutes while I was at it. All of that first-year experience helped me out in my second NHL season, because I got a lot more room on the ice and things started to turn around. I put in 42 goals, but still received around the same amount of penalty minutes.

I had no complaints playing for Quebec and I was proud going first overall in the draft rather than saying, "No, I'm not going to go."

A lot of kids don't even get drafted, so I was just happy with the fact that I was selected. I was treated well by the Nordiques although it was rough in my first year. We had a lot of young guys on the team and there were no veterans to help show me the ropes.

My first NHL fight was with Terry Carkner of the Philadelphia Flyers. He's a pretty big boy and I give him the edge in the fight but I held my own and stuck in there. During my first year I wanted to establish myself physically. I don't consider myself a heavyweight, but I will always show up.

The key is not whether you win or lose the fight — it's whether you have the balls to show up. That means more to me than winning or losing.

Some of my other first-year opponents were Garth Butcher, Doug Houda and Alan Stewart. I don't think I lost one fight among them. I was always in there on my feet exchanging punches. I won a few but I never clear-out lost one. I would say that most of my fights that year were draws.

When I'm getting into a fight it's more adrenalin than anything that keeps me from losing. I can take a good punch, which is another key to being a fighter. Having a glass jaw isn't going to help when you take on the big boys. You have to be able to take a punch and shake the cobwebs quick and get back in there.

Even in Juniors, I always held my own and never took a beating. The only player who ever cut me was Dean Kennedy, when he was playing for Buffalo. That was in my first year. I threw a punch but I didn't grab his strong arm and he came over the top with a right hand and cut me just over the eye. That's the only cut I've taken in a fight.

When Dave Chambers was coaching the Nordiques he never paid much attention to me. Dave was just trying to develop the team, and no progress was being made. When Pierre Pagé came in, things changed. Pagé liked my style of play and gave me a lot more ice time. He put me on a line with Joe Sakic and that helped my career. Joey set me up on a lot of goals and once I got them under my belt, I started to feel more comfortable on the ice. Being able to relax is a big key. When you want to score goals, you've got to be relaxed on the ice and not put added pressure on yourself when things start rolling.

I came into my second NHL season with more muscle and with an attitude that I couldn't do any worse than my first year. Everything was behind me and the chips were on the table, so I went on the ice relaxed and did what I could do. I started playing some of my top hockey and it helped that I was a lot stronger. I also was quicker with my reaction time, but the most important improvement was the things I picked up. I would watch other guys and ask them what to do in certain situations. It's good to have guys who you can talk to and will help you out.

The guy who helped me the most in Quebec is Joe Sakic, but it wasn't really from talking to him. The help came from watching Joe's style of play and what he does when he doesn't have the puck. I also studied Cam Neely, whose size and style is similar to mine. I studied what he does when he doesn't have the puck and what he does to get himself into the game. Cam gets himself into the game with a big hit or a fight, which is what gets me into games too.

Another guy who has that same style is Rick Tocchet. He also hits a lot and gets into the game physically. I'm capable of scoring 100 points and getting over 200 penalty minutes, like Rick has done. That's certainly within my talents, especially since I'm young and have already accomplished some things.

Intimidation had been a big factor in my game, but I don't think it's as effective anymore with the new rules. The fact is, if some opponents know that I fight and if they don't fight, they might not want to aggravate me. That's a good reason why I get more room, and I think that kind of intimidation helps. Fighting is important to me. It's something that I will continue to do. I enjoy it. I want to be known for being able to fight, although I don't think I will ever be a big heavyweight in the league. I just want to be known as someone who's going to show up, win or lose.

I could fight the big heavyweights, but I wouldn't be favored to win. I've done all right against some of the tougher guys in the league and I did well in a fight I had with Todd Ewen in the 1992-93 season. Fighting Todd is just part of the role that I have on this team. In this instance, Ewen went after my teammate Mats Sundin and I happened to be the only guy on the ice who fights. I took it upon myself to go after Ewen because that's part of my job — to protect the goal scorers. I just went in. I kept away from his right hand because I knew that he throws the right. I kept low and kept pulling over and held my own.

When I fight, I like to know what the other guy's strong points are. If he's right-handed, I don't want to be going in grabbing his left hand. It's better to have him throwing left hands than throwing his good hand. I like to know whether the guy's shirt is going to pull off when I grab him or whether he ties down or not. I try to know when I grab his arm if his sleeve is going to rip wide open. Fighting involves a lot of technique up here. It takes a lot of knowledge that you pick up just by watching different fights. The more you know, the more it's going to benefit you.

Before every game I tie down the jersey. I also cut my sleeve a bit and try and slide my elbow out through the bottom of my jersey. My right hand comes out and I come over the top with my punches and try to connect. If the guy slaps it down, I try a couple of uppercuts. If we're tied up and no one's letting go, then I switch to my left just to get it loosened up again and then I switch back to my right. I'd rather not trade off my left hand against someone's right hand, but if it has to be done, it has to be done. I can't see myself going toe-to-toe with someone throwing left-handed. I throw the left hand just enough to get the person thinking about the left and then I switch to the right.

A lot of my fighting style also depends on my opponent. If it's someone who I think I can beat — or should beat — then I do different things. If I'm fighting someone like a Terry Carkner, I have to read off him a bit more and watch what he's going to do. I might wait until he throws a punch and then return one myself.

What's really scary is when a guy takes his jersey off or it comes off during the fight. If a guy's coming at me half naked, there's not much I'm going to do. I can't grab his bare skin, so I have to wait until the referee comes in to break it up. When a guy like Bob Probert has his jersey off, it's time for me to start skating back to the bench.

In the off-season, I hit the weights a bit and work out on the speed bag and heavy bag. I've been lucky so far in my fights and in training, not having had too many problems with my hands. The hands seem to heal pretty quickly, but you have to remember that I'm no heavyweight in this league. I like to fight, but I think I'm starting to concentrate more on scoring goals now.

Surprisingly, I have some soft hands around the net. I'd have to say that my hands are the biggest asset I have right now in terms of my goal scoring. I have a hard shot and it's pretty accurate every time that I use it.

We've got a lot of scorers on the Nordiques, and my role is to watch out for the guys as well as do some scoring. I don't mind scoring, but it's good to have that kind of balance. I'd rather be known as a goal scorer and a fighter, than just a goal scorer or just a fighter. It's good for my character to have that status. That's why if I see something happpen that I think is a mismatch, I'll try and intervene. But I think teammates like Tony Twist should handle that stuff most of the time.

I've seen the Twister fight a few times now. He's the real man to jump in if things get a little out of hand. The thing that really impresses me about Tony is that he's a super guy off the ice. I would certainly not want to be on the receiving end of one of his bombs. That's exactly what they are — bombs. He doesn't throw any jabs and quick little punches. When he fights, it's back and forth and back and forth bombs. The other guy could have thrown four punches and he would throw just one, and if he connects, the other guy is going to get hurt.

I saw Tony fight a guy in training camp. They squared off and let them fly. By the end of the fight, we all gave the decision to the Twister. I wasn't dressed for the game and I happened to be sitting behind Detroit's bench. So I took a look at the other guy and his helmet had this huge dent in it from when Tony hit him. It was unbelievable, because he wore one of those hard CCM helmets. It's not the same as punching one of those soft little JOFA helmets. He literally dented and cracked the helmet. From that point on, I said that had to be one of the hardest punches I've seen in my life.

Another thing about Tony is that he loves to fight fair. I think if you're going to fight, then you should square off and start it that way. I do sometimes believe that you do have to get the advantage on some of the tougher guys in the league. If one of the heavyweights is running Joe Sakic, I'm surely not going to go up and ask him to square off with me in that instance. I'm going to jump him and try to get the advantage on him right away. I think it's a dirty way to fight. It happens, but I can't say I'm for that. It's more of a cheap shot if I fight that way, and I do prefer squaring off, but sometimes for a guy like me it's necessary.

I would fight anybody in the league if it came down to it. I think for me, whether the fight is right or wrong or I do good or not, it's the fact of showing up. If you show up, you get more respect from players than the guys who shy away from that stuff. Bob Probert is one of the toughest guys in the league and I would fight him if I had to, but I don't have to go out and fight heavyweights every night.

Joey Kocur is another heavyweight, but his hands are too messed up to be fighting all of the time. It's unfortunate and not something you like to see, but it's a definite disadvantage for himself. Louie DeBrusk is another tough kid who I played against in Junior. He was a big boy then and he's big now. Louie is a guy who uses a lot of technique in his fighting. Dave Brown is another one of the premier tough guys in the league, along with Probert. I never see too many guys want to fight Brownie.

There's been a lot of talk of myself having a dislike for Eric Lindros for what he did by not signing with Quebec. We had a little bit of a rivalry when we were in Junior, but that was the extent of it. When I played against him in Junior he was probably the best player I went against. I was also one of the better players in the league, and I guess the thing between us is more rivalry than anything. We would butt heads a couple of times but nothing really happened out of it. It's not a big deal on our team that he didn't sign with us. He was looking out for his own benefit and we didn't have any say in it and didn't care what he did.

Whether the league likes it or not, a good percentage of the fans likes the fighting. What are you going to do if something happens on the ice and there's no fighting? Guys are going to start spearing each other, and I think there's going to be a lot more injuries due to spearing than from fighting. I've never heard of a real serious injury through a fight. There are many more injuries due to high sticks and stuff like that, rather than from fighting.

I hope I can finish my career playing with the same consistency I developed after my first two seasons. I'm sure that sooner or later it will probably catch up with me and I won't be able to fight as much or score as much. But there's nothing that I can do about that now, and hopefully things will keep on going well.

I've set some goals for myself and one of them is getting over a 100 points in a few seasons. But one goal that not a lot of guys look to achieve is to get over 300 penalty minutes with those hundred points. That's something that I want real bad. When I'm playing a game, I like to get my penalty minutes up. It makes me a better player if I've got both categories going as well.

Chapter 2

THE HONEST HITTER: ADAM GRAVES

"I like to be familiar with a guy when I fight him, so I can adjust to players' styles. But the bottom line is that it doesn't matter how much I prepare, because you're always going to take a shot or lose a fight."

If Adam Graves is sometimes referred to as the Rangers' policeman, it could very well be that observers realize that he is a chip off the old block.

His father, Bob Graves, retired in March 1992 as a Detective Sergeant after 26 years with the Metropolitan Toronto Police Department. Thanks to Bob, Adam was able to persevere through the minor hockey system to become one of the most respected forwards in the NHL — and one of the toughest.

"It isn't shooting, skating and passing that makes you a winner," Bob Graves told Earl McRae of the Ottawa Sun, *"because a lot of guys can do those things. It's picking yourself up off the ice and showing heart and guts. That's Adam.*

"He gets it from me. He saw it in me. At family barbecues, playing touch football, I get out with the young guys and think I can do it all. I hate to lose. I don't give in anything to age."

Adam gives in to nothing, as anyone who has watched him perform first for Detroit, then Edmonton and, most recently, the Rangers, will attest. At times his checking is above and beyond the call of duty, as evidenced by the controversy surrounding him during the 1992 playoffs when his wood chop broke Mario Lemieux's hand during the Rangers-Penguins series.

The Rangers' camp argued that the whack was unintentional, but the damage was done and Graves paid the price in notoriety. Nevertheless, he returned for the 1992-93 season and played such a strong campaign that there were some who suggested that Adam — and not his hero, Mark Messier — deserved to be the Rangers' captain. In fact, Graves was named captain of Team Canada for the 1993 World Championships.

"I don't have any goals," says Adam, "except to play 100 percent every time. That's what my dad taught me. Play the present, not the end part. If you play 100 percent all the time, the rewards will come."

Graves discussed his life and theories on hockey after a Rangers' practice at their scrimmage rink in suburban Rye, New York. In his commentary with reporter Eric Servetah, Adam stressed that he preferred not to discuss fights, but rather that he wanted to talk about the game of hockey as a whole.

I started playing when I was four years old. My dad was a referee at kids' hockey games, and when one of the teams was short on players, my dad volunteered to let me skate with the six-, seven- and eight-year-olds. I was a roly-poly type of kid who could hardly skate.

My dad had played organized hockey through the Junior B level and then coached police teams. He helped me the most over the years. I can remember coming home from school and dad would be standing in the driveway with a baseball glove on and he'd encourage me, "Hey, take a wrist shot!" Hockey was the sport of the family and we were always having fun; all my buddies and my dad would be out there.

Sometimes I would play street hockey and, when I had a newspaper route for seven years, I had to get up at six in the morning, so I would strap on roller skates to make it a little quicker to get the route done. I'd put the newspaper bag over my shoulder and it would take me only 15 minutes on the roller skates rather than a half-hour on foot. Then I'd get back into bed and sleep for an extra hour before school.

I have two older sisters and three younger brothers. Plus, I have two foster brothers, so we have a full house to say the least. Surprisingly, there was no fighting in our family. We were very united as a group. When I played soccer, for example, they would come and watch my game and when we went on hockey tournaments, the whole family went. Everything we did, we did as a family.

After my sister got her driver's license, she began driving me to all the hockey practices.

My early life revolved around sports. I played a lot of soccer, a game that was good conditioning for hockey. All my hockey buddies played together on the soccer team and they were all my best friends, so I was hanging out with my friends and playing sports that I enjoyed. What made it easier for me was that the soccer field was just off from my house. After soccer practice, the whole team would come back and then we'd play ball hockey on the street for a couple of hours in the afternoon, then eat and everyone would go home because we had school the next day.

I have never been a tough kid. The only place where I'm really aggressive is on the ice. Away from the ice I'm not aggressive at all. I believe that you can solve a lot of problems without fighting — that's for sure. It takes a bigger man to walk away than it does to do something stupid or whatever. I don't think being aggressive away from the rink makes you a better person.

Sure, there are times when you have to stand by what you believe in, but most times you can do it without physical presence. The only way I'd get angry or upset off the ice is if someone did something wrong by my family or hurt my friends, and usually we try to avoid that.

I can remember getting into arguments and some instances where I'd get into the odd scuffle. I learned that you win some, you lose some and no matter how big you are, or how tough, you always take your lumps. There's always someone bigger and stronger.

I remember once, when I was a kid, my sister came home crying because an older guy had picked on her. My dad said that I had two choices. He said, "Tomorrow, when you get off that bus, you can fight him or you can come home and fight me." I was still small then so I figured the better of the two was to fight the guy from school. The next day we got right off the bus and started scrapping. I took a little bit of a shellacking but my sister was in there helping me. I got bruised but we stuck together and I knew I had done the right thing. That's what living is about: having people you care about taking care of each other.

By the time I was eight years old I was playing competitive hockey. Wherever I played, I was always aggressive although I wasn't very big for my age at all. I tried to work out to stay strong but I always tried to play clean, using the shoulder.

My thirst for hockey was unquenchable. There was a hockey school run by a retired referee that I went to for four years. I couldn't wait to go to that school. At the school I was a gopher. I'd tie up the kids' skates all day and get two hours of ice at night for eight weeks in the summer. I wanted a job there just so I could tie skates and get the two hours of nice ice free. I was fortunate to get the opportunity to get on the ice every night.

Besides that, my dad spent hours and hours with me but without pushing me. If I didn't want to do hockey at any given time, he'd say, "Fine," and that would be that.

My idol at the time was Darryl Sittler of the Maple Leafs. I remember standing in line at a mall for two and a half hours waiting for his autograph. I would have waited five hours, 10 hours.

When I was a kid I was told it would be impossible to play in the NHL, but I had a goal. Meanwhile, my dad was insisting that I worry about school. He wanted me to do well there and said that everything would take care of itself. And I did well in school — got Bs and As. I finished Grade 13 in Ontario and started university when I was in Juniors.

I got drafted by the Windsor Spitfires on the Junior B level and then made my way up to the big team in the Ontario Hockey League in 1985-86. Tom Webster, our coach, helped me out a lot. He's an excellent coach. I've been fortunate that through the years I've been surrounded by a lot of great hockey people.

Before I got to Windsor, I wasn't sure what to expect from Junior hockey. I remember that my goal was to score and play an all-around game, penalty killing and stuff like that. I worked hard in the previous summer, lifting weights and training hard to get ready.

My first fight was at age 15. It was one of those hold-on-and-do-the-best-you-can type of things. I had two more fights with the last one coming toward the end of the season. We both fell and I dislocated my shoulder in the process.

When it came to fighting, my philosophy was that I had nothing to lose. For every guy you beat, you get beaten yourself. I had my nose broken six times; I've had chipped teeth and stitches. I've seen stars and everything else, but my feeling is as long as you play hard, you won't allow yourself to be intimidated. That way you can never go wrong.

There are different kinds of fighters but the scariest has to be Joe Kocur. You've got to be crazy to fight the guy because he can hurt you. No one wants to fight him.

Some guys go into a fight and it's all or nothing at all. Some guys get mad and just go crazy; they can't remember when they fight. Myself, I try to stay calm and think about what I'm doing. I try to be smart. The worst part is that you might crack a bone in your face, get a broken nose, your teeth knocked out or stitches. For the most part, though, you don't get hurt too much in a hockey fight. If I can stay in strong enough shape, I may not be able to control the other guy in a fight, but I'll be able to defend myself. I'm not going to hurt too many people; that's not what it's about. You show up and do the best you can.

In Junior I couldn't just tough it because I'd get killed. I had to do a little bit of everything. Being aggressive is part of the game and it's something that I had to work at a lot. I worked at my conditioning, staying in good shape and staying strong. On the ice I worked on my shot, my stickhandling and my skating.

My last year with Windsor was the 1986-87 season. I played in 66 games, got 45 goals and 55 assists and 70 penalty minutes. I was getting confident and felt better about my game. My hitting came naturally but I had to work harder at shooting the puck and making the right play.

Tommy Webster wanted me to play much the way I play now: be a team player and go to the net; chip in some goals, play aggressive and be a persistent forechecker. The most important thing to me is the respect of my team. You have to play for your teammates whether it means taking a hit for the team, giving a hit, sticking together when you have to, throwing a check, blocking a shot or scoring a goal.

I don't think I've ever jumped a guy. When someone has hit my teammate the wrong way, I've jumped in to fight. I'd come in, grab onto him and then he'd drop his gloves and we'd fight. But I don't think I've ever come in from out of the blue.

When I got to the NHL with Detroit in 1987-88, I wanted to make it so badly that I felt that I had to do whatever it took to stay, even if it meant getting beat up. I didn't care. I took my lumps, that's for sure. I wanted the coach to know I was on the ice. I wanted to make sure he knew I was on the ice whether it was trying to stir up trouble or whatever. I just wanted to get attention and maybe get a second shift so I could use my skills. I was willing to do what it took to play more and more.

I remember in my first camp that I weighed only 180 pounds and management said they wanted me to be a little stronger for the next training camp. So I worked really hard at the weights over the off-season and I came back into camp at 210 pounds. I was really strong and I guess a little less mobile. I don't think it helped my game, but they realized that I wanted to play and do whatever I could.

I played nine games in that rookie year with my first game in Edmonton. I remember being intimidated by my first shift. I was with Shawn Burr and we were supposed to be checking the Gretzky line with Jari Kurri. To me, Kurri was fascinating. I didn't want him to blow by me so I waited at the blue line. I picked him up — really just walked into him — and held onto him the best I could. I was intimidated in the sense that I didn't want to get scored on. Another star I kept my eyes on was Stevie Yzerman. I liked to watch the better players to see how they approached the game and made the big play. They gave 110 percent no matter what. Whether they were having a good game or not, they always showed the effort. Nine times out of 10 you're going to play well if the effort is there.

My second year in Detroit was 1988-89 when I played 56 games and spent the other 14 with Adirondack in the American League. I came back to the Red Wings for the playoffs, was in five games and then I went back down to Adirondack. We played Hershey in the semis and then New Haven in the finals and we won.

When I came to the Red Wings' camp the following September, I was a little more confident, but I knew I couldn't relax. I had to keep going, going, going. I made the big club and played 13 games and then I was traded to Edmonton along with Petr Klima, Joe Murphy and Jeff Sharples in exchange for Jimmy Carson, Kevin McClelland and a 1991 fifth-round draft choice.

I started fighting the most after I got traded to Edmonton. There was one fight with Joel Otto, a really strong guy. Well, I survived but I don't really like to talk about it too much. I think I've improved at fighting, but I don't know if I'm good at it. I just go out and play aggressive and I'm not afraid to do it because it's one of those things that you go out and do what you can do. I don't sit back and think about fighting.

When I'm fighting, I'm aware of what the other guy tries to do in a fight. I like to be familiar with a guy when I fight him, so I can adjust to players' different styles. But the bottom line is that it doesn't matter how much I prepare, because you're always going to take a shot or lose a fight.

It's like the fight I had with Rob Ray in Buffalo, when he was out there running a bunch of our guys. Ray is a tough guy, a hard-working guy and he's done a great job to get where he's at. He works hard for his ice time and people should respect him for that.

This incident was one of those things where I was on the ice with Mark Messier and Ray was running him and a few other guys. I have a role to play other than scoring when I'm on the ice and that's to look after the guys. You need everyone to do his part on a team and fighting is one of my parts.

We couldn't have Messier being run, because we don't need him injured and I kind of started the fight with Ray. Boys will be boys and no one really gets hurt too badly from a fight. I'm sure if I ran Pat LaFontaine, he'd try to do the same thing to me. I wound up doing well in this fight, but it could have been the other way around.

I was very lucky with Edmonton. I played more with the Oilers than with the Red Wings and we went on to win the Stanley Cup in 1990. I have a lot of respect for the teammates I played with on that club. We had a lot of skilled players and I was a young guy who had to pay his dues. As the year went on, I learned a bit more and got more opportunities to play. If a team does well — as those Oilers did — every individual does well and everyone seems to prosper because of it. And I don't mean that in a financial way — I mean that in a championship way.

In the last 15 or so weeks of that season I played on a line with Joe Murphy and Martin Gelinas, which proved to be a great opportunity for me. Both were great guys and we had a lot of enthusiasm. We had no pressure to score or anything else. We were just out there after a penalty kill or after a powerplay or any lull or after we scored a goal, just to maybe change the momentum and put it in our direction. All we did was get the puck deep, play aggressive and work together. Murph is a very skilled hockey player and Martin was really strong on the puck in the corners. I tried to read off them and play aggressive when I could.

I enjoyed my two seasons in Edmonton but I wasn't happy about what I saw happening with what had been a good team; I mean they were dismantling it, whether it was because of salaries or whatever. When the Oilers decided not to sign me to a new deal I wasn't upset because there was the offer from New York. I had become a Group One free agent and was signed by the Rangers in September 1991. With the Oilers, the most points I got was 25 [7-18] in the 1990-91 season. During my first year in New York I more than doubled the total [26-33-59]. The reason was that I had the opportunity to play on a line with Mark Messier and Tony Amonte with Brian Leetch at the blue line. In that sense I was really fortunate. I was given a lot of empty nets to shoot at and I got chances and the puck started to go in for me. I felt better about handling the puck and, to my mind, 90 percent of the game is mental and the other 10 percent is physical. I attributed a lot of my improvement to having Mark alongside me because he's helped so much.

I've been asked how I define my role between toughness and goal scoring; when to do stuff and when not to. It's hard to answer because hockey is an emotional game and I play with enthusiasm. I can't go out and say, "Well, on this shift, I'm going to do this and on that shift I'm going to do that." I just go out and play as hard as I can and do what I can and play on instinct. It's too quick a game just to be sitting back. It's not like football where you make up plays and then you go and execute them, then come back and talk about the execution.

One thing I learned is that we all make mistakes. I know I make a mistake every time I step on the ice, whether it be losing a draw or not picking up my man or making a bad pass or missing the net on a shot. I mention that because it reminds me of an incident during the 1992-93 season when Basil McRae was giving Mark Messier some grief and I stepped in very early in the game and got thrown out of it by referee Denis Morel. It was just one of those things where I didn't necessarily agree with the call, but then again Morel is a good referee and, as I said, I know that I make mistakes. These things are going to happen in a hockey game. McRae is a good hockey player and a great team guy. He's a tough guy who will fight anyone.

I didn't hold a grudge against him because I knew that he was doing his job and that's the way it is. Obviously, I wasn't happy getting thrown out because I love playing and I didn't relish going to bed early. I was all psyched up and then, 17 seconds in, I got kicked out. I felt I didn't deserve to get the heave-ho but, hey, that's the way it goes.

Mark told me that I have to be smart about stuff like that, which I understand. On the other hand, my feeling was that we didn't need to have Mark injured. For us to be successful, we need him healthy. If the other team is going to take runs at him, trying to take advantage of him, or players like Brian Leetch, and they hurt them, then we're going to be in a little bit of trouble. That's why I jumped in.

I have been watching how the league is moving on the fighting issue over the past couple of years and my feeling is that I don't think fighting should be taken out of the game. If the NHL did that, there would be no return for guys taking advantage of the better players, and all the better players, unfortunately, would start getting hurt on a more consistent basis. It would take away from the skill level of the game.

I've yet to see anyone get seriously hurt through fighting and, for the most part, every guy in the league is pretty much fair in the way he fights. I don't know of any player, off-hand, who jumps other guys. Everyone seems to square off and when it happens like that, I don't think it hurts anyone and it's a good release for all of them. I'm not saying there should be 10 fights a game, or anything like that, but if you've got to fight, it doesn't hurt.

Fighting is part of the game and you're going to have people who like it and others who don't. It's like you're going to have voters who like Bill Clinton and people who don't. You have people who like watching television and others who don't. Whatever subject you pick, you'll have pros and cons. It's funny, but while there's so much talk about rough hockey, I see brawls in baseball all the time but I don't see brawls like that in hockey anymore. Hockey got branded with that fighting image years ago.

But every so often there is a big hockey fight that gets quite a play in the media. During the 1992-93 season we had the Tie Domi-Bob Probert confrontation. It so happens that I know both guys real well. Tie is a really good friend of mine and I know Probert from Windsor where I have a place in the summer. I played with Bob in Detroit and he's a super-nice guy just like Tie. And I'm sure that if they met off the ice they'd be good buddies as well, but on the ice they play hard and they had one heck of a battle. I don't think anyone left his seat in the whole building. What's more, I don't think either of them got hurt so I found nothing wrong with it. I mean boys will be boys, and while you don't like to see premeditated fights, by the same token, no one got hurt and that was good.

Chapter 3

INTENSE TO THE NTH DEGREE: CHRIS CHELIOS

"My belief is that when it comes to fighting, anybody can beat anybody else on any given night."

It hardly surprised anyone that Chris Chelios was a popular choice as 1992-93 Norris Trophy winner. At age 31, the former U.S. Olympian was at the very top of his game. One of the hardest-hitting of the modern defensemen, Chelios also had carved out a reputation as one of the most ornery — and talented — backliners since Eddie Shore.

What makes Chelios such an intriguing character is the manner in which he has so expertly blended his skill game with his harsh behavior on the ice. Winnipeg Sun reporter Brian Smiley said it for many others when he noted in January 1993 that Chelios rates "as public enemy No. 1 in Winnipeg, a dishonorable distinction brought on by a temper tantrum Chelios threw in the Winnipeg Arena, a tantrum which rated a 10 on the temper meter."

According to witnesses, Chelios charged that a) Winnipeg didn't deserve an NHL franchise; b) the Jets would fold in the playoffs; and c) Teemu Selanne was a coward for not fighting. Chelios, for the record, later issued a denial.

Right or wrong, this was not the first time Chelios was at the center of an NHL firestorm. During the

1989 Canadiens-Flyers playoff, Chris detonated an international controversy when he heavily checked Philadelphia's Brian Propp into the boards, knocking the forward unconscious.

Opponents claim that it was a vicious check, finished off by an elbow to the head. Teammates — and Chelios, of course — suggested that it merely was a typically robust hit that should not even have been penalized.

In point of fact, Chelios has been hitting that way ever since he laced on a pair of skates, the difference being that his intensity has found its logical terminal on NHL rinks and no team would ever turn down an opportunity to acquire the Greek-American.

"Chris is one of the most competitive players I've ever coached," says Lou Vairo, who directed the 1984 U.S. Olympic squad on which Chelios, Al Iafrate and Pat LaFontaine played. "He'll do whatever he can to win hockey games."

Chelios was a member of the 1986 Canadiens Stanley Cup champions and appeared destined for a long career in Montreal until the Habs mistakenly traded him to Chicago for Denis Savard because it was politically correct to have another French-Canadian on the squad.

As a Blackhawk, Chelios surfaced as the team leader and the man most responsible for Chicago's high estate in past seasons. His disdain for the opposition is constant and almost legendary.

"Chris cares about his family and his team," Blackhawks' ace Jeremy Roenick once said. "After that, he just doesn't give a damn."

Questioned about the subject during a TV interview, Chelios would not deny that his teammate had sized him up as well as anyone. For further insights into the charismatic defenseman, Chicago reporter Keven Friedman sat down with Chris at Chicago Stadium.

I have one brother and three sisters. When they were younger, my sisters were into track and swimming. My brother, who plays hockey in the minors, is pretty much the same as me. My father, who is in the restaurant-bar business, played soccer on the Greek National Team, so I figure that that helped get us involved in sports.

When my mom and dad got me started with hockey in Chicago, the Blackhawks were the hottest club in Chicago and every kid wanted to play hockey because Stan Mikita and Bobby Hull were on the team.

After my first couple of years on skates, I began to play pretty well and I wound up on the best team every year. Eventually I made it to a traveling squad, and that put quite a burden on my parents.

They put in a lot of hours, took off from work a lot to drive me out-of-town. My sisters suffered the most because my parents were always spending time with me. My mom says I was not a peaceful kid.

I compare myself to one of my own sons. He's just wild and you have to watch him all the time. He's fearless and has no conception of danger. He'll climb on anything. One day he cracked my other son in the face with a book. I have two kids, Dean and Jake. Dean is the one who thinks before he does something. Jake is really sharp for his age [two years of age at time of interview] and he's not afraid of anything. If he thinks he's going to get hit, he's going to hit first whereas Dean, if he gets hit, is probably going to whine about it first and then do something.

Besides hockey, I played a lot of baseball when I was young. It was one or the other; if I wasn't playing baseball, I was playing hockey and vice versa. During my high school years I had a job in a supermarket — probably 30 hours a week — just to have spending money. It ended up being a really good job.

After we moved to San Diego, I happened to be on the beach one day and I met a kid who was interested in hockey. He had been playing for the university in San Diego and we got to talking and he gave me the phone number of a Junior coach in Moose Jaw, Saskatchewan. I called him and wound up getting a ticket there for a tryout.

Playing Junior hockey in some ways was just like playing pro. I still wasn't very big, physically, so I relied on my quickness and adjusted to the physical part. As I got bigger, I played more aggressively and there were fights all the time. I had maybe 70 fights in two years. I was the only American in the league that first year, so that had a lot to do with it.

I felt lucky just to get a tryout and I did anything I could just to stay on the team. Up until then, I had been a forward but as soon as I got to Moose Jaw, I realized that they needed defensemen, so I played defense. I just switched.

At that time I was still considered a finesse player — one of the better players in the league. But since I was a defenseman, I had to be aggressive and I had to know how to handle myself. I had done some boxing in high school, so it came pretty easy.

Bear in mind that being tough doesn't necessarily mean fighting. For me, being tough is being able to take a hit and give a hit. I fought quite a bit in my first four or five years of pro. By then you've gotten your respect and you don't fight as much. I'm more valuable on the ice than off and the way the rules have changed, it's a lot tougher to go out and fight.

When I was still in Juniors, one of my toughest bouts was with Garth Butcher who was fighting everybody, not just me. He was a tough kid. We were 17-year-olds and he gave me two or three pretty good ones, but I've fought him a couple of times and did pretty well. My belief is that when it comes to fighting, anybody can beat anybody else on any given night.

After Juniors, I moved on to the University of Wisconsin and found quite a difference in the hockey there. College was more of a developing system; you practiced all week and then played only two games on the weekend, whereas in Juniors it was more of a pro-type season.

After I got to Wisconsin I was still growing and learning a lot about the game, the position and playing a team game. College hockey helped me a lot. I went from collegiate hockey in 1982-83 to the U.S. National Team in 1983-84 and, finally, the Olympic team.

The whole year leading up to the Olympics in Sarajevo was really exciting, partly because of what had happened [the Miracle at Lake Placid] in 1980. Everybody treated us well and we had a big following, but the Olympics itself was a disappointment in that we didn't win the way we had hoped to. Still, when I look back, I feel that I was lucky to be able to play and represent my country and, really, that's what it's all about.

As my hockey career evolved, my attitude about toughness was always there. I enjoyed the intimidation part of the game; it excites me more to give a big hit than scoring a goal because that [hitting] is a big part of the game. Playing defense, I don't score as much but I like the big hits. I guess if I was playing center, and scoring, I'd feel differently about it.

Needless to say, I've had problems over the years with my style of play, and there have been incidents such as the episode with Brian Propp. The fact of the matter is that I just hit him and he hit his head on the partition. Since it happened in the playoffs, they made a big deal of it. The Boston media in particular inflated this reputation of mine. I was supposed to be a premier player, an All-Star, and they made a big stink about it all the time.

I know Propp and I have no problem separating what happens on the ice with what happens off the ice. We have a lot of friends in the league, but on the ice, you're not thinking about friendships. You just see a different-colored jersey and not the person in it.

I've been asked if there is any person in the league who I wouldn't fight and my answer is that there's nobody I wouldn't hit, but there are guys who I wouldn't try and hit to hurt them and really hit them hard. In the playoffs I would do anybody. I would do anything to anybody in the playoffs, but during the regular season it's pretty difficult for me to play against someone I know.

My first couple of years in the NHL were played in awe. Being on the same Canadiens team with guys like Larry Robinson, Bob Gainey and Guy Lafleur was really something special. I just kind of sat back and watched everything happen. I played hard and learned a lot from these guys.

The most important thing they taught me was their winning tradition. Winning was the most important thing and to do so you had to set aside your personal goals and play as a team. I could have been a totally different player had I started somewhere else. Some young players go to other teams and they find everybody's selfish; they just play their own way, their own style and don't adjust to team play. In Montreal, they didn't allow that to happen.

Once I got to the NHL it took me a bit of time to get used to the fighting because there was so little of it in college. You win a couple of fights, as I did, and you get more confident and then you don't worry about it too much. As the years went on, I tried to be more disciplined. My biggest downfall now is with the referees. It's not so much me taking bad minor penalties and leaving my team shorthanded as it is taking 10-minute penalties and leaving my team without me. The new rules have left me frustrated because of the adjustments that had to be made. I like to think I can adjust to any type of play so I have to learn to control myself, although sometimes I lose it a little bit.

There's been a running debate about fighting in the NHL. My feeling is that if they take it out, they take it out; and if they don't, it's fine with me, too. Fighting has been a part of the game since I've been playing. It doesn't bother me. But with the rule changes, you don't get away with as much as you used to, and what it comes down to is that I'm not going to go out there and do something that would put me in jeopardy of losing money.

I've been beaten in fights. I got the tar beat out of me by Larry Playfair. Fighting against a guy like that, I realized how big and strong some of the heavyweights in the NHL really are. He had hit our goalie and I just grabbed him. Before I knew it, he was just giving it to me.

There are guys in the league who can be intimidated; the finesse players you can intimidate, and a lot of the Europeans don't like to be hit because they're not used to that. You go out of your way to hit them.

Some talk goes on on the ice but I don't like talking too much because it always ends up being a yelling contest. There are some guys in the league I just plain don't like, but I'm not going to be a jerk to anybody. I'll say, "Hi" to him, but I'll never be the best friend of someone I don't like.

In 1992-93 I had a problem with the Winnipeg media over a confrontation I had with Teemu Selanne. He's their best player and my job is to defend against him. I'm not going to beat Selanne trying to skate with him because he's too quick and talented a player for that. So I had to go after him physically and take him out with my body. If I could sit in the penalty box with Selanne, that's a good match-up and fine with me. But the Winnipeg press made a big stink about it.

If I could go out and play a game like Brian Leetch or Phil Housley, with my offensive skills alone, that would be great. But I wouldn't fit into the Blackhawks if I played that way and I wouldn't have fit into the Canadiens either with that style. Besides, I don't have the kind of offensive skill that a Leetch or Housley possesses.

There is yet another side of me. I do some charity work with Jeremy Roenick. We have a summer hockey school and donate some money into a charity called Cheli's Children. In 1992-93 we gave a $30,000 check to cocaine babies, buying cribs for them. When they are going through withdrawal they need to be held and the cribs provide a motion that makes them feel that they are being held.

II

ESTABLISHED HEAVYWEIGHTS

Chapter 4

ALGONQUIN ENFORCER: GINO ODJICK

"We were playing Edmonton one night when Louie DeBrusk went out on the ice for them. He looked at me and said, 'It looks like we're going to have to go.' I said, 'Yeah, no kidding! We're not out here to dance.'"

A full-blooded Algonquin Indian, Gino Odjick established himself as one of the most boisterous and arresting big-leaguers almost from the day he put on a Vancouver Canucks jersey during the 1990-91 season.

The 6-foot-3, 210-pound left winger banged his way to a top-heavy 296 penalty minutes in only 45 games as a National Hockey League rookie but, more important, gained a spot on the big team. In fact, he dressed for six playoff games in his freshman year.

Canucks' president Pat Quinn perceived a pugnacious quality that, in some ways, reminded the boss of his own NHL days as a hard-hitting defenseman with the Toronto Maple Leafs and other clubs. In 1991-92 Odjick played the entire season with the Canucks, managing four goals and six assists and a hefty 348 penalty minutes.

Tri-lingual — Gino speaks English, French and Algonquin — Odjick became an instant fan favorite at Pacific Coliseum and an idol to native people. Interestingly, when Pavel Bure signed with Vancouver, the youthful Russian turned to Odjick as his buddy and hockey's odd couple became close friends in no time at all.

During the 1992-93 campaign the Canucks took over the top of the Smythe Division and remained there through the spring. While Odjick never could be accused of scoring prowess, he was a factor in the club's ascendency to first place.

Vancouver reporter Sandra MacPherson interviewed Gino during a break in the action during the 1992-93 season.

I was five when I first laced on a pair of skates. My older sister took me skating and instead of hockey blades, I wound up wearing figure skates. I had five sisters and I fell in third in the family. We got along quite well. I never bossed them around. In fact the only thing I can think of that we argued about was over the television. But that was about all. I didn't have any brothers but there were lots of cousins in the family and we were all very close.

My interest in hockey started early, partly because my dad started coaching me on the Algonquin reserve and I became one of the better players from the earliest days. We used to play on outdoor rinks and it got pretty cold. You really felt it when you weren't actually playing. To beat the cold we'd wear an extra pair of regular gloves inside our hockey gloves and a toque under our helmet and away we'd go. We were having so much fun we didn't really realize how cold it was.

We played pick-up games and in the winter we lived to play. We'd play all the time and have tournaments all over. In the summertime it was softball, and it was always just for fun all the time.

At home we'd watch the games on TV and there always were big arguments because half of us were fans of the Boston Bruins and the other half cheered for the Montreal Canadiens. My favorite Bruin was Stan Jonathan, a small but tough forward who was a native player. After Jonathan retired, I started cheering more for the Canadiens.

Jonathan was a good fighter. Me, I had a fight on the ice when I was 14 years old and got beat up really bad. I got caught at the end of a shift and was pretty tired. I had no wind and the other guy was fresh. He just caught me good. I didn't have another fight on the ice until I was about 17.

When I played on the reserve, I played just for fun; I never really practiced. That changed when I got called up to Junior hockey. Unfortunately, I was a little behind on some things so I just figured a good way to stay with the team was to just start duking it out and stuff.

I was 17 when I went to play Junior in Hawkesbury and I guess they needed a physical player. I was quite willing to do it and that's how it all began for me on an organized basis.

One of the smaller players on our Hawkesbury team had called me a goon and a dummy, and one night when I was on the ice a tough guy on the other team grabbed our little player and beat him up bad; the poor guy suffered a broken nose and his eye was knocked out of the socket. And I just let him get beat up because I wanted him to know that it was important to have a player like me on the team to protect him and that he shouldn't have called me those names. Of course, I felt bad after what happened to him but I also wanted my teammate to know that he needed me.

By the time I got to Junior A hockey I was tall but not that big in the sense that I was lanky. I guess I was about 6-2, 185 pounds in my first year of Junior. I played two seasons for Laval in the Quebec League. I had become friendly with a former Montreal Canadiens player named Gilles Lupien who had turned hockey agent.

He said that maybe I could make a career out of hockey and explained what I had to do. He said I didn't have to fight all the time but that I should prove myself as a player. Lupien knew what he was talking about because he had virtually the same job as me.

Then, I got drafted by Vancouver in 1990. I was picked in the fifth round of the draft, 86th overall. The Canucks sent me down to the International League and I played 17 games with Milwaukee. The night before they called me up to the NHL, the Canucks had played Calgary and got an awful pushing-around from the Flames. That's when Pat Quinn decided that Vancouver needed me.

I knew what the Canucks wanted and I knew what I had to do to stay around, so I decided I'd just start right away. My first fight was with Dave Manson who was then playing defense for the Chicago Blackhawks. I did all right. I threw a couple of punches and then fell down.

After that, I had a really good fight with Stu Grimson and, from there on, I stuck with the big team. The Canucks knew I wanted to do the job. If they bring you up as a tough guy and they think they need a little more toughness in the lineup, just have a few scraps in the first 10 games and make a presence. You plan it. And then you show that you can play more and more.

Having a fight in front of a big crowd was some kind of rush for me and I was really happy with the way I played. But then the next day comes and you have to prove you want to stay. I took it that way for my whole first year.

Nowadays when young guns come up, I tell them that if they have that [enforcer] kind of role, they should just show they want to stay. Just have a couple of scraps when they come up because there are lots of guys who are going to score.

A few people helped me improve enough to compete in the NHL. One of them was Paulin Bordeleau who played in Vancouver [1973-74 to 1975-76]. He taught me how to turn right and left and how to make a pass. His passes were great. He helped develop me as a player in terms of skills and that. Paulin worked with me in Laval during my first season there, then Pierre Creamer took over. He had coached the Pittsburgh Penguins previously and told me what to expect as a tough guy in the NHL. He told me not to try too much; just go up and down my wing.

So, I was really lucky. I had one coach who really helped me with my physical skills and another who really helped me with my mental skills and, all in all, it ended up working. I got to play my first year as a fifth-rounder and that doesn't happen too often.

The first thing I noticed when I arrived in Vancouver was that the Canucks didn't have a really tough team. They had a lot of small players. I was smart enough to realize what I had to do to play in the NHL. And Brian Burke, who was our assistant general manager, would say, "Dance with the girl who brought you to the dance." Which, to me, meant that guys like me who were tough had to play that way.

When they sent me to Milwaukee I knew I had to improve as a player and still contribute with the rough stuff here and there. That's what I did and then they called me back.

The role for a big guy is easier to play in the NHL. Here, things are a lot more positional. All you've got to do is pick up your defense and pick up the man going wide. Whereas in the minors, there's a bit more running around and stuff. The big guys are stronger in the NHL and they're smarter fighters than they are in the minors.

My feeling was that you have to be aggressive for the first 10 NHL games. Fight and do whatever you have to do to be more aggressive. Then, you know that will buy you time to show them bit by bit that you can be a player.

Sometimes big guys come up and they want to show that they can play before they show why they're really here. Those usually end up going down pretty quickly to the minors.

When I got to Vancouver, the former Canuck, Ron Delorme — who was a terrific fighter — gave me a few pointers. He showed me how to use hand speed and urged me to lift weights. Now I usually get five-pound weights and throw them as fast as I can. Fifty times with the right and 50 times with the left. Every day. Just for the speed.

There are a lot of guys in the NHL who can throw a lot of good punches and take them. To become a good fighter you have to fight smart. You can't go all out and try to kill the guy. It's a combination of trying to protect yourself and hitting well. If you lose, just lose a little bit. If you win, just win a bit. Never get too beat up or beat up too much. Just being consistent and smart about it is the way to go.

Bob Probert has the best fighting trick. He lets you grab on and then he starts skating backwards and his whole jersey comes off. Then, you've got nothing to grab onto and that's why he's so good.

With anybody else, when their shirt comes off, you can usually neutralize them a little bit and slow down their punches and stuff like that. But with his shirt coming off, he can still throw big and throw freely.

Sometimes when I'm in a fight, I'll let the other guy tire himself out and then get a good position on him and start throwing them. There are different ways of doing the job. Some guys get quick starts and never let the other fellow back in it — like Craig Berube. He throws a lot of punches and doesn't let the other guy get balanced. There are different ways for different fighters.

Marty McSorley uses that big shirt. He's always trying to knock you off-balance so you can't get too much on your punches. And, of course, it's hard to hold on to him because of that shirt. He's got great stamina, too. The three big guys are Probert, McSorley and Dave Brown.

Then there's Tie Domi. He's really tough. He's a small guy who can take as many punches as you can throw at him. He's really, really ballsy. Mind you, he's not a Probert, or a Brown or a McSorley, but he's right in there; a tough guy to fight.

When Tie came into the league he fooled a lot of people. He was throwing lefts. Then he got into a little song and dance after his fights but when he does stuff like that, he's hurting himself because, in this business, there's somebody who's going to beat you. As Domi found out in 1992-93. Bob Probert just beat the living daylights out of him.

There are 84 games in the regular NHL season and because of so many games, you might win one fight but you might lose the next one and that's something Tie has to learn. It has a little to do with maturity and, I'm sure, he'll mature. Right now he's a good shit-disturber and he pisses everybody off. He's good at what he does but he's going to have to learn that you can't go around doing what he does for long, otherwise he'll learn the hard way. For sure.

Another tough guy for whom I have a lot of respect is Shane Churla. He's not very big but he's what you want in a tough guy on your team. He comes and hits everybody, every night, and it doesn't matter who you are — he'll hit you. He may not have a lot of talent, but Churla sure has a lot of heart.

The best fights I've ever had were with Dave Brown because I had to use everything that I had. Dave is a really strong guy who can hit hard. When I fought him I was at the max as far as my strength goes. I don't know if it was the same for him but I was always right there with him. That was where I used more of my strength.

In our first fight, Dave gave it to me pretty good, so I went right away at him the second time. I felt that I didn't do as well as I could have or, maybe, I didn't fight him the right way. That's why I went at him a second time in the same game. That was all right. The third time he was fooling around and punched our defenseman Garth Butcher in the head. When that happened, I came in and jumped on him and started fighting. Then he was mad because he didn't think he did as well as he could have, or should have done. I had given him a shiner.

The next time we met he came out on the first shift when I was out there, so I knew right away that he wanted to fight and we did. In fact, we fought twice in that game and didn't get anything resolved. That was the end of our battles.

At that time Dave Brown had quite a reputation for fighting but I always tried not to worry about things like that until the fight started and then it was too late to worry about it. The exception was the very last fight when I had heard through the papers and stuff that Dave was mad at me.

Domi has been a problem because of the way he fights. Once he hit me with a left and I didn't know that he was a lefty. He knocked me down and I got right back up again and started throwing punches, but the ref got in the way.

Was I affected by it? I just brushed it off. I said to myself that I had made a mistake and the next time I won't make the same mistake. Then again, you can't be losing too often. It's just like anything else. You don't want to make the same mistake twice and I try not to do that as a fighter.

My mistake with Domi was in thinking that he was a righty when, in fact, he was throwing with his left.

Another time I got hurt was with an elbow thrown by Jay Caufield of the Penguins. That was one of the things in my career that upset me the most because 95 percent of the time, the big guys in the NHL are honest. If they want to fight, they'll fight. Caufield caught me with an elbow and I think he wanted to stun me and then fight me. But the thing was, he hit me too hard and broke my cheekbone. He came skating in and popped me with the elbow; then he was ready to throw off his gloves and fight instead of just saying he wanted to fight me, or let me know right off the face-off.

I was disappointed in Jay after that, but then we had another run-in and I fixed it. I don't have any grief with him now. I got my revenge and that's it.

But he had broken my cheekbone and I was out for about 10 games before coming back for the playoffs. In my first game back I wasn't wearing a visor. We played Los Angeles and I got into a fight with Jay Miller, who could handle his dukes. I got confident that everything was all right and then I went from there.

After the broken cheekbone I wore the visor only in practice. It's not fashionable for a fighter to wear a visor during a regular game. If I have to wear one, I'd rather not play because I wouldn't feel comfortable with it. I'm too proud to do that.

I understand that my opponents are trying to beat the tar out of me, but I have nothing but respect for them because I know, first-hand, that they don't have an easy job.

It's pretty rare when I'm really mad at my opponent. You know, things happen. All the little guys go out and stir up all the trouble and then they put on two big guys who sometimes haven't played too much and haven't played one shift against each other. They go put out the fire and calm everybody down. That's the way it is. Most of the big guys don't get too mad but Tie Domi has a way of making all the big guys mad because of his cockiness.

There's a general pattern that shows why every team needs some-one tough to protect the artistic players. Take Winnipeg as an example. Early in the 1992-93 season they didn't have anybody big to help skill guys like Phil Housley and Teemu Selanne or Evgeny Davydov, the Russian. I'd cross-check Davydov and all their good players. I didn't care; there was nobody on their team at the time who was going to stop me. So, when I cross-checked Housley, I didn't have to worry about fighting someone. Then, they went out and got Domi and Kris King, and the Jets' stars got a lot more protection for the rest of the season.

It's the same way with my team. If something happens to one of my players, then I have to do something about it. That's why it's very important to have a big guy on your team.

After a few years in the NHL, I got to know how the other guys play and how to handle them. Some nights both guys [enforcers] will respect each other and then other nights some other guy will do something stupid and it's always the big guys who have to put out the fire.

Quite often words are passed before a fight starts. I'll give you a for-instance: We were playing Edmonton one night when Louis DeBrusk went out on the ice for them. He looked at me and said, "It looks like we're going to have to go." I said, "Yeah, no kidding! We're not out here to dance."

We both knew the score because of the way their coach, Teddy Green, had sent Louie out on the ice. We both knew we had to go. He didn't do anything to me that night and I didn't do anything to him. I didn't run any small guys and he didn't either. But the way the game was going, we had to go and we went. We did it honestly and there was no problem.

There is such a thing as fighting smart. Sometimes I let guys come after me. If we're down, 2-0, or it's in the third period, or if it's the first period and your team doesn't have any jump, then it's a good time to fight.

I've been asked whether I worry about some young fellow coming up and taking my job and my answer is that, as a native, growing up on the reserve, my parents taught me that I can't worry about things that I can't control.

The only things I can control are the things that I do. All I can do is try my best. I'm sure that if somebody comes along and is better than me, then I'll be happy for him and he'll get his chance. Right now, I'm not worried about that.

Chapter 5

BAM-BAM OF THE BIGS: TODD EWEN

"My priorities are like this: I do what's best for the team and, after that, I hope I can take care of myself."

Well-spoken and sensitive, the off-ice Todd Ewen is far removed from the pugnacious puckmeister who split his National Hockey League career between St. Louis and Montreal, but has since moved to the Mighty Ducks of Anaheim.

In his spare time, Ewen has written a children's book called A Frog Named Hop *and poetry, and has displayed a bent for the literary life. He is anything but the caricatured bad guy once he removes his skates and padding.*

More than that, Ewen has shown that he possesses skill to accompany his repertoire of body checks and police work. When, at the start of the 1992-93 NHL campaign, the league asserted that it would de-emphasize brawling, Ewen smoothly made the adjustment, lifted his artistry level while, at the same time, retaining all the gusto that has endeared him to fans and teammates.

A native of Saskatoon, Todd served his apprenticeship with New Westminster of the Western Hockey League, Maine in the American League and Peoria in the International League before clicking full-time with St. Louis in 1987-88. He was dealt to Montreal in December 1989.

Until the 1992-93 campaign, Ewen was more an enforcer than an offensive force. His most active season had been 1987-88 when he played 64 games and totalled four goals, two assists and 227 penalty minutes. In

1989-90 he played 41 games for Montreal and compiled four goals, six assists and 158 penalty minutes, which was his most productive output until 1992-93.

Ewen neatly made the segue into the de-gooning process and, under the new regime, developed into a more well-rounded performer. He played in 75 games in 1992-93, scored five goals and nine assists for 14 points while collecting 193 penalty minutes.

At 6-foot-3, 220 pounds, Ewen is an imposing personality during an interview or on his right wing. However, in person he does not appear anything like his nickname, "Animal." Amiable, literate and a devoted family man with two children, Todd was a cooperative subject during his meetings with reporter Eric Servetah in the lobby of the Marriot Glenpointe in New Jersey the evening before a game against the Devils, and in visits to Nassau Coliseum on Long Island.

When I began taking my hockey seriously in the Western League at New Westminster, I realized that there was a "ladder effect" in terms of climbing up among the tough guys. I knew when I got there that a lot of tough players had come from the WHL and I soon discovered that if you wanted to work your way up that ladder, there were certain guys you had to "go" [fight] with. I had to fight these guys and it was as fair as fair could be most of the time.

I would stand back, take off my helmet, throw down my gloves, pull up my sleeves and away we would go. That's the way it started. There was no running around, no cheap shots and we all had the same idea of how it should be. If you check the *NHL Guide* you'll notice that a lot of [tough] guys I played with and against — Craig Berube, Dave Manson, Link Gaetz — made it to the NHL. It's cool that we all came out together and we all had the same idea of how it should be.

It's interesting to wonder how I'd feel about fighting some of those fellows since we go back so far. But if the situation came up and knowing that we have to do a job, the first consideration would have to be my team and what's best for it. I can't be selfish about something like that and I can't be tentative about fighting anybody. If I get into a fight and I get beat up, so be it, I get beat up. But the important thing is that I'm trying and that's the best I can do. My priorities are like this: I do what's best for the team and, after that, I hope I can take care of myself.

I grew up in St. Albert, Alberta, right by Edmonton. It also was the home of Troy Murray, Greg Hawgood and Rob Brown. I was into every sport you could name. I played baseball, football, hockey and lacrosse. I was a competitive swimmer ever since I can remember and I've done everything that dealt with sports. I loved sport, and my mom was into art, so I would fool around drawing sketches. I can draw but I wasn't into it as a big deal during my youth because sports was so big with me.

My dad was into body building and was drafted by the Hamilton Tiger Cats and the New York Rangers simultaneously. That accounts for my sports orientation. When I was 15, I got the opportunity to play hockey for New Westminster, but played Tier II hockey for the Vernon Lakers for a year.

In New West I was with some neat players like Cliff Ronning, Bill Ranford, Brian Noonan and Craig Berube. Funny thing is that I really didn't get into fighting until I was in Juniors, and I can only recall one fight outside of hockey.

The first hockey fight I got into was strange and difficult to put into words. I was tentative at first because I had that fear that I was going to get hurt, and until you get hurt, you don't understand that it's really not as bad as it looks. You have to get in there and actually get something busted and get hit in the face. You don't know if you're going to drop like a fly or if you're going to get up there and get right back into it.

Frankly, I wasn't a very good fighter at the start in New Westminster, but I didn't quit and I didn't lose too many. When I fought guys like John Kordic and Dave Manson, I took a couple of punches. Once I was heading off the ice after a whistle when Manson came at me from behind and hit me in the back of my head with a sucker-punch that broke my helmet in half. It was such a hard hit that I even felt in on the inside of my head. I turned around and we went right at it. It was very funny.

Not that fighting itself is funny, especially since the process of establishing yourself in the league is a long and tough one. There's a never-ending cycle; you're fighting to become a player, and you want to make it among your peers. After a while, you fight so much, the opponents' names go in and out of your head. For me, it was all part of the game that was there.

It didn't hurt that my coach in New Westminster was Ernie (Punch) MacLean, and he was one of the toughest around. He had been at New West a long time going back to the days when Barry Beck played for him and they had one of the most fearsome teams in the West. Even when I played for him, if there wasn't four or five fights, it wasn't a hockey game. I knew up front that I had to go out and be aggressive, and I like that.

Some players have idols when they're young but when I was 17 and 18, I didn't have any except for Clark Gillies, the big left wing who played for the Islanders when they won the four straight Stanley Cups. I like the way he looked — big, and rangy like me — I like the way he played and I like the way he fought. He was one

NHL player I really liked to watch and tried to learn from, otherwise I didn't know many players in the majors.

Funny thing, but the year before he quit, Gillies played for Buffalo and that was my first year in the NHL. One night we were playing the Sabres and, whaddya know, I'm out on the ice, look up and — I couldn't believe it — there was Gillies standing next to me. I bumped him once, did my job and finished the shift. For one split-second I was in awe, but I had my job to do and he had his, but we never did fight each other.

I was fortunate. In all the years I've never really been beaten up. Sure, I've wound up in some bouts where you'd score it a draw but never have I been wasted. Part of the trick is mental, not wanting to lose a fight is important. If you give up, you lose.

This reminds me of one of the first fights I had when I came up to the NHL — with Bob Probert; it's the one everyone talks about. I came down the boards, we dropped the gloves and I one-punched him to the ice. I hit him right at the end of the chin and he went down. I dazed Bob with that shot and it's one of the only times that he's been hurt bad in a fight.

As soon as we came out of the penalty box, it was back to center ice where we swung and turned and kept swinging until his jersey ripped wide open and I had nothing to grab on to. Finally, I went down, and then got back up and he went down and got back up. That was a great fight. I don't think I lost and I don't think Probert could say that he beat me up.

That was memorable but it wasn't my first "official" fight. Chicago Stadium was the site of what I consider my original NHL test. It developed after I had skated into the corner and the Blackhawks' young defenseman, Marc Bergevin, was there with the puck. I didn't know him and he didn't know me. I hit him once in the corner and then we came around the net and I gave him another good hit. He came back at me and cross-checked me on the side.

At the time I was too young for that kind of stuff so when somebody would do that to me, I automatically said, "Okay, let's go!" He was willing, so we went at it and I beat him up; simple as that.

I had a lot of run-ins at the beginning. It seemed that there was a cycle with me fighting guys in our division — Probert, Kocur, Probert, Probert, Probert, Kocur. Every game there was something, but Joey Kocur was difficult because it's hard for someone like me, with long arms, fighting a guy like Kocur who has short arms and is really strong and has a knockout punch. I could hold him out at a distance and I could win or he could pop me one and put me down.

Most of the time we ended up throwing little rabbit punches on the inside or against the boards. The thing with Joey is that it's hard to get away from him, especially with the lock grip on the inside of your elbows. So it's hard to get back and swing a good right with him.

Some players have a set style but mine is simple: WIN. Win at any cost. The one thing I keep saying all the time is that if you stop, you're going to lose. Of course, I get in trouble a lot of the times because I don't stop. For example, Kocur and Tony Twist will take a barrage of punches and then try to unload The Bomb. Me, I just get in there, get the job done and let's go! If you want to go, you go. If you want to stand back, then you stand back.

I don't do much talking before a fight starts. If you don't say anything, it makes the opposition a little more hesitant because they don't have a grip on you. If I stand there, yelling and screaming, "You're a jerk; let's go!" the other guy will think, "Shut up and do it!"

One time when I do remember talking was when I went up against Craig Berube. He skated out on the ice and said, "We're going; we're going." So, I said, "Okay." They dropped the puck and we went at it. It was a good fight and I had fun fighting him again. In a case like that it's kind of hard to keep from laughing while we're fighting since, to me, fighting Craig is like fighting my kid brother, Dean. Me and "Chief" had been pretty close during our years in New Westminster. Yet, we'll still fight when necessary.

My brother and I used to fight plenty, especially during the summers. We played together briefly. It was my last year in Juniors and his first. One night a big defenseman named Brent Severyn, who was 20 at the time, beat the snot out of him. I mean he kicked Dean's ass all over the ice. So after the time in the penalty box, my brother came back to the bench and was shaking his head, "I didn't do good; I didn't do good."

The best thing for me is grabbing my opponent anywhere in the body. I'm a strong skater, so I pull and push into my punches. As soon as I can get you off-balance, the better. The best place I can fight is against the boards or close to the boards. I like my opponent's back near the boards because I can pull him up along the boards and I can pull him down. And there's always a chance that he's going to fall down and be unstable and I can start racking away.

Don't get the impression that all this fighting is easy, because it isn't. It's tough to go out on the ice and fight 100 percent every time because you just don't want to do it. That's why I have so much respect for Dave Brown since he's done it for so many years.

In the first couple of years all the fighting is great, but then you want a little bit more out of your hockey. You want to contribute more to the team. After a while it became more difficult for me going out there, knowing I was getting only one shift and the coach would say, "Go — this is it. It's your one chance to get out on the ice. Go over there and take that guy out."

During my last training camp with the Blues [1988-89] I got fed up. Brian Sutter was coaching and every morning we would have four different teams and hold a morning and an afternoon game. I would always be switched to the team opposite the rest of the fighters, like Tony Twist, Kelly Chase and Herb Raglan. We would have fights — stick fights, three-on-ones, it was unbelievable — and I couldn't believe that they would set it up like that.

But every morning I was changed to a different team and we went at it. Frankly, I thought it was disrespectful to me for what I had done for the team up until that point. They put me in that position because they wanted to see a couple of toe-to-toes and see who would come out the best, and that person would get the job. I figured since I played for four years for the team that they would have some commitment to me. I did a good job up until then but then they started treating me like a piece of meat and that's when I lost respect for the team.

Which perhaps helps explain why I respect Dave Brown, because he's done it for a long time and has gone through so much and is still there — still hanging in at an advanced hockey age.

It's funny because people like us [the ice cops] are working with million-dollar players, but we're still segregated on the bench. We have to be quiet, not cause problems and simply do our job. What's helped, of course, are the new rules.

In 1992-93 I went through a long stretch of the season without fighting. I just went out there bumping and grinding because I knew that the new instigator rule would make life difficult. The hard thing with it is that they're now taking money out of our pockets. Since I'm not among the higher-paid players on the team, it's hard for me to justify going out on the ice and being an insitgator, maybe get kicked out, suspended and then lose money to protect million-dollar players. That's wrong.

On the other hand, I'd feel bad if I didn't do anything to protect, say, a Denis Savard, and he got hurt. That would kill me because it would have meant that I didn't do my job that I've been doing for years. I understand what the league is doing. The NHL wants to ensure that the really gifted players do their stuff. But nowadays, with so many players wearing visors, you get guys like Ulf Samuelsson hurting players and getting away with it because he's protected from retaliation by the visor.

In the older days, you could rough up the big boys, push around and drop the mitts and there's an old-fashioned fight. Now, with the visors, so many players have no fear. A guy like Samuelsson puts on the armor, comes around, hits anybody where and when he wants to and then, when someone goes after him, he's not afraid to "turtle."

Which brings us to the question: How do you get a guy like that? How do you protect your teammates against him? It's not easy. You try to hit him but it's hard to get a bead on him because he'll dish the puck off all the time and then duck. A player like that is the kind that you could sucker-punch without any compunction.

Two years ago Samuelsson took Brian Skrudland's knee out and knocked him out of the lineup. I could go over and slap him in the head for that right now but it still won't help Skrudland. It's not going to go away for as long as he's on the ice. Samuelsson should be suspended for doing something like that, but he never is. He's wrecking guys' careers and is shortening others and more knees are being taken out.

Meanwhile, if I go too far, I'll get fined and suspended. And if I get fined, you can bet that it'll come out of my salary. People think the team can get around it and pay us, but if they tried to pay me back and got caught, they'd get fined $500,000, so it's not going to happen.

Mind you, not all the tough guys have to be big, physically. Teams need players like little Keith Acton and Mike Keane, who can get away with a whole bunch more because they're not 6-3 and they don't have a reputation as an animal. Teams need a universal set: goal scorers; little guys who get in there and muck; and the big guys who have to hit a defenseman and turn over the puck. A fellow like Keane is useful. He's a good hitter, a good fighter and scraps all the time. A guy like him adds to the chemistry which is a key word in hockey nowadays.

But times are changing and I have no idea where the league is going with the fighting crackdown. All I can say is that it's hard to believe that they're going to eliminate it completely because by the very nature of a hitting game like hockey, tempers will flare and fights will erupt. They simply aren't going to get rid of it, although they might level such a drastic penalty that you could lose your livelihood because of it. Personally, I think the hockey is good now and they shouldn't change it anymore.

For me, it becomes more and more important to get out there and play as opposed to sitting on the bench. That's why, at the end of the 1991-92 season, I asked to be traded; I wasn't playing enough and it bothered me. I wanted to have the opportunity and I wasn't getting it while Pat Burns was our coach. Then, Jacques Demers got the job and before the season started, he phoned me.

"Todd," he said, "stay, and I'll give you a chance but what you do with the chance is up to you." I took him at his word and he was good for it. I played more and more and finally felt that I was contributing.

I have two children. The oldest is Tyler and the youngest is Chad who is a monster. He tripled his body weight in three months; he's simply going to be huge, like his daddy. He'll be driving a truck soon, and I'm having a weight bench put into his room. I play rough with Tyler and tackle him, and now that he's in school it's more difficult for him to adjust to playing with kids. He got sent home from school one day when the kids were playing with their toys and he went over and grabbed one kid who had his toy and body-slammed him. So he's only three and he's getting thrown out of school. He's having fun and he has a temper, but he can control it.

One of these days my kids will be able to read a children's book that I wrote. It's called *A Frog Named Hop*. The problem was, when I wrote it my kids were young and I didn't quite understand how capable they were of understanding an advanced language. So I didn't know how hard to make the book and as my kids progressed I learned that children progress much faster than I give them credit for. So I have to keep on rewriting the book to keep up with them. If Tyler's the average kid, then I'm way off-base, so I keep on rewriting it. The first couple of rewrites were still way too simple for children because it doesn't keep their attention, so it's something that I have to work on. Children like to be challenged, and I didn't know that before, but I'm learning it now. So it's been rewritten three times and I do want to get it published. I want to give it a try, and each time the story changes it's getting to the point now where it's pretty close and I have to start looking for a publisher. I've been trying to reach [ex-Canadien] Ryan Walter to see what he has done with his children's book. He's got some really good ideas and I want to throw them around with him.

I also draw. I've done a bunch of pictures of the team. I've always had the talent to draw and I like to screw around with it once in a while. During a game in the 1992-93 season against the Islanders, a bunch of the players on their bench were heckling me about my drawing. They were saying, "Hey Todd, draw me up or come over here and make me a sketch." It was pretty funny and especially when I looked over and saw Mick Vukota laughing hysterically with his head in his hands on the bench.

As for hockey, I know that I'm getting older. Looking at the team we had in 1992-93, I figured that we had a good chance to win the Cup, and we did. We had a lot of talent that didn't blossom until the playoffs. So, as long as I can stay injury-free, I should be alright. The thing is, though, you never can tell with injuries and I've had some bad ones going back to my days with St. Louis where I had a fight and busted my hand. I've broken every finger on both hands at least once from fighting. After I broke my hand a second time, I was sent down to Peoria and I got traded right after that.

I actually came up to Montreal with a broken hand, but I still played for the rest of the season although it always was swollen and I had to ice it down every day. I had to get the adrenalin flowing before I could use the thing, but it's incredible what a person can do when he is really psyched-up, and that's the way I was at that time.

Playing with the broken hand gave me some weird feelings and it wasn't so much how it felt when I was fighting because, in a fight, you're so pumped up that you don't feel anything until it's over. The strangeness came from shooting the puck. I'd come down the ice with the puck and then would want to take a snap-shot and I'd feel the bone move across the other way. It was being pushed in and pushed out. I could feel everything inside my hand moving around.

Another weird incident involved my nose. I got into a fight with Greg Smyth and I grabbed him then began tossing him around the boards. I was holding him with my left hand and feeding him right hand after right hand. Then he reached out — and, to tell the truth, I don't know how he did it — but as he was falling he hit me on the nose. Meanwhile, I kept hitting him while he was on the ice until the linesman picked me up.

Smyth stares back up at me and says, "Look at your nose; look at your f....n' nose." To that, I shot back, "Hey, I've just been beating the shit outa you for 20 minutes."

After that, we both went back to the dressing rooms and I was waiting for the doctor to arrive. Meanwhile, I'm saying to myself, "I can't believe he hit me; I can't believe he got me on the nose."

I was so pissed off and finally looked in the mirror and, sure enough, my nose was all twisted. So, I put two fingers in my nostrils and snapped them up into my nose and, sure enough, it snapped back into place and that was it. The nose began bleeding but I put some ice on it and that was it — done!

The hand wasn't so easy. Doctors told me it would heal over the summer and it did, but just on the outside of the bone. It didn't heal in the middle. Anyhow, one day after the new season started, I was carrying some grocery bags, along with my son, and we're coming down a hill. I was wearing dress shoes and slipped on some ice. Boom! I hit the ice and my hand popped again. I dropped the groceries and the kid landed on my chest. When the kid came falling down, I put out my hand to break his fall and that's when the hand broke. I missed the rest of the season and then had more surgery. This time they put a wire in my hand and now I'm left with a pinky finger that doesn't go straight and a big scar. Otherwise, the hand feels fine.

Injuries are part of the business. I also have a wire in my temple — a broken orbital bone — courtesy of Al Secord, who's now retired. While I was playing the puck in the corner, he dropped his mitts and nailed me with the first punch right on the side of my eye. It was at the point where we were just running at each other, the puck came loose, I knew we were going to fight but the puck was right there. He just suckered me and away we went.

He nailed me with the first punch and we went at it. Everybody has his wounds and this just added a broken orbital bone to my collection. It took a couple of weeks to heal and then I went right back at it again.

The NHL changed it's attitude toward the ways referees handle fights. Explaining it is difficult because we're not supposed to say anything against the referees or we'll get fined for that. The league wants to cut down on fighting. So the refs are trying to break the fights up early and the problem with that is that more of the linesmen are getting hit than the players because they are trying to get in there so quickly. Before they let you go until you burned yourself out and they just dragged you to the box. That was the good old days and that's fine with me, but it's not happening anymore.

See, we can use some of the rules to our advantage now. One night Mick Vukota wanted to come at me and I said, "No, I'm not going to fight you today." I did this because it was a 0-0 game and there was no point for me to fight when it could have been costly and we were working the puck good in their end of the ice. Mick was just trying to change the game and I had to hold back. But it was tough because we were watching fight films all day and it brought back the good old days. I had been pumped up watching the guys fight and seeing myself in some of them.

I have seen my share of frightening things on the ice. By far the worst was the Clint Malarchuk ripped-throat episode. I was with St. Louis and we were playing Buffalo when Steve Tuttle of the Blues crashed into [goalie] Malarchuk and Tuttle's sharp skate blade sliced across Malarchuk's throat.

I happened to be in the crowd, watching the game from the press box which was directly about the spot where it happened. Blood just spurted out of the wound in a big oval and everyone in the crowd just went dead while the entire Sabres bench was freaking out. They were running around and pounding on the glass and, luckily, the medics got to Clint in time, bandaged him up and got him off the ice. It was shocking to see an accident like that with the blood spewing and then the place going completely quiet. So much blood flowed out of his neck that if he had been on the other end of the ice, none of the medics could have gotten to him in time and he would have been dead. It was scary stuff.

Then again, you see some funny stuff on the ice as well. Early in the 1992-93 season we had a game against the Flyers and Dave Brown went after Lyle Odelein of our club. Lyle is one of the gamest fighters I've seen in a long time. He'll fight anybody and, of course, Brownie has been one of the best for a long time. Anyway, on this night Brownie should have gotten an "undressing penalty" because he took off his helmet, his jersey and his gloves and then challenged Odelein.

I couldn't believe my eyes. I mean there was Brownie half naked at center ice. And I'm yelling at Dave, "What the hell are you doing?" It reminded me of the movie *Slapshot* where the guy takes off all his gear at the end.

Mind you, I have no objections to Brownie taking off his jersey so that Lyle had nothing to grab on to when they fight, but my philosophy is this: if you are going to lose a fight then you lose. Personally, I'm not scared about losing. I'll be back; I'll be there again.

Chapter 6

THE BIG "P":
MIKE PELUSO

*"I don't think I'm in the top five of all
the league heavyweights, but I will be
there every night. I'll take on the
heavyweights and that, in itself, is
good enough for me."*

*At 6-feet-4, 210 pounds, Mike Peluso symbolizes the
hulking hockey player of the 1990s. That size — and
a modicum of skill — has enabled the Minnesotan to
hedge-hop from the University of Alaska at Anchorage to
Indianapolis of the International League and then
Chicago, Ottawa and New Jersey.*

*Peluso never made any bones about his style and his
penalty minutes (320 with Chicago in 1990-91 and 408
the following year) attest to Mike's approach to the game.*

*Under Blackhawks' coach Mike Keenan, Peluso was
encouraged to play a hitting game and was rewarded
with consecutive 53 and then 63 game seasons in
1990-91 and 1991-92, respectively. Perhaps more
significantly, Keenan showed his faith in Peluso by
playing him in no less than 17 playoff games in 1992
and thrust Mike into a pivotal role against the champion
Pittsburgh Penguins in the 1992 Stanley Cup finals.*

*With expansion and the addition of the Tampa Bay
Lightning and the Ottawa Senators in 1992-93, Peluso
had the opportunity of expanding his horizons. At first it
appeared that Chicago would retain his services, but the
firing of Keenan no doubt cost Peluso some support and
he was exposed to the expansion draft.*

*Peluso was claimed by the Senators on June 18, 1992
and emerged as one of the better forwards on Ottawa's
new NHL team. He eschewed some of his old rough-house
play to concentrate more on scoring. The result was a
respectable total of 15 goals, 10 assists and 318 penalty
minutes, considerably more than Peluso's six goals and
three assists in his previous NHL campaign.*

*"Mike is the kind of player who fights for his team, and
he's not worried about who he fights or how he does,"
says Ottawa teammate Brad Marsh. Despite his assets,
Peluso fell into disfavor with Ottawa management and
moved on to New Jersey for 1993-94.*

*In separate interviews with reporters Richard
Middelton in Ottawa and Eric Servetah at New Jersey's
Brendan Bryne Arena, Peluso candidly discussed his role
in the NHL as well as his development into a big-league
hockey player.*

I'm from a small town in Minnesota called Pengilly. It's up north
and the environment there is much like it is in the central part of
Canada. The winters are cold and there's plenty of ice. We had a lot
of outdoor rinks and that's where I learned to skate.

I have three older brothers — Frank, Joe and Gino — and they
were really hard on me. I was a short, heavy-set kid and they'd take
me out in the front yard, be it winter or summer, and would throw
me the football and make me run up the lawn and take shots at
nailing me. Considering some of the situations they put me through,
it's a miracle that I'm still alive.

Sometimes they'd put me in an inner tube and roll me down a hill
onto one of the bigger highways in town. Once they put me on a sled
on a snowy hill of a golf course and pushed me down the slope. I
crashed right into a tree and had a skull fracture. They always made
sure that they tested the waters with me before doing anything. I
remember once when they had just gotten BB guns one day. They
sent me running off, pumped up the BB guns and shot me right in
the ass. Man, were they ever hard on me.

I may not have liked it at the time but what they did was instill
competitiveness in me. My brother Gino and I would fight and
wrestle all the time, but I knew that I could never beat him. You
could never beat your older brother. But I put up a good fight and
made sure that he got it, too. If that didn't work, then I'd scream for
my mom or dad to come to my aid. All three of my brothers were
better athletes than me, but I learned from them, especially the
hatred of losing. If they lost, they still would put up a fight. After
getting my ass kicked by them, me and my younger sister, Julie,
would get into some good battles, but it was all in fun.

In our town we had a guy named Mike Gordovich, who was the godfather of hockey up there. He'd flood the rinks for us and get us going on the ice so that we could play pick-up hockey all day.

Once I got a little older, we got into competitive hockey and, quite frankly, there was nothing else to do but get on the outdoor rinks and bang the puck around.

After a while, I made it to high school hockey and when I reached that level my eye was on Division I college scholarships. By that time I had developed a competitiveness that comes with the outdoor hockey in northern Minnesota. A lot of guys I grew up with have that hate-to-lose spirit which, I believe, comes from the environment. That cold winter has a lot to do with it.

For most of my life, I played defense. I had good rink sense and was a big kid though a bit on the slow side. Where I come from, they usually throw the big kids back on defense. My two older brothers were forwards and my two younger brothers were defensemen.

I didn't make the transition from defense to forward until my first year of pro hockey. It was the exhibition season under Mike Keenan and our team needed a little bit of spark. He threw me up front and I got some big hits and everything seemed to work out that way.

I just stayed up front, although I think I'm a better defenseman than a forward. But as the years went by, I figured that the only way I was going to make it to the NHL was if I made the transition to forward because of the fact that the players are so much faster now with the lateral movement and whatnot, and the forwards are moving quicker.

There were times in Chicago when Mike Keenan would throw me back on defense. If he felt that somebody wasn't clearing out the opponent or there wasn't any banging or crashing going on in the corners, he'd put me back there to get the defensemen doing their work. I didn't mind that a bit.

I was drafted 10th (190th overall) in the 1984 NHL Entry Draft by the New Jersey Devils, but they wanted me to go to school rather than turn pro. The more I returned to school, the more I realized how important my college degree was and I'm not at all bitter about that decision.

After the Devils' opportunity went sour, I went to Minnesota's camp and got turned down there. Then I went to the Blackhawks whose organization demands hard work, loyalty and honesty. They gave me a chance to play and I just took it from there. All I wanted was a chance. I got it and everything has been a bonus for me ever since.

Although fighting is prohibited in college hockey, I got into it because of my size and competitiveness. I hate losing and in college I played dirty and tough. Granted, they don't have the fighting, but I got away with as much as I could get away with and that was due to my competitive nature. I hate getting embarrassed and I hate to lose.

Anybody in the NHL has to have a sense of competitiveness and a sense of hating to lose. If you have that determination, that desire, you're going to go a long way because the coaches are going to see that.

Speaking of coaches, the ones who helped me the most were Darryl Sutter and Mike Keenan in Chicago. They gave me a chance to play and anybody who knows me or who played with me or coached me, knows that I can play the game. I had big numbers in Alaska-Anchorage in a Division I league.

Playing 30 or 40 minutes a game against top Division I schools is sure to improve you. The blessing in disguise was going to Alaska. I stepped right in, played four years and had 30 or 40 minutes a game against top Division I teams. I had to improve because I had to keep up to the pace.

Darryl Sutter was the one who drew out the most in me and helped put me on track in the NHL. He'd help me or boot me in the butt if I needed it and he pushed me. He was a big influence on my career, as was Mike Keenan.

When I got to Ottawa, Rick Bowness gave me an enormous amount of ice time and put me in different situations including special teams. Having all that experience in college helped me polish my tools. But I still go out and hit people and look them in the eye. I do whatever I think the team needs for a spark on any given night.

As a lefty, I have an advantage as a fighter. I know that it's harder and tougher for me to fight a lefty, so being a lefty I know that my style throws people off-guard at first. When I fight, I try to get off to a good start, keep my head up and my arms punching and just go. I don't really have a style. I just try to go out and get revved up and on certain nights I realize that it's not going to go so well.

Knowing what you are going to have to do that night has you preparing early in the day. When the fight comes, you are aware of it. If you go into a hockey game not prepared for a battle, then certainly the other guy has an advantage over you because he's preparing over there. If you get scared early enough in the day, it will work out for you.

I still have to work on my balance a bit and I don't think I'm in the top five of all the league heavyweights, but I will be there every night. I'll take on the heavyweights and that, in itself, is good enough for me.

Naturally, it's been harder for me in Ottawa although I won my good share of fights in 1992-93 because I was prepared. During my last year in Chicago it was easy for me because I had Stu Grimson as a teammate. Grim is a good man and we had a close-knit pairing that I didn't have in Ottawa. As far as I'm concerned Stu is the toughest guy in the league although he doesn't get enough credit for what he does for the Blackhawks.

Night in and night out he's the cheerleader, getting the guys going. He is one of the honest fighters and we certainly have learned a lot from each other. When we were in the lineup, we were a tandem and one of the best in the league. We looked out for one another and read off each other. It didn't hurt that each of us was healthy all year.

Stu and I had some good battles in the Norris Division. Certainly, when you have a guy like him to go into battle with, it makes life a heck of a lot easier. Some nights, if he wasn't going, then I'd do it and if I wasn't going, he would go. So it was nice to have Stu along with me in the Chicago Stadium wars. Playing on that smaller ice surface with those roaring crowds and the big organ in the background was incredible. It's a tremendous feeling to win a bout in Chicago Stadium.

In Ottawa, I had to do it all by myself. I had to go to war every night against three or four tough guys on the other teams. Some nights I had to go against all three and they knew that I was all by myself. That makes it really tough to handle. I can't fight three times a night all year long. I was in that position a few times during the 1992-93 season. There were times when I fought twice in the first period.

At one point I had planned to follow through on boxing lessons but I dropped it. I felt that with the rule changes that preceded the 1992-93 season I wouldn't be doing as much fighting, but it turned out differently. Boxing is something that I still plan on looking into because having the lessons builds your confidence and helps your balance. It's good, hard training and excellent for conditioning.

I've had my share of good fights with Tony Twist, Basil McRae and Randy McKay. Randy is a tough man; someone you would really love to have on your team because he's going to work for you. He'll be there when you need him.

It seems like every time Randy and I met in a game we wound up fighting. The wars from our days of playing in the Norris Division carried over. It seemed like whenever we ran into each other on the ice, we'd make eye contact and the gloves were dropped. Whenever you put two tough guys on the ice at the same time, there's always a set-up for something to happen. There's not much room out on the ice and you're going to run into each other at some point during your shift. When that happens usually an altercation is going to take place.

My first NHL fight was against Basil McRae when he was with Minnesota. I had just been called up from Indianapolis the night before we played in Minnesota and there was a pre-game brawl. Then we went to Chicago and the same thing happened in the warm-up. That was the fight where Wayne Van Dorp got hurt and wound up sitting out against Shane Churla. That's when I knew there was an opportunity for me to step in and show what I could do. It was my first fight against McRae and it lasted a long time, going from one end of the ice to the other. It was a good opportunity for me to better myself and my chances of staying in Chicago. I took him on and it worked out for me.

One thing I've learned is that you don't brag about the fights you win because there's always someone out there who will give it to you the next night. I stay away from rah-rah-ing it up after a fight. I go to the penalty box and mind my own business. I don't like to brag because bragging will come back to haunt you and other players will back me up on that one. I keep my mouth shut and do my job.

I've changed my fighting style somewhat. I don't tape the back of my skates so I have much better balance than I ever did. I used to tape the heck out of them and now I have much better balance. Dave Manson helped me out on that, telling me not to tape my skates as much because at one point I taped the back of my skates completely so my ankles wouldn't even move. The change has helped me a lot.

Sometimes in a fight a player will catch you off-guard because you may not know him or you might not be sure that he wants to go. Once I had a fight with Mike Eagles, who was a teammate of mine in the minors but was on the opposite side in the NHL. He surprised me because I felt that he wasn't going to want to fight but he did. I also had a fight with Bill Guerin of the Devils. I wasn't sure that he wanted to go so I had to wait, wait, wait but then I got caught a bit off-guard. Sometimes that split-second could make a difference in a fight because the first punch is the key. If you get that first lick in, chances are you're going to win the fight. My brother Frank always told me to get the first one in — even if it's a sucker-punch — and go from there.

After I got to Ottawa my point total went up. I had some great opportunities to put the puck in the net and hit a couple of pipes. But I don't really go out to try and score. Mainly, I try to get offensive chances. I pick away and pick away, work hard, forecheck and cause friction out there. It certainly paid off for me in 1992-93.

My penalty minutes went down as well. When I was with Chicago in 1991-92, I was lining up against team's fourth lines and players who had the same role as me. I was up against Bob Probert and Troy Crowder when we played Detroit. Against the North Stars, I had to face Shane Churla and Basil McRae. St. Louis had Darin Kimble and Kelly Chase. The difference now is that teams don't dress two tough guys like they normally would. When they cut down all the fighting and instigating, it changed the game.

In my case, it was a matter of getting more ice time and getting to play in more different situations. When it came down to the crunch for the Blackhawks and who they were going to protect, it was a choice between me and Rob Brown, and they decided to let me go.

I was sad in a way because I had a lot of friends and great teammates there. Going to the Stanley Cup finals with them and not winning put a bit of a damper on things because we had a gruelling series with Pittsburgh.

On the other hand, coming to Ottawa was a blessing in disguise because everything fell into place with my career. The people in Ottawa were great, supportive and knowledgeable about hockey — similar to fans in Chicago. They expected the team to work hard and take a physical stand when necessary. My personal popularity was great. Every time I hit the ice I could feel the intensity of the crowd.

Ottawa fans like a hard-working player. If they think you're willing to pay the price, they'll back you. They pay money to come watch a game that's going to energize and enthuse them, and I felt an obligation to do something for them that they liked. To win the fans' hearts I had to go out and hit, score and, if necessary, fight.

Sometimes you have to know when not to fight. I recall a game we played against the Devils in Ottawa. We were leading 1-0 when Ken Daneyko dropped his gloves and wanted to go. His gloves were off before I even knew what was going on and he squared off and looked me in the eyes. But I knew we had the lead and I figured that we could get a powerplay and be up by two. Sure enough, that's exactly what happened and we had a 2-0 lead going into the second period, which was a good lead for us because I know how hard it is to score goals in this league.

One thing that really bothers me was the constant stories in the Ottawa papers that I didn't do my job physically and that I was trying to play too much of a finesse game. I totally disagree with that and I don't know what player those reporters were watching all season. I had over 25 majors for fighting in 1992-93. I finished all of my checks and I looked people in the eye. I was out there playing hard every night and I went to battle myself most of the time. In retrospect I believe that it was more a case of the reporters not knowing what they were writing about, or just trying to put stuff in the paper.

When the league took on a new direction as regards to fighting and the officiating of the game at the start of the 1992-93 season, I thought it would make a difference. But gradually the referees began slipping away from calling things tight, and by the end of the season, teams were back to putting two or three tough guys in the lineup.

The biggest advantage for a hockey team is to have a guy who can throw them on any given night but who can also play the game. It's a big plus if you can be an effective player on the ice and also fight. It's a hard commodity to come by and the guy who I think does it best is Cam Neely of the Bruins. That guy would go to work and battle every game, but he can also score 50 goals in a season. He's the kind of guy I look up to. The player from the past who I would only compare him to is John Ferguson. John was my idol. He could play the game and also break your jaw. That's the kind of player that I want to be like by the time my career ends.

Chapter 7

DON'T CALL ME "CHARLIE": DAVE MANSON

"My decision to drop the gloves and go will not be decided by the crowd; it will always be on my terms."

It long has been an NHL axiom that you cross Dave Manson at your own risk. This rule-of-thumb suggestion is rooted in the defenseman's Junior days when he starred for Prince Albert and totalled more than 600 penalty minutes over three seasons of Western Hockey League fury.

Through his early National Hockey League career with Chicago, Manson was considered borderline unmanageable and certainly unsuitable for anything remotely close to Lady Byng Trophy consideration. During the 1988-89 season, he amassed 352 penalty minutes and had become the scourge of the Norris Division.

But as the seasons unfolded it became apparent that Dave Manson also could play hockey and do it well. He packed a powerful shot, knew how to patrol his own end of the rink and began putting up offensive numbers that arrested the critics' attention. In short, he became a winner and the Blackhawks' successful playoff performance in 1989 and 1990 was in no small way due to the Prince Albert, Saskatchewan native.

In October 1991, Manson was dealt to the Edmonton Oilers in exchange for Steve Smith. He continued playing well and finished with 79 games under his belt which were good for 15 goals and 32 assists, not to mention 220 penalty minutes.

Unfortunately, Manson's career was bedevilled by two totally unrelated incidents. An on-ice accident resulted in damage to his vocal chords and, while he was able to continue his playing career, he suffered through the 1992-93 season with a barely audible voice. Dave also was the center of a contract squabble with the Oilers, and his name was mentioned in trade rumors as much as any single NHL player. However, by the March 1993 deadline, Manson still was an Oiler and remained so through the rest of the 1992-93 campaign.

Despite his problems, Manson has emerged as one of the most coveted backliners; a veteran who has become one of the true intimidating forces in big-league hockey but who accompanies his rugged play with an artistry that belies his image.

In separate interviews with reporters Dan Carle of Edmonton and Eric Servetah in New York City, Manson details his life and NHL career.

My first taste of high-level competitive hockey came in 1983-84, which was the initial season I spent in the Western [Junior] Hockey League with Prince Albert.

I was 16 years old when I came into the WHL and I knew that I had to establish myself, so I went out and fought because we had four other defensemen who were going to play regularly. I knew my time would come and I would get my ice, so it was a matter of me going up there and establishing myself around the league.

That's what I went out to do and then, in the next season [1984-85], my ice time increased and I got a few goals (8) and a few points (38) and improved even more in my third year (14-34-48).

In 1986-87 I was called up to the Chicago Blackhawks and played 54 games as well as six games for Saginaw in the International League. Chicago is a big market for sports and, in a sense, I was lucky. As important as the Blackhawks are, they were last in the eyes of the fans because of the popularity of the Cubs, Bears, White Sox and Bulls.

People didn't know too much about the Blackhawks except for the fans who came to the games. As for me, people looked at my last name and my past record and, automatically, there was that "Charlie Manson" stuff. When the scouts build you up as a physical player, the fans immediately expect that kind of stuff from you, whether it be fisticuffs or smashing bodychecks. The fights did come and "Charlie Manson" just followed after that.

I wasn't an especially gifted athlete so my route was relatively traditional in that I had to go out and earn my stripes in the best way I could, which was by being aggressive. That was one way for me to do it because we also had defensemen who were going to play all the time, play the power play and, for me, to cut into that ice time, I had to earn my stripes, and playing tough was one way of doing it.

During that first season with the Blackhawks, we had a game at Joe Louis Arena in Detroit and the Red Wings beat us something like 12-0. Our coach, Bob Murdoch, felt it was time for a couple of us to go down to the minors and gain some confidence so they sent me to Saginaw. I played six games down there and played pretty well.

After the sixth game, I was recalled by Chicago and played against the Bruins and Blues. I thought I played pretty well. I tried to get into a fight but nothing really happened and then, after the St. Louis game, Murdoch wanted to send me back down to The I [International League] but [general manager] Bob Pulford stepped in and said, "He's not going back down."

So, I stayed in the NHL, got into a couple more fights and, after that, Murdoch started sitting me out again. Maybe if I had stayed in the minors during the period, I might have gotten lost in the shuffle but here I was still with the big club and, for that, I have to credit Pulford for saving my NHL career.

Craig Berube once said, "Sometimes it's tough when I know I have to fight." The fact of the matter is that there's no question but that the fighters have the toughest job in hockey. The goal-scorers and even the coaches will tell you that because there are people the coaches know they can take advantage of, and if somebody out there is getting pushed around, then I have to go out there and stick up for them.

In some cases that's the right thing to do. However, there comes a point in time when a guy has to stand up for his own rights, too. But if a teammate of yours is the underdog and is in a mismatch, then it's my right to be there and that goes for Craig Berube, Bob Probert or whoever. You have to be there to help out your teammates.

The most penalty minutes I ever got in the NHL was the first year that Mike Keenan coached the Blackhawks, 1988-89. I really didn't know what was expected of me, and then I had a little tiff with Keenan after a couple of games into the season. By that time I already had about 150 minutes due to some misconducts and a couple of things like that.

I asked Keenan, "What do you expect of me?" He answered, "I want you to play hockey." After that, I set my mind to playing hockey and then I had a little incident in Vancouver where I was in jeopardy of being suspended for 14 games because of an altercation, but the league overruled it. After that, things started going my way. I started scoring some points and got some goals and my confidence started to build and things just carried on from there.

Not that I stopped fighting, but I found that a fight interests everybody. Look around the league and you can see the way general managers structure their teams. Every one has the so-called "physical presence" simply because you need it. It's that simple. On the Blackhawks, for instance, they don't want a star like Jeremy Roenick pushed around and beaten up night in and night out. He's the guy who's going to carry them into the playoffs, so a Stu Grimson knows his part in Chicago and he knows when it's time. He's smart enough to realize that.

There are plenty of rough customers in the NHL but I would say that the two toughest guys in the league are Bob Probert and Dave Brown. I've been hit by some good ones including Joey Kocur and Randy McKay, to name two. In every fight I've been hit so it's really a matter of who hits you harder and who you remember.

Sometimes I'm goaded into a fight. But if I'm getting a lot of ice time it doesn't make sense for me to take off after a guy who's playing only five or six shifts a night. That's something that the coaches have tried to explain to me, and it's helped my game. Ronnie Low [Oilers' assistant coach] has said to me, "Act. Don't react." That advice has really helped my game.

My decision to drop the gloves and go will not be decided by the crowd, it will always be on my terms. If someone is out there taking advantage of my teammates, I'm going to be there because if I allow it to happen once, it will happen again in the next game. You have to set a plan to see that they're not going to be able to push around your team. Sometimes if you don't want to, you still really have to do it.

I've been aggressive all my life so even at this point in my career, I can't change my style because I get a few points or a few goals. If I'm not aggressive then I'm not going to be effective for my team. I have to make sure that I'm out there taking the body and bumping and grinding. I get my chances on the power play and I've got a good enough shot that if I can get it away I can score a few goals and keep my confidence up. But I remember what got me here and if I ever forget that, I'll probably be out of the league next year.

I'm an intense kind of guy with a physical presence to go with my personality. If you are an intense person in hockey, the physical part will come. You don't see too many goal-scorers who are real intense guys who bump and grind along the boards. In my case, I realized early on that I wasn't going to be like Ray Bourque, Brian Leetch or other of those finesse types. My target is to use my physical attributes to my advantage and everybody who knows me understands that that's part of my game. But they also know that I can play hockey.

For example, I have talked to my wife quite a bit about the game and she has learned plenty. She knows when it's time for me to play aggressive and she doesn't get too worried about it when a fight does break out because I've been in that kind of situation before. My mom used to have a hard time with that stuff, but it's something that she's gotten through.

Not that the incidents are easy to digest. One of the most publicized was the game in Toronto when I was still with the Blackhawks. It was one of those five-on-five situations that broke out in our end. I didn't pair with anybody because the linesman got one of their guys over to the bench.

It was a case where I was standing there and Denis Savard, who was then with the Blackhawks, was fighting with Gary Leeman. At that time the linesman had told me to go over by the net near the exit gate, and so I did. But they thought I had gone off the ice — which I never did. I just stood by the goal crease and I saw that Leeman was beating up Savard, who was our premier player.

That was a mismatch and I felt I had to be in there. I got in there but the league didn't approve. As far as I'm concerned the league exercised a double-standard and suspended me for 10 games, claiming that I had been off the ice and had then returned to get into the fight. The videotape didn't clearly show me going off the ice. It was a case of them thinking about who I was and therefore punishing me. I got punished more for my reputation than anything else. When I came flying in there, I bumped and hit into the linesman Ron Finn. The collision knocked him down and it got me an additional three games. The league must have figured, "Let's give this guy everything that he could get because he did that to our linesman."

There still are plenty of good fighters in the NHL and Dave Brown is a guy who I respect because he doesn't go out there and look for it, but he's more than willing to go if he's challenged. He's not a cheap-shot guy and he's always been fair. Wendel Clark is another pretty tough kid. There are guys like that who play hard but are not out there cheap-shotting the opposition.

Under Mike Keenan, I had mixed feelings. To be honest, I wasn't very comfortable with my role with Keenan, but he was a coach who made me better. I respect him for that. What I had to do in Chicago was look at where my career was going and decide to play as consistently as possible. That's what I set my mind to doing. I wanted to be the kind of player who would deliver the kind of game my coaches could count on, night in and night out.

I wanted to be a hockey player first and foremost and even though I was cast in a different role, it was important to me to build up my skills as much as possible while at the same time realizing that I still had a role with the club. I wasn't upset with my role in Chicago because I knew that I had to get into the NHL any way I could. I had set my mind to that a long time earlier and that's what I did. But once I started to mature in Chicago, I proved that I also could play hockey, and that's what I've done ever since.

My hockey life changed after I was traded to Edmonton in 1991. From Day One with the Oilers, the coaches looked me in the eye and said, "We expect this, this, this and this from you," and it's been that way ever since. They've never B.S.'d me in Edmonton. It was very easy playing for Ted Green, Ron Low and Kevin Primeau.

The Smythe Division is different from the Norris. The Smythe is more wide open; they let you skate and you don't get the same kind of bump-and-grind that you get in the Norris where a lot of fights take place. Not that there weren't fights in the Smythe, but I didn't go looking for them and when I fought it was on my time, when I was ready.

I've had a few memorable fights, like the one with Scott Stevens. The first fight was just a case of finally having enough, so we dropped the gloves. We started fighting and then the linesman jumped in and Stevens started to gouge at my eyes when we hit the ice. When you have fingers in your eye it's not too pleasant and you'll do anything to stop it. So, I head-butted him a bit. The next time we squared off was in Chicago and Scott was playing for St. Louis. We had a beef at center ice and had a chance to fight each other because the linesman wasn't able to get in between us.

My philosophy on fighting goes like this: I don't want anyone to tell me after a fight that I jumped him. I like to be fair. If you're going to lose a fight, lose fair. If you win, you should win fair. That's the way I see fighting.

If you check fighting tapes you'll see that things have changed since the 1960s and 1970s when guys would just stand back and throw them. The first guy who went down, went down, and the other guy would be the winner. Now you see guys grabbing each other's arms instead of standing back and seeing who really is the toughest guy. Times have changed.

Another thing that's changed is the way some players actually adjust their sweaters for fighting and have the sweaters tied down. I say players should all wear the same type of sweater and they should not allow guys to cut their sleeves off at the elbows. A player like Marty McSorley wears a sweater that's 14 sizes too big so he can win a fight.

The thing is, if one guy is going to do it, everybody wants to do it. You don't want to have one guy with an advantage who can get the better of you, so then you're forced to do the same thing. Maybe that explains why Dave Brown — one of the NHL's best fighters — resorted to taking his jersey off before a fight. He was forced to do it. I'm sure Dave would love to stand back and throw them, too, because he's pretty punishing both ways.

One of the bits of strategy that I've learned over the years is when to turn away from a fight to help your team. During the 1991-92 season I came to the Oilers and they really didn't care if I played tough or not, but they knew I would be there when they needed me. Anyhow, on this night we were playing Winnipeg and I knew what was coming with Shawn Cronin before it even happened. He wanted to fight and I figured that our team could use the power play — with him getting the instigator — instead of me getting into the fight. I was right. Cronin got the penalty; we got the power play, scored and won the game because of it. The thing is, before you fight, you have to read the situation and I'm a lot better at it now than earlier in my career. Now I'm allowing my team to use situations like that as an advantage.

Let's face it, there are times when you have to skate away from incidents and, on the other hand, there are times when you just have to fight. When I do fight, I like to stand back and throw them. But the way things are, guys don't want to get hit so they tie up my right arm and I'm forced to tie up theirs, and that's the way it goes. If a guy gives me a punch, I have to take the punch, and if I have a chance to give one, I have to make sure to capitalize and give it back.

In recent years the league has gone about changing the rules to suit the goal scorers, and I don't think that's such a good idea. The NHL must remember that not everybody is a goal-scorer. There are players who got to the NHL by bumping, grinding and otherwise playing hard. Even the tough guys in the league are hockey players first. They are not goons, not policeman nor any other of that bullshit. They are hockey players primarily and didn't get to the NHL by just fighting. A lot of people like to stereotype them and say they did it with their fists, but a player has to skate, shoot and stickhandle before he can get to the top. That's number one.

My message to the kids is not to worry too much. Sure, it's fun to have a hero and you may idolize a guy like Bob Probert or Dave Brown or that type of guy, but don't try to go out there and be exactly like them in a midget game. That type of game is not there anymore and it won't be fun to try it.

Kids should go out and work hard and learn if they want to make it in the Juniors or the NHL. They have to change with the times.

Chapter 8

THE GRIM REAPER: STU GRIMSON

*"The mental approach to fighting
in hockey is hard to establish
immediately. It's a tricky thing and it
has taken me a long time to work it out.
Fighting can be a very intimidating
thing the more time you seem to spend
on it: preparing for it, worrying about
your opponent. It can be all-consuming."*

*A towering 6-foot-5, 220-pound left wing, Stu Grimson
attended the University of Manitoba before being drafted
by the Calgary Flames in 1985.*

*An eighth-round, 143rd overall pick, the Kamloops,
British Columbia product cut his professional puck teeth
with Salt Lake City in the International League. He
finally emerged in the NHL with Calgary for a single
game in 1988-89. He didn't score a goal in his debut, but
exited with five minutes' worth of penalties.*

*A year later he played three more NHL games while
spending most of the season in Salt Lake. This time his
NHL score sheet read no goals, no assists, no points and
17 penalty minutes.*

*The Flames gave up on him in October 1990 where-
upon he was claimed on conditional waivers by the
Chicago Blackhawks. Teamed with the equally robust
Mike Peluso, Grimson raised the level of the Chicagoans'
thumping ability and won the favor of GM-Coach Mike
Keenan.*

*Perhaps the greatest show of faith by Keenan was the
decision to promote Grimson and Peluso to first-line*

status at various times during the Blackhawks- Penguins Stanley Cup finals of 1992. The strategem didn't exactly reap big dividends but it certainly aroused the media and inspired more than a little controversy.

Otherwise known as "The Grim Reaper," Grimson became a Blackhawk mainstay in 1992-93 while his sidekick Peluso was left unprotected and eventually found himself exiled to the baby Ottawa Senators. Stu was interviewed by reporter Eric Servetah early in the spring of 1993 during a Blackhawks visit to Nassau Coliseum. Additional material was obtained by Chicago reporter Keven Friedman at Chicago Stadium.

As a kid I played a lot of sports. I was into golf at a fairly early age; I enjoyed soccer and played junior high football. In the winter I managed to get in skiing as well.

There were two kids in our family; myself and a younger sister who wasn't overly athletic. She was more interested in the arts, craftwork and stuff like that.

I played Junior hockey for Regina in the Western League. I was fortunate to be in a Junior organization which was very dedicated to educational performance as well as on-ice performance. When I was a 17-year-old Junior I was in the 12th grade and was able to graduate while still playing another two years of Junior hockey.

My first hockey fight in Juniors was quite a learning experience. We were playing the Winnipeg Warriors and this was my first month with the team. The other fellow wasn't a real, tough guy, but he was a middleweight and could hold his own. Of course, I didn't know anything about him when we collided and I just decided to take him on late in the shift. He filled me in royally, and embarrassed me because I was quite a bit bigger than him.

When I played for Regina I was away from home for the first time and on my own while enjoying a pretty high profile position in the community. I kind of walked around with a chip on my shoulder and wanted people to know who I was. It was a real immature phase for me and it got me into a lot of trouble. At this point I did a lot of things that I regretted.

One night, for example, a friend and I had a little too much to drink and we had been partying a little bit and came into contact with another crowd who had been partying as well. For some reason, we took exception to some immaterial and irrelevant thing this group had said about us, and I wound up getting a little over-exuberant about the whole thing. I took a swing at the other guy and ended up pushing him through one of the doors at the party.

I played three years for Regina and then, through a friend, was able to get into the University of Manitoba where I got in a good year-and-a-half of college hockey and also got a pretty good start on my education. I certainly gained a lot by being at the university. For one thing I got to first meet the lady of the family who would become my future in-laws and soon after I met my future wife. The entire family has had a terrific influence on my life and it was through them that I was able to learn a lot more about Christianity, which has become very important in my life.

Before that happened, the Flames had drafted me in 1985 and I even went to their training camp for a week but left it then because I was immature. The Flames still had my rights in 1987 and that's when I went back to their camp and eventually turned pro with the Calgary organization. The Flames assigned me to Salt Lake and that's where my character developed as a player.

Everyone who goes into hockey's minor league system has it in his mind that he has to prove something and I was no different. I believed that I had to prove myself, physically, at the start. Besides, the Flames made it very apparent to me that they wanted a physical presence and I wanted to prove that I could do the job for them, first and foremost.

At the same time, I wanted to prove that I also had playing skills and it was important to me to prove to them and myself that I wouldn't be a liability to the club as a player.

Once in the minors, I discovered that it was easy to get into a fight. There were a lot of guys willing to tangle and I could fill up my dance card just about every night, if I wanted to, because everybody down there is hungry to prove himself.

The mental approach to fighting in hockey is hard to establish immediately. It's a tricky thing and it has taken me a long time to work it out. Fighting can be a very intimidating thing the more time you seem to spend on it: preparing for it, worrying about your opponent. It can be all-consuming. Basically, I go into every game waiting to be ready. If something needs to be attended to, I want to be in a position where I'm ready to respond.

By the same token, I can't be overly aggressive or too finely-tuned to the point where that's all I'm worried about. I've got to be able to go out there and put my anxieties on the shelf and be able to play the game at the same time. If I'm worried about who is on the ice and who is not on the ice and what's going to happen next, I'm not doing the job either offensively or defensively.

What I've boiled it down to is this: if I fight, I fight. If it's going to happen, it's going to happen. At one time, earlier in my career, it was a very consuming thing that was very emotionally draining. But I kind of got to the point where I said, "Okay, worst-case scenario, I go and fight!"

So, what is it? At the most, it's 30 seconds of work; a 30-second sporadic instance and that's all it's going to be. By boiling it down to an isolated little incident, it takes a lot of pressure off me.

After a while, I was able to categorize fighters since different players have different tendencies. Some like to go and bomb while others like to tie up their opponent. Then there are those who have a power hand — a left or a right, it's different for each guy — and if you face one of those, the smart thing is to tie up his power hand.

In my experience, Dave Brown has been the heaviest hitter I've encountered, with Joey Kocur right up there. Technically, Bob Probert ranks among the most skilled fighters partly because he's a threat with both hands and is certainly one of the busiest fighters and one of the hardest to defend against. Going up against Probert, I have to be sure I'm staying busy and I don't want to find myself where I'm trying to get away from his punch and have my head down or something like that because he'll just overwhelm me. Bob is very quick in responding to a weakness which is why it's good to take away his power hand. He's better with his right than his left, and he has a tendency to throw his right more often, so I want to stay away from that and keep busy with my right if I can. After that no brain surgery is needed.

Looking back, I would have to say that the first time I fought Probert was the toughest. Part of that had to do with reputation because I had spent a lot of time hearing about fighters and the stories about him had already become legendary. Perhaps I went into the fight more psyched about him than somebody else; which is not to say that Probert wasn't worthy of the heavyweight title people bestowed on him. In any event our first fight was a fairly long one, pretty well a back-and-forth, punch-for-punch event that was probably a draw.

It's all business on the ice. Certainly, I don't look forward to fighting with a player on another team with whom I have a certain personal relationship. But when it comes to whether I have to fight or not, the bottom line is that it's all business out there and friendships are forgotten on the ice. It's a difficult thing to do but it has to be done if we're competing at the highest level of our intensity. These types of confrontations happen and I'll give you an example. Bobby McGill and I are very good friends going back to the days when we were teammates in Chicago. After he got traded to San Jose, we got into a fight. But that was perfectly natural because we're both physical players. No negative feelings are harbored by either side. We understand the situation without even having to say anything.

I don't think I've ever been involved in a fight where someone has taken a cheap shot at me or tried to gouge my eyes or pull my hair or anything like that. Players at the NHL level are experienced enough to understand that when a fight is over, it's over. We have an unwritten rule that after the ref and linesmen have broken up a fight, there are no cheap shots, dirty tricks or anything like that because those things can come back and haunt you.

No doubt about it, hockey has changed to the extent that fighting majors are down and you don't see bench-clearing brawls anymore, or five or six fights at the end of a hockey game after the score has been decided. Personally, I don't think anyone wants to see an all-out brawl because that's when people get seriously hurt. Nobody wants to see the last three minutes of a game go on for half an hour.

The way hockey is now there are fewer players running around looking for trouble. It goes back to clubs once having two or three players on each team playing that role where now one guy can handle it, and that's me on the Blackhawks.

In any event, the effects of hockey fighting have been exaggerated by the media in the sense that you never see anybody paralyzed after a hockey fight. But if the critics really want to be concerned, they should take a serious look at football. I mean they've got some real problems with that sport; young men having their lives completely changed because of the nature of the sport. You never see that in a hockey game.

There's a fair amount of talking on the ice and sometimes it's meaningless. I can remember a game against Winnipeg when I was having words with Randy Carlyle and Tie Domi intervened. Frankly, I didn't catch what he was saying but what I said back to him didn't make a lot of sense either.

There are occasions when I'm probably more vocal than I should be, but I don't get too abusive. On the other hand, if someone on the opposition takes a good hit from one of our players, I may let them know that he is coming again, or something like that. But I don't get into those personal conflicts, talking trash with other players, because that doesn't serve any purpose.

The worst injury I ever suffered from a fight came when I was playing with the Flames and Dave Brown was with Edmonton. Actually, we fought a couple of times, the first time being when I was called up from the minors. I fought him once in Edmonton and did pretty well and then we returned to Calgary and he got the better of me there. With a series of left hands, he broke my cheekbone in three places. It was pretty quick and I think he was motivated because I had done pretty well against him in Edmonton. In any event, he just skated straight over to me off the face-off and said, "Let's go!", so we dropped the gloves and went at it. As a result, I was out for five weeks and the doctor had to put a stainless steel pin in my cheek.

When we had that fight there still was a great rivalry between Edmonton and Calgary. I still have a lot of respect for Dave because he is a hard hitter, a good fighter, a stand-back-and-throw guy, but the secret to doing well against him is to grab hold of his left arm. If you can't do that, you're in trouble.

Another one to watch is Joey Kocur who I fought a couple of times in Junior hockey and once in the pros when he was with Detroit. He's pretty fair with his left hand but his right is his power hand. Also, Joey is pretty good at keeping out of range and keeping his right arm free.

Kelly Chase is another smart fighter, technically very good but not the kind who is going to kill anybody in the heavyweight class. You rarely see him get hurt.

I had a fight with Dennis Vial when he was with the Red Wings. It was during an exhibition game before the 1992-93 season. Dennis is a real competitor who can both throw and take good punches, which is a tremendous asset. A lot of fighters — Vial, Tie Domi among them — are underrated because of the strength of their chins. I've thrown some of my best stuff at guys like that and they just took it and kept on going. I have a lot of respect for Dennis and Tie and I know that they have a tremendous advantage being able to take punches the way they do.

The fight with Vial was a good and long fight which took a lot of endurance and adrenaline. We both fought and extended ourselves beyond what we thought we could. All of a sudden, when the altercation was over and we were winding down, I began thinking about what had taken place and I realized how tired I was. It only goes to show you how far adrenalin can carry you — much beyond what you normally would accomplish.

It's either the fear of being hit or the fear of being humiliated that gets you past the point of fatigue. In this particular case, the fight was at Joe Louis Arena in a game that was less meaningful because it was an exhibition. What I find now is that I get less and less involved in pre-season fights. I no longer feel a need to make myself known or get myself established. People know that I'm capable of holding my own.

I don't like fighting smaller guys like Domi. Most bigger players feel the same way. Lots of times when I go out to fight, I do it to give my team a lift, especially if we're not playing too well. But if I go out and fight a smaller guy, it doesn't do a lot because A) if I win, I'm beating a smaller guy; B) I'm beating a guy I should have beaten; C) if he happens to land one on me and looks better than me, it works against me. So, from a technical or tactical standpoint, fighting a little guy doesn't do a lot for me.

When I did fight Domi, it was a good one. He didn't throw a lot of punches and I threw probably a half-dozen, so it wasn't terribly long as fights go. It was a case where Tie had me by the jersey and was kind of holding me and wasn't returning a lot. Meanwhile, I wasn't able to get at him for some reason. He must have had my right arm tied up and the fight ended when I pulled his sweater up over his head and the ref and linesmen jumped in. What I learned is that Tie has a supremely hard head and he takes punches as well as anybody I have ever fought.

Ted Green once said, "A lot of guys could fill Tie Domi's skates but not many could fill his helmet," which is a good quote. I don't think it has a lot to do with his chin or jaw structure, if you're talking technical. I know that guys with fleshier faces have a better time taking punches and that seems to be it. Vial has that round head and the two of them, Vial and Domi, have a lot of similarities when it comes to the cranium and chin.

Another tough one is Mick Vukota. He's a big, strong guy for whom I have a lot of respect. He's balanced on his skates and when you have that and you're well-developed in your upper body, you can hurt someone. I saw him give Al Secord a good beating before Al retired. That had to be a highlight for Mick because Al had been one of the NHL's premier fighters.

Vukota has a body slam that doesn't really bother me. Everybody has his different style, but if Mick is more comfortable with getting his shots in and then taking you down to the ice, well, that's a percentage way of fighting. Guys like that don't get hurt and, consequently, they probably last longer.

Even though my right is my power hand, I don't mind throwing my left and am comfortable enough with it to use it on quite a few occasions. But I feel better with my right.

Sometimes fighting interferes with my hockey. An example was the 1993 All-Star Game at Montreal. I was supposed to represent the Blackhawks in the Skills Competition for hardest shot. I had the fourth-best rating for hardest shot in the Campbell Conference and I was looking forward to participating. But in our last game before the All-Star break, we played against the Red Wings and, near the end of the game, I got into a pushing match with Gerard Gallant. I gave him a shot and he came back at me and I pushed him again and he came back only this time taking me by surprise because he dropped his gloves.

I dropped my gloves and he threw a punch. I don't think he intentially meant to gouge me but he got a finger in my eye. What I remember was having my head down and, all of a sudden, bringing it up to try to get at him and I was unable to see. It was a sensation where light was hurting my eye and it was badly tearing. I went over to the penalty box but still couldn't see that well.

After the game I put some ice on the eye and then the doctor examined it but found no damage to the retina or the surface of the eye. It just had a bruise and by the next day it was swollen and totally shut. I couldn't see out of it at all. Both the doctors and I decided that it didn't make any sense for me to go to the All-Star Game under those circumstances because I was also having a lot of problems with balance. When you have just one eye, you don't judge depth very well and you're a bit off-center. I was very disappointed that I couldn't participate but it will only serve to make me try that much harder next time around.

I don't know if I would have been able to shoot the puck as fast as [the eventually winner] Al Iafrate who got it up to 105 miles per hour. I had a 97 mph shot, but since then I've lengthened my stick and tested my pattern of swing. Consequently, I've increased my shot by a couple of miles per hour.

During my NHL career I've worked with some good fellows, one of them being Mike Peluso who teamed with me on the Blackhawks until he was picked up by Ottawa in 1992. In Chicago, Mike and I shared equal duties although he probably played more than I did. Peluso is a warrior who straps on a lot of intensity and emotion before a game. Mike Keenan expected both of us to bring that to the locker room. We were not only there to play but to spark the team as well and get involved in as much contact as we could.

Keenan never communicated anything verbally about going out on the ice and getting into a fight to Mike or myself. We knew how the game was going and we were bright enough to know that there were certain instances where we were expected to assert ourselves that way. When the team was down and we were having liberties taken against our team, Mike was very sensitive to these things. He liked us to carry the tempo physically. So, if we were being abused, either myself or Peluso — or both of us — would see ourselves on the ice against a guy like Probert a little more. We were left to assume from that that we were expected to get involved.

It was a fun part of our job and part of our responsibility. Some nights it may have been [done] begrudgingly because we may not have played a lot on that particular night and it's tough to get involved when that situation arises. It's difficult to get off the bench stone cold, maybe having played only one shift or two prior to that — especially when it's late in the game — and then get involved. On those nights I would feel a little unsure of myself.

I felt comfortable working alongside Peluso because I knew that when a situation arose, one of us should get involved in it and a lot of the times he would. And I'm sure that he felt the same way. I never felt that I was in a situation where it was just me and only me and I would be the only player who had to go.

The scariest thing I've seen in terms of a hockey fight took place in the minors in a bout between Mark Janssens and Martin Simard. Martin was able to grab Janssens underneath the trousers and just kind of pull his feet out from underneath him. Janssens' helmet flew off and his head hit the ice without any protection. Janssens swallowed his tongue at that point and his jaw locked. The trainer had to go in and break his teeth and dislodge his tongue since he was suffering convulsions. It was frightening for everybody out there witnessing the episode.

Janssens spent some time in the hospital and even more in rehabilitation waiting for a blood clot to dissipate in his brain. That was a scary time. That was the bad news. The good news was that he came out of it and he played just a few weeks after that.

In terms of my feelings, scoring goals is still the fun part of the game for me. I fully understand that by the nature of my role, I may not be given the goal-scoring responsibility very often, but when I'm given the opportunity, I like to provide whatever I can, even a goal or two. But when all is said and done, the physical part will always be an aspect of my game that has to be apparent. The fact remains that my physical abilities and strength from an enforcer's standpoint are my biggest asset. I have to be able to push myself and be a sound defensive player and good when I'm in the offensive zone. I need to be able to provide contact and good forechecking when I'm on the offense.

Hockey isn't my only interest in life. I've kept up with my college studies and do correspondence courses during the summer. I'm majoring in Economics, heading for a Bachelor of Arts degree which I want to complete before I'm finished playing. Then, I hope to go on to some post-graduate work, depending on what kind of things are happening at the time.

Chapter 9

THE CHIEF OF WASHINGTON: CRAIG BERUBE

"My role hasn't changed from the Philadelphia days. I still do the same things — hit, play hard, go to the net and stir things up. If I have to fight, I fight, but I try to play tough, intense hockey out there."

One of the most durable of the NHL ice policemen, Craig Berube has been an asset to every club for which he has played. Nicknamed "The Chief," the native of Calahoo, Alberta has skated for Philadelphia, Toronto, Calgary and, most recently, Washington during a seven-year big-league career. He actually had been dealt from Philadelphia to Edmonton in 1991, but was sent to Toronto before ever playing a regular season game for the Oilers.

Gregarious and articulate, Berube broke into organized hockey with Kamloops of the Western Hockey League and later played for New Westminster and Medicine Hat. The Flyers signed him as a free agent in March 1986 and he made his NHL debut in the 1986-87 campaign.

Until 1989-90, Berube was like a yo-yo going up and down between Philadelphia and Hershey of the American League. He finally clicked with the Flyers and became a Spectrum hero until he was acquired by the Maple Leafs in 1991-92.

Although Maple Leaf Gardens fans took Berube to their hearts in 1991-92, the Leafs traded him to Calgary in January 1992 in a mammoth deal that sent Doug Gilmour to Toronto.

*As a member of the Flames, Berube helped preside
over the club's renaissance in 1992-93. But at the start of
1993-94 he was skating for the Capitals.*

*"The Chief" has not lost any of his zest for battle but
maturity has made him a more intelligent player and
one who should be skating in the NHL for several more
seasons.*

*Craig has developed into one of the most respected
fighters among his peers. He fights fair, utilizing strength
and incredibly quick right hands. "The Chief," who also
was featured in the original* Bad Boys, *provided fresh
insights into his profession during an interview with
reporter Eric Servetah at the Long Island Marriott Hotel
prior to a game against the New York Islanders.*

I've had to change my style somewhat now that the NHL has altered
its fighting rules. I'm able to play the game now and my penalty
minutes are down. I haven't had as many fights.

Not that I approve of everything that the league has done because
I have found that guys have gotten away with a lot of stuff out there
and the referees have generally not done anything about it. That's
the worst thing about the way the rules have been changed.

Sure, it's great to play and play the game hard, and if a fight breaks
out, that's the way it is, but nowadays guys get away with stuff that
you used to be able to go out and handle. Now it's tough to take care
of that stuff without getting kicked out of a game.

Start a fight now and you get kicked out of the game. That
has changed the game a lot, and for the worst in my mind. Players
are being run from behind and have been sticking each other and they
get away with it because there's no respect in the league anymore.

The trade from Philadelphia to Edmonton was disappointing, but
I went into camp with my head up. I had a few fights in exhibition,
one of which was a good one with my old pal, Todd Ewen. Things
were looking good, but I got caught in a deal going to Toronto. I
knew that Edmonton was going to make a trade to get rid of Glenn
Anderson and Grant Fuhr and that Toronto needed some toughness,
so Glen Sather ended up throwing me into the deal.

I enjoyed playing in Toronto because I got a lot of ice there and
proved to everybody that I could play and score some goals. With
the Leafs, I was playing the best hockey of my life, plus I was fighting
— doing it all — but I would up getting caught in another big trade,
going to Calgary.

Getting traded three times in a year — from Philadelphia to
Edmonton, even though I didn't play any regular season games for
the Oilers, and then to Toronto and finally Calgary — was tough.
But I got to enjoy Calgary right away because I got to play.

My role hasn't changed from the Philadelphia days. I still do the same things — hit, play hard, go to the net and stir things up. If I have to fight, I fight, but I try to play tough, intense hockey out there.

When I do fight, I like to tie up the other guy's punching arm while throwing with my other arm as fast as I can. I try to throw them fast to keep the guy off-balance. I fight to the other guy's style. I try to learn about my opponent's style and adjust to do something that I know will be effective.

Like any other fighter, I don't like to go down. If I do get floored, I try to get up and keep going and do the best I can. If I can get up, I will, and I'll stay in there.

With some fighters, you have to be very aware of their assets. Take Tie Domi, for instance. If I want to fight defensively against him, I have to worry about his left because he throws a big left haymaker. So, I'll start throwing the rights quickly and know that eventually he's going to come back with the big left. If I'm smart, he will miss with the left and I'll continue on with the rights. Another thing about him is that you can't really hurt Tie. You throw a lot of punches and hit him but you're not really hurting him and, then, all of a sudden you get whacked with his big left. I have to watch him coming in with that punch.

It's tough for me to throw uppercuts against a smaller guy like him. I'd be coming right into his range by throwing an uppercut, and then he'd really be able to hit me. So I try to stay back and hit him with straight rights.

I took up boxing when I was a youngster playing Junior hockey. Since then, I've boxed every summer for training and still do it because it keeps me in good shape. It also helps my fighting in that it keeps my hands fast and keeps my senses together.

Before every game, as a precautionary measure, I tie my jersey down. If my jersey would come completely off during a fight, then I wouldn't tie it down. But since it can get stuck sometimes over my head, it's better to have it secured.

I've tried the Dave Brown technique of taking the jersey completely off before fighting, but my shirt tends to get caught going over my head and I don't like that feeling. So I decided to forget that and keep it tied down all the time.

I was lucky in Calgary having Ronnie Stern as a teammate. He's a really tough guy and was great to play with. He hits hard and stands in there with everybody. He's solid, skates well, dumps the puck in, hits guys and backed me up. Matter of fact, we backed each other up and that's why I enjoyed having him on my side.

Every training camp there are new tough guys to contend with in terms of people wanting to make the big team. My theory is that if they're going to take my job, then they're going to take my job, but they have to beat me to take my job. But in training camp, September

1992, our new coach then, Dave King, didn't allow fighting in training camp so nobody had a chance to dethrone me and I didn't feel any pressure from the younger guys.

Hey, I've had a long amount of experience in fighting. When I played in Juniors in the Western Hockey League, I used to fight heavyweights like Ken Baumgartner and Rudy Poeschek. Guys like them were on almost every team and I used to have a lot of good-square-off-and-adjust-your-sleeves kind of fights. People didn't back down then and it didn't matter who you were, they fought you.

Me, I like to square off when I fight. I want to stand back and fight with a guy and, to tell you the truth, I don't think I've ever jumped anybody. It's not necessary for me to annihilate an opponent; I don't think it's that important. I like to win a fight but getting out of there without getting hurt and doing well is the most important thing. I don't think I've had any great victories or anything like that, but just getting real keyed up and doing well enough to get the victory is what it's all about.

Before a fight I don't do too much talking, although I did a lot when I was new to the NHL. But not anymore. For me to fight, I just have to go out and play hard, hard, hard, and make the other guys want to fight me. That's what I want to happen. I don't go up to the other guys and say, "Look, I want to fight." I don't do that anymore. I just go out and play really hard and, if a fight comes, I'm ready.

Every so often I've heard the suggestion that coaches tell tough guys to go out and fight but nobody ever told me to go out and fight. For the most part, we know when we have to do it. I've always known when I've had to fight so that's probably why I haven't been told.

Both Mike Keenan and Paul Holmgren helped me a lot. Keenan gave me a chance to play when I was young and he taught me how to go out and win. He taught everybody how to win and play hard. Paul Holmgren also gave me a chance to play and even more of a chance to prove that I was a good hockey player. Both were good coaches.

We all want to become better players and my formula has been to work hard every day in practice. I practice skating, puckhandling and stuff like that. You just have to keep doing it and doing it and try to get better. The more you play, the better you get.

My advice for guys coming up who play tough is to make themselves noticed. You have to go out and do something like getting into a fight to make yourself noticed. If you're not noticed, you won't stay, and if you're noticed, it doesn't matter what else you do — that's points for you and you'll stay up. The best thing to do is get at it right away and play hard. If you play hard enough, you're going to get into fights and that will get you noticed.

Most coaches understand our roles. Dave King liked me to play hard and, if I did, then he let me play. He knew I had a job to do, fighting-wise, sometimes, and that was fine with him. He played

Ronnie Stern and I more when we were playing hard and he sat guys who weren't playing hard. It didn't matter who you were and that's what I liked, because if you're not playing hard, you're not helping the team. He gave guys who worked hard a chance to play.

In an article written by George Johnson of the *Calgary Sun*, Dave King once said of my game: "Chief's demanding on himself and those around him. I like that. He's a competitive person. I like that too. We've got him working with a weight vest, trying to improve his quickness and agility. He's receptive to things like that."

Personally, I think I'm capable, skill-wise, of scoring 15 goals in a season. I've gotten the chances but I just haven't put them in. My hockey is more disciplined than before and I'm not taking bad penalties. I try to stay as focused as possible on the ice and keep calm. I don't get as many penalty minutes as I used to, so I'm always conscious of making a bad play and getting called.

The Smythe Division [now called the Pacific] has had a lot of tough guys over the years: Marty McSorley, Gino Odjick, Tie Domi, Louie DeBrusk. Lots of them can really fight and, because there are some keen rivalries, there's a lot of action.

Mind you, I loved the Patrick Division and I loved playing for the Flyers. And now I'm back east with Washington. I can't change the past and I can't change the future. I play where they like me to play and I'm happy.

Every year, some new, young fighters come along and one of them is Louie DeBrusk of Edmonton. He's tough and likes to grab and throw. He's a strong kid who knows his job and tries to do it every night. There was a stretch during the season where Louie had dropped the gloves in eight of 10 games, and we decided to square off. Louie may have been in a groove up until that point, but in this match I clearly came up as the winner.

Edmonton has another good one in Shayne Corson. He gets in tight and moves quick. He throws uppercuts and comes over with some. He's got quick hands and he's a tough guy. He fights when he has to and he's a good player. The thing with Corson is that he can't be going out and fighting all the time since he's too good a player. He has to fight only when the time is right. He knows what to do and he does it well.

When I was younger, I used to prepare for a fight before a game but I don't do that anymore. Now I prepare for the hockey game and what I have to do to be successful. I don't think about having to fight this guy or that guy. If it's going to happen, it's going to happen.

It's like when we play Winnipeg and Tie Domi is on the other side. I just go out and hit him hard and if we fight, we fight. I'm not worried about it. I don't mind trading punches with Domi. I've fought him three times now, twice when he was a Ranger and once since he became a Jet. I've found that I don't have to worry about his left and trying to stop it although I admit he is tough and won't back down.

There are lots of tough guys around. I remember when I still was with Philadelphia and we had Jeff Chychrun and Tony Horacek. They were good hitters, but Troy Crowder of the Devils did some damage to them in three separate incidents. We had a home-and-home series, and Troy had beaten Tony in New Jersey the day before. So now we were in the Spectrum and we were losing the game with the Devils, so I had to go out and take on Crowder. The thing I remember most about this, was that my right hand at the time was really banged up and Troy had been on a roll with the fighting. I had a job to do and I had no choice but to spark the team and do my job. Troy landed the first couple of shots, but I got inside and I threw the last nine punches of the fight, landing a couple.

Bob Probert of the Red Wings is real big and strong and tough. He has no fear. Once he gets his gear off and comes after you, he's tough to fight, especially when you have nothing to grab. Many years ago I fought him and I did pretty well because his jersey stayed on but, when it comes off, it's trouble. Once in a more recent fight, he got his stuff off and I was just trying to swing. He was swinging and we were twirling around and I fell.

After that fight, we had another and I caught him with a couple coming in and then he hit me with a few when he came in. We threw a couple more at each other and then we fell. They were a couple of good fights, but I'll tell you what — Bob Probert is tough to beat. He can take a punch better than anybody in the entire league. I've hit him probably as hard as I could hit him and it doesn't even hurt him. He's tough and honest. If you want to fight, he's ready to go and he's fair about it.

I've had a few with Marty McSorley. He's big, strong and tries to maul you and wrestle. We once fought in Los Angeles in 1992-93, and he hit me a bunch of times behind the head — but he was trying to put on a little bit of a show for the fans. Marty is a good fighter and when he goes, he's always ready. He likes to punch and pull and keep you all wrapped up and, in that sense, he's a different kind of fighter. Marty also wears that oversized jersey, and it makes it difficult to get a good grip on him.

In my mind Dave Brown is the best. Dave could kill you. He throws that big left and all I can say is that I'm glad that I know him and we're friends.

Chapter 10

THE CHICAGO CRUSHER: DARIN KIMBLE

"I got into the first fight I ever had in hockey, swinging for about half a minute. When it was over, the crowd went crazy and I thought to myself, 'Well, this could be the job for me.'"

Like so many of the scrappy National Hockey League individuals who display an old-time Canadian spirit, Darin Kimble has the rugged mark of a Western Canadian. Born in Lucky Lake, Saskatchewan, he learned his stickhandling trade in such renowned precincts as Brandon, Manitoba, Calgary, Alberta and Prince Albert, Saskatchewan.

A 6-foot-2, 205-pound right wing, Kimble was drafted by the Quebec Nordiques on their fifth pick (66th overall) in the 1988 NHL Entry Draft and played 26 big league games in 1988-89, his rookie season. The Nordiques also had him hone his skills at Halifax of the American League where he played 39 games that season.

For the following two years, he bounced back and forth between Quebec and Halifax. The Nordiques eventually dealt Kimble to the St. Louis Blues in February 1991 for Herb Raglan, Tony Twist and Andy Rymsha.

In June 1992, he was dealt to Tampa Bay with Steve Tuttle, Rob Robinson and Pat Jablonski for future considerations. Darin never played for the Lightning. In September 1992, the Boston Bruins obtained him from Tampa Bay, but he eventually wound up with Chicago at the start of 1993-94 season.

Before Kimble could make a mark with the Bruins, he
was involved in a terrible auto accident which nearly
killed him. At the impact, Kimble's right hand smashed
through the windshield, leaving major damage that
required extensive surgery.

"I'm a physical player," said Kimble following his
hospitalization, "and I've got to be banging. I've got to
take care of my teammates. That's how I've always
played the game. I'm not going to change."

Kimble underwent rehabilitation and finally returned
to the Bruins' lineup in December 1992. "When I first got
out of the hospital," he recalled, "I thought it could be all
over. If my hand wasn't going to be good, then I couldn't
play."

Resolute, Kimble made it back to the bigs. In an
interview with reporter Brian McDonough at Boston
Garden, Darin described his climb from the kids' ranks
to the NHL.

I grew up in a little town of 300 people, so at any given time we only
had eight or so guys playing on the local hockey team. That meant
I got a lot of ice time and scored some goals. I was big for my age
and that proved to be an asset in the sense that things went pretty
well for me.

Off the ice, I was a happy-go-lucky person who was friends with
everybody. At times, in school, I was a bit of a troublemaker but I
never did anything too serious like fighting a lot. As a matter of fact,
I hardly fought at all.

As a kid, I admired Guy Lafleur more than any other big-league
player. He was with the Montreal Canadiens at the time and every
Saturday night I'd watch them on television. I was also a fan of
Bobby Nystrom when he played for the New York Islanders. I liked
his "tough-as-nails" style of play. No question: Nystrom inspired the
brand of game that I play today. Nystrom did all the dirty work and
was instrumental in the Islanders' success.

It wasn't until I reached the age of 16, playing Tier II in Swift
Current, Saskatchewan, that I began to play a rougher brand of
hockey. It was then that I got into the first fight I ever had in hockey,
swinging for about a half a minute. When it was over, the crowd
went crazy and I thought to myself, "Well, this could be a job for
me." I've done it all the time ever since and I've always liked it. It
never bothered me. In Juniors I fought Tony Twist about 16 times a
year. In our first fight he broke my nose but, overall, we came out
about even.

When I came up to Quebec in 1988-89 it was good for me because
I was a young kid and there was an opportunity. I felt I had to make

a name for myself and the best way to make a name for myself, in my case, was fighting. At that time the Nordiques were always losing and I was always trying to do something to spark the team, so I got into a lot of fights and got my name around the league.

The first NHL fight I remember was against Perry Anderson who played for the New Jersey Devils. He was a hard-skating, tough customer and I recall that it wasn't much of a fight — more a wrestling kind of thing. After that I fought Dave Maley, also with the Devils, and that was a pretty good one.

My most memorable fight was with Troy Crowder, who was another Devil, and who had established quite a reputation after fighting Bob Probert and doing very well against him. I still think Probert is the toughest guy in the NHL and he's been around so long. Not too many guys beat him. Ask around — they'll tell you that he's ranked number one and rightly so. I fought him once and didn't do well.

I understand that some people criticize fighting, but my view is that it gets the fans involved. They pay a pretty good price for a ticket and if a fight is going to get them standing up and cheering, then it's good for them.

Fighting also keeps the sticks down. The skill guys like Mario Lemieux, Adam Oates — people like that — won't get run at if there's someone on their team to protect them.

Of course, you don't want to fight if you're going to get your club in trouble, and by that I mean, nowadays, they're calling more instigator penalties. If you get an instigator, you're hurting your team so you have to watch yourself and not hurt your club with that kind of penalty.

The media play a big role in creating the image of a tough player. You can see what happened in New York with Tie Domi. He's a tough kid and I have nothing against him. He's a small person but he'll fight anybody. The only thing I don't like about Domi is that he always has something to say. He's always in the paper saying how tough he is and how he wants to fight guys and that. He just gets himself in trouble by doing that.

You don't hear guys like Dave Brown and Bob Probert saying how tough they are. But Domi was in the paper saying he wanted to fight Bob Probert and then Probert went in there and beat him up. If someone like Domi keeps going to the papers saying he wants to beat guys up, he makes himself look like a fool when he gets beaten up. I think Tie learned a lesson and will keep his mouth shut in the future.

There are a lot of tough players in the league, and Randy McKay is one of them. McKay is not a very big person, but he's tough. He can play the game and get you a bunch of goals. Randy fought a lot over the last two seasons and he reminds me of Bob Probert. He may not be quite as tough as Bob, but he always comes to play and he does both parts of the game.

Another guy I respect is Craig Berube. He's a tough guy who's always involved in the game. He doesn't lose too many fights and he's been around for a couple of years. But the biggest reason I respect Craig is his ability to fight fair. If a guy isn't fair about his fights, then I'll have no respect for them. I haven't dealt with Gino Odjick, but I've heard that he jumps players once in a while.

Lots of players get stuck with labels and they stick. I've been labeled a fighter and it's going to stick with me. There are dirty and cheap fighters. If a guy jumps somebody from behind — or suckers somebody — that's not fair fighting. I'd rather just see two guys stop, drop their gloves and stand back and see who the best person is; there's nothing cheap about that. If someone has to go around suckering guys, he isn't that tough.

Injuries are a part of the business. Over the years I've had a couple of broken noses, a broken hand and a couple of broken knuckles, but they have all healed.

The way the NHL has changed its rules enforcement, a player obviously will not be able to just sit on the bench and then go out and fight. In the old days, you might be expected to just go out on the ice and fight but it's not going to work that way. You've got to be able to play the game now, and if you're not able to play the game, you're not going to be around.

I've felt pressure because I know what my job is and lately we don't know if the league is just going to say, "Bang! Everyone gone!" I hope that doesn't happen, but I don't know what they're going to do. After all, that's my job they're talking about so, if they kick it [fighting] out, I'm gone. Definitely there's pressure.

Being a fighter certainly isn't the easiest job in the world and I wouldn't tell children to go out and just be a fighter because it has its hazards. You get a lot of broken noses, your hands get all cracked up and all that.

As for myself, I want to be remembered as a person who came to play every night. I want to be known as an honest person who wasn't jumping other players from behind or cheap-shotting people — nothing like that. I hope fans remember me as an honest person who came to play every night.

III

NOT-SO-LITTLE
TOUGH GUYS

Chapter 11

HIS MIDDLE NAME IS HARD WORK: KRIS KING

"When I try to hit someone, I don't think about not hitting them hard enough to hurt, but I'd be devastated if I actually did hurt somebody."

Originally scouted and signed by the Detroit Red Wings, Kris King was a minor figure in the Motor City organization until he was dealt to the New York Rangers in 1989.

Under coach Roger Neilson, King developed into a pestiferous and eminently effective checking forward. In 1990-91, he reached a career high 11 goals and 14 assists for 25 points in 72 games. He also scored twice in six playoff games.

Neilson and King formed a strong bond and in 1991-92 Kris was a factor in the Rangers' march to the President's Trophy for the best overall record in the league. He played 79 games over the regular season and 13 playoff games during which he scored four goals and an assist, admirable for a defensive left wing.

King's hustle, chatter and ability to disarm the enemy were qualities that seemed to ensure a long career on Broadway, but the Rangers' slothful start in 1992-93 caused general manager Neil Smith to make changes. In one sweeping move, King and Tie Domi were dealt to the Winnipeg Jets for Ed Olczyk. Significantly, the Rangers plummeted out of the playoffs after the trade whereas the

*Jets regrouped and pulled themselves into a playoff berth.
A few weeks later — after Neilson was removed as coach
— Roger admitted that he opposed the trading of King.
    At 5-foot-11, 212 pounds, Kris packs a wallop when he
connects with bodychecks and can find the net from time
to time. He is just now reaching the prime of his career.
    Kris was twice interviewed for this segment. The first
such encounter was handled by reporter Rita Gelman
when King was new to the Rangers. An updated interview
was handled by Reg Jenkins and John Ploszay in Winnipeg.*

I grew up in a small town where there were only about 900 people and there are only about 300 more now. It was a bit northeast of Thunder Bay, Ontario, quite a ways up North. The winters were long so there was very little to do but play hockey. My mom and dad always took us to the rink, mostly by snowmobile, because the roads would be covered by snow.

My first position as a hockey player was goalie. I played between the pipes until I was about nine years old, and one day I just decided to leave the nets and try to play up front. I got a couple of goals and found that it was a lot more fun than just standing around for the whole game. So, I moved up front and was pretty good; not a great skater but able to score a fair amount.

If we weren't playing at the rink, we were playing on the road or on the lakes and I grew up watching the Maple Leafs on television. I always wanted to play in the NHL — for the Leafs. One year Darryl Sittler, who was a Toronto star, came to speak at a banquet and really grabbed my eye, because he was such a nice guy. Meeting someone like Sittler reinforced my desire to be in the NHL. I was just a kid who loved the game and wanted to play in front of everybody.

My first experience with organized hockey came when we moved to Gravenhurst, Ontario when I was 13. Our teams would travel to such places as Toronto and other cities. I wasn't very big then; not even 100 pounds and I got pushed around a bit at first but I started putting on weight when I got to be about 17. When I got up to the Junior A level with Peterborough I began worrying about my conditioning.

Until I reached Peterborough, I had never had a fight on the ice. The first time I remember fighting in Junior I kept my gloves on because I didn't know better. It was an awakening experience for me, to say the least.

When I played for Peterborough, the toughest guy in the Ontario League was Rick Tocchet. He's become a great scorer, but when he played Junior he was one of the tougher guys. Then there was Bob Probert, and I don't have to tell you about him. The Ontario League has always been known for its tough players and there was a fair share when I was there.

My first big fight in Junior hockey took place in an exhibition game against a guy on the Guelph Platers named Greg Royce. I was 17 and he was about 19. It all started when he pushed me behind the net. We kind of looked at each other and he dropped his gloves and started beating on me. I still had my gloves on and I took a few punches until I finally realized that I couldn't punch a guy and hurt him with my gloves still on, and that lesson stayed with me.

With Peterborough, I learned that the team had a special chemistry and each fellow had his role. I realized that if I was going to be drafted, the only way I'd be noticed would be by playing a tough, two-way game. The physical part of my game was the key.

In my draft year, I was rated in the eighth round and Washington picked me — in the fourth round. That was quite a surprise on account of the earlier ratings, but the Capitals needed some toughness because Scott Stevens was their main enforcer and they wanted him to play a more offensive role and stay out of the penalty box. They gambled on me, hoping that I would develop.

I went to three training camps with Washington and always went back to the Juniors because I had eligibility remaining. But after my final year in Peterborough, I went to camp and was assigned to their Binghamton team. At the time, Washington was sharing the team with Hartford so they were only able to ice seven forwards each and that kept the chances for players like myself very small.

I started the year there and played about two months and then they decided to send me to Fort Wayne. I was on a three-way contract and would only make $11,000 in the International League. I couldn't live on that so I made a big decision and decided to go back home so I could weigh my options. When I did that, the coach in Peterborough found out and phoned me. He asked if I wanted to come back and play as an over-age Junior. So, I contacted Washington and they were pretty upset with me. Maybe that's why they gave me my release and I was allowed to play as a free agent. I wound up having a pretty good year and was scouted by Neil Smith, who then was working for the Detroit Red Wings.

Smith saw me because I was playing against his Adirondack team. I had also met Colin Campbell who was an assistant coach in Detroit. He had seen me play Juniors as well. Both Smith and Campbell went to [Red Wings' vice-president, general manager] Jimmy Devellano at the same time, saying that I was a free agent and that maybe they'd sign me for their American League team. That persuaded Devellano and he signed me with Detroit.

I could have gone with four other clubs but I preferred the Red Wings because they had that one American League team in Glens

Falls, New York [Adirondack] and I felt I had a better chance with them than if I got into another situation like the one I did with Washington, winding up in the International League.

My first experience with the Red Wings was in 1987-88. I had a two-way contract and played only three games in Detroit and 78 with Adirondack in Glens Falls. I played constantly there and got some good experience, winning the rookie-of-the-year award for my team. My numbers were pretty good; 21 goals, 32 assists and 337 penalty minutes.

I went to the Red Wings' camp the following year and Jacques Demers was the coach. They were having some trouble with players so that gave me an opening, and since I had a good camp, Demers took me on the big club.

At first, I played regularly until the other players came back and then they had me here and there. I'd get ice once every week or two weeks and when I did play it amounted to two or three shifts a game. I played in a total of 55 games and scored two goals and three assists. It was hard on me because I wanted to contribute more.

What happens in a situation like that is that you want to make an impression so you run around hitting people or get into a fight and that's what I did most of my first year in the NHL. With the limited ice time, I still managed 168 penalty minutes.

Still, I learned a lot about the politics of the game and what it was going to take to play and play more. I went home that summer and worked as hard as I could to get ready for the next year. As it happened, Detroit felt that I couldn't play there the following year, so they traded me to the Rangers for Chris McRae and future considerations.

In a way I was surprised by the trade because I had spent the summer getting mentally and physically prepared to be a better player with Detroit to become a regular. It was a tough summer in the sense that I kept telling myself that I was going to play and play a lot, but there always the thought in the back of my mind that I could end up back with Adirondack after a full year in the NHL, and I didn't like that idea.

The break for me was when Neil Smith was named general manager of the Rangers. He was the one who signed me with Detroit and always was a big backer of mine. Then, Roger Neilson got the coaching job. Roger and I had always been close friends going back to the Peterborough days.

A week before the trade, my father said to me, "I figure you're going to New York." He was joking, of course, and I still was with the Red Wings at the time. In fact I packed my bags and headed for Detroit with my family because we were looking for a place to live and I was staying with Gerard Gallant of the Wings.

Just a day before training camp opened, Jimmy Devellano phoned and told me I was traded. At first I was shocked because I wanted to play for the Wings, and I had good friends in Detroit.

So, when I arrived in New York, I didn't know a single player. I didn't know anybody but the general manager and the coach, but everything turned out okay after a slow start. I played only two out of the first 10 games and didn't know where I was going or what was going on. I thought, maybe, I was going through the same thing again but Roger was a new coach and he had to take time and evaluate what kind of players he had and what kind of team he could ice.

Pretty soon I was playing regularly and was used in all kinds of different situations. I definitely knew that the Rangers wanted me to play physical because that's why they traded for me and the Patrick Division always was a tough place to play. About halfway through the year I started playing with Darren Turcotte and I became more of a protector for him, and then they started getting me into a checking role. I'd be out there to watch the other team's top player. When Jan Erixon, one of our other checking forwards, got hurt, I was given even more of a role as a checking forward.

This was both challenging and rewarding because my ice time increased and the job was important although not as glamorous as scoring goals, but it sure meant a lot in terms of the team winning. I began to feel more confident with my ability to handle the puck and make plays. I knew that with even more ice time and practices, I'd get even better and establish myself as a pretty good checker.

I was very happy just to play and play regularly and it didn't hurt that we had a winning team in New York. That's one thing that keeps you coming to the rink; knowing that you're part of something that could be big. It was very rewarding.

We had some other physical players on the Rangers at that time, so that made it a bit easier for me. There was Lindy Ruff and Randy Moller, who had been around for a while, and Troy Mallette, who was young like me.

I played 68 games in my first season with the Rangers [1989-90] and got 286 penalty minutes. A year later the penalty number dropped to 156. It didn't hurt that Tie Domi stepped in.

Personally, I enjoy the physical part of the game. I love to hit and I kind of enjoy instigating things. Not to the point of talking a lot but just for the way I play. I don't really enjoy the fighting part and I'm not in the same league as some of the bigger fighters. Naturally, I'd like to score more but hitting is what I do and I'll continue doing it. Hopefully, it will keep me in the league for a long time.

I liked playing in New York. I'd be downtown, walking with my wife, and fans would come up and talk to me, always wanting to shake my hand and give me a high-five. That's pretty cool in such a big city with so many sports teams and so many people; for them to know who I was.

Where we lived — near the Rangers' practice rink in Rye, N.Y. — it was a very rich area and people were not into the Rangers as much, so we were pretty much left alone. Which was good since we played in the city and then we'd come home to rest. We didn't need all the hassle all the time.

I enjoy being with kids and don't mind giving autographs. I still remember when I was a kid and was really thrilled to see an NHL player. They would give me autographs and now I can return the kindness. Kids will appreciate the gesture because that's what it's all about.

As far as the playing is concerned, there are a lot of mental techniques used and, of course, one of the most important factors for me, as a player, is to know the referee. After a while, a player comes to know how a particular referee handles a game; his attitudes, moods on different nights. Older players know exactly if they can get away with an extra shot here and there or if they can say an extra little bit.

We have a funny relationship with the referees. Sometimes we're cursing them and sometimes we're begging them to stay in the game. But it's a relationship that requires smarts because it's up to them how much you play.

Sometimes it's the difference between a two-minute and a 10-minute penalty. As for fighting in hockey, it's a subject that has become a very popular one over the past few years. In my first NHL year fighting is pretty well all I did. If there wasn't fighting then, maybe I wouldn't have gotten the chance to stay in the league and develop as a player. Some players come into the league as physical forces for that one reason and then, after lots of practice and games, they develop into better players. Had fighting been banned when I broke in, I might never have gotten the opportunity that I did get.

On the other hand, it's good to see the amount of fighting has really dropped dramatically over the years. That's a good sign that the NHL is curbing it, but you have to remember that fans still do enjoy fights and that hockey is a very physical and emotional game.

You can't take that release of emotions which comes with fighting out of the game without something else getting more severe; it's quite possible that stick work would increase. That could be a little more dangerous than just two guys wrestling or throwing punches.

I know that some people are very much against fighting but the sticks ARE a very dangerous thing and if sticks are your only line of defense, the game could get a lot worse. Usually when there are altercations involving two guys, they aren't going to severely hurt each other with their fists.

When I played for Peterborough in my later years — when I was 20 — Domi had come along as a 17-year-old rookie. He was the young fighter and I was the old fighter on the team and we developed a pretty good relationship.

I also had a pretty good relationship on the Rangers with Darren Turcotte. Before the referee blew his whistle to start each period Darren and I had a little act we'd go through. He would stand off in the corner and the players would file by me and touch gloves and then Darren would wait until the goalie was ready and skated by me, slapped my hand. I would slap him in the behind with my stick and then I would go over to the goalie and slap his shoulders and his head and his pads and then do the same with the backup goalie. The funny thing was that until somebody really pointed it out to us, we never even realized that we were doing the ritual.

Fights sometimes take funny turns. I remember once when I was with the Rangers and Mick Vukota was playing for the Islanders, we got into something. I had put a clean hit on Mick and then he tripped me but I kept my cool. Then he knocked me down and I still kept my cool, and then he took a swing at me and finally I went with him.

First, the background on this: the year I had gone to Binghamton, Mick had come as an invitee to the Washington camp and we were both looking for the same job. Still, we got along pretty good but he didn't even get to play in Binghamton. Since then, Mick has done pretty well for himself and knows what his job is.

Before the clash we had in that Islanders game, the Islanders were down by one and Mick was trying to get something going. I was hoping to let him instigate the fight so that he could get an extra two-minute penalty and we would have the power play; so I restrained myself. But after taking one, two, three shots from him I figured I had to do something about it. We could have fought but we said to each other, "Okay, not this time." We were standing right beside each other and it was a case of mutual respect. We could have gone at it but we wouldn't have gained anything and probably would have gotten thrown out of the game. You learn how to respond to situations like that.

You seem to sense when it's the right time to fight; sometimes when your team is down and looking for a boost, maybe you have to get things going. You look at the scoreboard and if you're down by a goal or up by a goal, you don't want to get an instigator penalty and be shorthanded just for the sake of fighting. You have to look at who you're going to fight; if you haven't done well against that guy and you have a feeling that the guy might get the upper hand on you, well, it's going to knock a little bit of wind out of your team as well as yourself. So there's a lot to it.

Figuring when a fight is over and when to stop is an interesting question. First of all, you start with the concept that nobody on the ice really hates anybody on the opposition; or at least they shouldn't. The game is played on the ice and that's where it should stay. It's a business and we realize that so it isn't very often that guys really try to hurt other guys. Once the linesmen get in there and things look like they're done is when you end a fight. You just say, "Okay, that's it."

Most fighters are respectful of the linesmen and referees and each other. They know when to stop and they also know that if they want to fight again, there will be another time. It's something that's pretty universal among the players. Which is not to say that every so often you won't have some character take a shot at you after you think the fight is over. After all, guys do get heated up and I know that I get people mad at me. You learn to control your emotions and be a little bit smarter.

I've been known to get under the skin of opponents. Once, when I was with the Rangers and Dino Ciccarelli was with Washington, the Caps were on a roll and we were in a slump. My job was to check Dino that night and I bugged him like I usually do. We were talking back and forth and I got his attention. He finally took a shot at me and we both got 10-minute misconducts and there was only nine minutes left in the game. So, he was gone. For me to take Ciccarelli off the ice is a pretty good trade-off for our team. Besides, we wound up winning the game.

Stick-swinging is something the league has been cracking down on over the years and, to tell you the truth, I don't think I've really swung a stick in anger — where I actually meant to hurt somebody — in all the years I've played in the NHL. Everybody slashes but I don't think it's with the intent to hurt somebody. You often see guys just get really frustrated and they use that stick and lose it for a second and just forget that they could really hurt somebody. It's usually the smaller guys who use the stick as their only defense. If you have a short fuse, you can cause some damage.

You can hurt someone very badly if you hit him from behind. That's something that shouldn't be allowed. Kicking with your skates can hurt people. A lot of things happen but the stick is the worst because a player is in control of that and has to be in control. It's very sharp and it can hurt.

When I try to hit someone, I don't think about not hitting them hard enough to hurt but I'd be devastated if I actually did hurt somebody. A few years ago Kevin Hatcher got hurt from a hit of mine. I was using my knees. It was nothing I did on purpose but it was very unfortunate. I wrote Kevin a letter, apologizing because there was no intention on my part to hurt him. I wasn't very happy with myself over that.

There has been talk over the years that some of the superstars — Wayne Gretzky and Mario Lemieux, for example — are not to be hit as hard as other players. I don't think that's right. If you hit those players, you're getting attention from all the players on that team and getting their mind off the game.

When I was younger, my most memorable fight took place when I was with the Red Wings. We were playing in Chicago and Bob McGill and I had been running at each other all game. We had a fight right at center ice and it lasted a couple of minutes. It was a really good fight. We exchanged punch for punch, but there wasn't any clear-cut winner. It ended because we were dead tired, stopped, looked at each other and skated to the penalty box.

Many fans who come to the games are under the impression that those of us who play tough hockey have tough personalities away from the rink, but that isn't the case. People who know me on the ice are surprised to see me off the ice. My family and my wife are everything to me. I'm a laid-back kind of guy. After the season, my family and I head right back to our cottage in Ontario where I love to fish. I try to do a lot of charity work and I spend as much time as possible with my family.

In my earlier days, the first thought people had about me was that I was a fighter, a goon. I've gotten away from that because I took on more roles, and that's good. Everybody who plays the game wants to be known as somebody who is a well-rounded, contributing personality and not necessarily just a fighter. I want people to respect me for that. I'm proud that I play and I'm proud of who I am off the ice. I want people to know that person, too.

I'm not blowing my own horn or anything, but when I was in school, I was always an 80 student. I always loved my schoolwork and I was in university when I was 18 years old — and I had three years before I came to the pros, which isn't easy for a player coming out of Junior hockey. I was always really good in school and took pride in it and that was because of my family. My grandmother was a teacher and my mom always brought me up to respect education. That was something that's been instilled in me and that's the way I am.

There's the family relationship and then there's the relationship we build on the hockey team which is a very interesting one. Any hockey player will tell you that when the season is over, win or lose, he doesn't enjoy leaving the team. After all, we go through a nine-month struggle together and when summer comes we miss the routine of being with the guys. We get into a routine where we get up, go to the rink to practice, come home and keep repeating it. Granted, a lot of us can't wait until the off-season, but when the schedule is over it's almost natural to sit around and mope for a while because it's really hard to re-adjust.

When I was traded from the Rangers to Winnipeg in 1992-93, I had to make quite an adjustment. The machinery for the deal went into motion after we had lost a game in New York. When I was with the Rangers, Roger Neilson always was in control of the meetings. On this occasion he was sitting in the back of the room and I could tell that something was wrong because I've known Roger for a long time and we're friends.

Up until that point I had heard rumors of a trade involving Winnipeg, only now it was actually happening. I was told to come to Neil Smith's office and he said straight out, "You've been traded."

This was quite an emotional experience for me and I became angry, especially because I would have to leave so many friends. But I phoned [Jets' coach] John Paddock and he made me feel real good about the situation. I also had a very emotional conversation with Neil Smith because it was Neil who had given me my break with the Red Wings in the first place. I knew that it had been hard for him to tell me that I had been traded.

I went home and packed, met the guys for lunch at 2:30, then a car came and picked me up and at 5:30 I was on my way to Winnipeg.

The Rangers got Ed Olczyk for myself and Tie Domi. Smith said he needed scoring and the Jets needed toughness. I know that a team needs more than just scorers. You need guys who are going to grind it out in the corners and I know that Roger Neilson opposed the trade right from the start.

You wonder what caused Smith to make the deal and, in a sense, I think it was partially motivated by what had happened the previous summer when the Flyers got Eric Lindros in that controversial case when, for a short time, the Rangers also thought that they had had him. I had discussed this with Milt Dunnell [*Toronto Star*], my favorite writer, and we talked about the same thing. He thought it stemmed from a feud between Roger and Mark Messier, but I know that that was blown out of proportion.

I think the Rangers' problem stemmed from a breakdown of a family situation. When we heard that our top players — Darren Turcotte, Tony Amonte, Doug Weight, John Vanbiesbrouck and James Patrick — could be part of that deal and could be gone, it ripped apart the whole family feeling that we had on the Rangers. The guys began to feel, "Oh, shit, they [management] don't care that much about us." That was mentally hard on the players. Let's not forget that hockey is such a mental game, so something like that is going to have an impact. Likewise, the Mark-Roger thing didn't help.

Of all the players in the league, the one who intrigues me is Rick Tocchet. I played against him in Junior hockey and I've watched him develop into quite a scorer. I remember thinking that I'd like to play like Rick because a guy like that is dangerous. He was a leader in Philadelphia and now he's a leader in Pittsburgh. And he's chippy. Doug Gilmour is another like that. Those are the guys I like best.

When I'm finished with hockey I want to be remembered as a player who worked hard, was honest and gave the best he could every night; someone who established himself as a good team player and had character.

Chapter 12

THE ST. LOUIS "CHASER": KELLY CHASE

"I can't be intimidated anymore. I've gotten beaten up so many times by so many guys that, honestly, taking a beating doesn't faze me. I don't have qualms about having to fight — and I'd fight anybody."

Kelly Chase is the foot soldier among hockey's hard guys. Of modest size (5-foot-11, 195 pounds), the native of Western Canada's plains usually confronts hitters bigger and often stronger than himself but never has backed down from anyone.

He was plucked from the Saskatoon Blades of the Western Hockey League in 1987-88 and assigned to the St. Louis Blues' International League farm team in Peoria. After a couple of cups of coffee in the bigs, Chase finally established himself as a full-time NHLer in 1991-92.

Chase, who admits that he was a finesse player as a youth, has no qualms about his assignments and handles them with the efficiency of a Mario Lemieux scoring goals.

At one point in the 1992-93 season, the Blues were toying with the idea of putting Chase on a line with Brett Hull and Ron Sutter. "It would have given us some forechecking," said Hull. "It's not the threat of Chase fighting. It's the crashing and bashing that he does which would make the line work."

During an interview with reporter Eric Servetah between periods of a Blues game with the New Jersey Devils at the Brendan Bryne Arena in New Jersey, Chase revealed himself to be a thoughtful and personable young

man who relishes his NHL job and understands more
than most how fortunate he is to be a major leaguer.

I was born in a very small town — Porcupine Plain, Saskatchewan — where everybody was into sports simply because there wasn't a lot else going on.

My parents owned a farm which my father looked after when he wasn't taking care of the local arena. In the wintertime he didn't have a lot of livestock to watch so he looked after the arena, which had a curling rink as well as the skating rink.

I was fortunate since my brother and I got to the rink every day and put in a lot of time on the ice. I loved it out there and my love of hockey as a kid made it easy for my parents because they always knew where I was even after my dad left the farm and bought a service station in town.

After they closed up the station, they went straight to the rink and there I was playing hockey with the kids and sometimes with my younger brother, Kyle. The two of us had a great relationship and fighting wasn't big with us although, like all brothers, we fought a bit, but never very hard. If there was trouble, we were at each other's side.

My father died when I was 14 years old, and at that point in our lives my brother and I got really close. Matter of fact, we still are — as is our whole family. I took on the role of father figure, but Kyle didn't want anyone thinking that I was going to look out for him. He made sure that everybody knew that he was his own person and he was as tough as he was and he didn't need me to look after him. But still, older brother that I was, I made sure that I did look after him and, as a result, we caused some disturbances. I always had to fight for everything for the family and I was always real quick to stick up for the family.

One of our heroes in those days was Barry Melrose, who came from a town called Kelvington, which was just a few miles down the road. We admired Barry because he had made it all the way to the NHL and was playing for the Winnipeg Jets at the time. We all wore Melrose hockey pins and it was a big thing that his sister happened to be a teacher in our school.

But Melrose wasn't the only hero. Joey Kocur and Wendel Clark also came from our area and Wendel's brother, Don, played hockey with my cousin on the Junior level. We looked up to all of those guys and when someone like a Barry Melrose made it in the NHL, it gave all of us the incentive to try and do it ourselves.

As a youngster, I wasn't particularly interested in fighting and don't even remember the very first fight I ever had. Yeah, I got into a lot of bouts, but no, I didn't like them. Some kids like to fight but I wasn't one of them. The only time I fought was when I felt the need to stick up for something I believed in. If somebody said something derogatory about my family or my friends, I would fight. The more I grew, the stronger I got — what we call "farm strong." I didn't work on weights and stuff like that but, I built myself up doing chores around the house.

Hockey came early in life for me and the best thing was that my parents were really great about it. Most of the games we played were 20 to 60 miles away — an hour's drive — and my parents would take our vehicle every time. It was hilarious because sometimes we would have three games in a week and we had 12 or 15 kids on the team. If we were short a car, I'd phone them from a service station and say, "Hey, listen, we're short a vehicle; we need another car." Even if they couldn't go, and another one of the parents was going, they'd say, "Here's our car."

Four of us would pile into the car, throw our equipment in the trunk and away we would go to the game. Nobody had to tell me that I was lucky to have parents like that, who were willing to go out of their way to help us kids play hockey. They were always there.

As a kid, believe it or not, I was a finesse player. Part of the reason for that was because I came from a small town, got to play a lot and was able to develop my skills early on. We had two lines on the team so you didn't have to wonder when you were coming up next because you WERE up next.

The whistle would blow and I would get right back on the ice. At that age, it looked like I had a lot of talent because all I did was score goals and have fun. When I was 16, I was good enough to move away to Humboldt, Saskatchewan to play Junior hockey. It may have occasionally embarrassed me to say so, but at that time I wanted to become a professional hockey player.

In Humboldt, my coaches were Don Clark, Wendel's older brother, and a fellow named Bernie Lynch who had been a finesse player and who had coached the Swedish National Team. We had a lot of skilled, younger players and I wasn't so sure how I would fit in with them.

I wanted to prove that I belonged but, on the other hand, I didn't want to tell them straight out that I wanted to become a professional hockey player. They would have looked at me and said, "Yeah, right!" I always told everybody that I was going to be a school teacher. At first I was scared that they were going to cut me because I didn't add enough offensively. After all, I was a 16-year-old playing with 20-year-olds. I figured that I had to add some other dimension to my game and, since I always liked to hit, I decided to play physical. Even though I had some finesse moves, I always banged and they knew that I was always going to bang and run at guys.

In the beginning, I didn't fight. I'd wear my mask, hit hard and play tough, but I didn't fight until Juniors. When I got to Humboldt

I decided to fight. Right away I got into a couple of bouts and I did fine. My first fight was against a guy from Yorkton and I just basically went into it with my head down and swinging. I hit the guy a good one and cut him. Actually, I did great in the fight and, of course, the team thought I was going to be a tough guy and they were expecting me to fight more and more.

It was kind of scary because once you get into that mold, you never get out of it — and for the most part I have never really gotten out of that. The funny thing was that I don't think I won another fight for about three years.

I always showed up and I was never scared of anybody. Of course, there were guys I had to be careful with and guys I had to respect more than others. It may sound arrogant but it isn't — I can't be intimidated anymore. I've gotten beaten up so many times by so many guys that, honestly, taking a beating doesn't faze me. I don't have any qualms about having to fight — and I'd fight anybody.

What could be worse than what happened to me in Tier II in Humboldt? A guy named Darwin Sommerville was a 20-year-old who just beat the hell out of me. He knocked me down; I twisted my knee when I went down and my eyes were black. It was so bad that I actually couldn't open my eyes the next morning and I had to keep a hot washcloth on my face. I had my knee and my black eyes plus scratch marks all over my face and, besides that, he also broke my nose. Still, as bad as the beating was, it didn't bother me, honestly. I just went out and did my own thing. One licking out on the ice was no big deal. And nobody has to tell me that there's far worse ways to earning a living, and having somebody give me a beating on the ice for 30 seconds wasn't going to worry me.

In that season I played 57 games, had 18 goals and 18 assists but also had 270 penalty minutes because that's what was expected of me. Eventually, I received invitations to Junior camps and when I got there the coaches did interviews and they were saying, "Yeah, we have some young, tough 17-year-olds" and I would hear my name mentioned because they all wanted a physical presence.

After a year in Humboldt, I played the next season in Moose Jaw with Tim Cheveldae. They told us that we didn't fit into that league and that we should go back to Tier II and try to get a college scholarship rather than play in the Western League because we weren't going to fit in. So the two of us went to Saskatoon and we made the Western League team there. We finished third and Moose Jaw finished eighth. The year after, we finished first and Moose Jaw was seventh. We were pretty fortunate that Moose Jaw didn't think we could play in the league because we went to a team that was a better organization and in a better hockey town.

The WHL was a no-nonsense type of league; there was no place to hide. If you played the game honest, you weren't going to have any problems because everybody was honest with each other. What made it easier for me at Saskatoon was that our coach, Marcel Comeau, was completely fair. He didn't care who you were — a first-liner or a fourth-liner. If a guy wasn't pulling his weight, he'd get benched, which meant you always had to be prepared to play. If you came to play every night, you were in business.

I worked for Marcel and it paid off. In my first year [1985-86], I got 25 points, then 46 the next year and 55 in my final year of Juniors. Marcel knew that I knew what my role was and the more he played me, the more I did what I was supposed to do.

You learn pretty quickly what to do and what not to do. I mean you don't go over to Bob Probert or Joey Kocur — tough guys like that — and smack them in the back of the head and jump them, and expect that it's over after you've hit them. You lose your respect right then and there.

People aren't stupid. They know when somebody is being honest or dishonest. You can't trick people. If you're working hard but you lose the game, generally people are going to say, "Hey, you know, the guy is honest about what he does." It's the same thing as if you're working in a factory. If you work hard, you get a break. Well, fine. If you don't, well, okay you don't, but you've got to be working hard to be able to earn bread. Generally, guys who work hard get the breaks because, sooner or later, people catch on. If you're honest on the ice, people will see that and appreciate it.

In Juniors I was in maybe a hundred fights. I fought guys like Ken Baumgartner and Craig Berube and some other tough people. During the 1987-88 season I signed with St. Louis and went from Saskatoon to their farm team in Peoria. I wanted to go in and prove that I wasn't going to take any crap from anybody and that I was going to be an honest player. I did that and I had almost 280 penalty minutes in my first year in the minors.

I played hard and got my chances. I caught a break with the Blues when Herb Raglan and Todd Ewen both got hurt and they needed somebody to fill the gap. I just wanted to make the best of it and didn't want to get sent back down.

My first game was under Brian Sutter and it was fine. I went out and banged around and into anybody. I didn't know any guys except Tony Twist who played with me in Saskatoon. We went out and banged into as many bodies as we could, tried to play physical and let them know that we were excited to be with them and in the NHL.

It was good to have Twist alongside since we had played many years together in Juniors and Peoria. We fought a lot of battles together and I have a lot of respect for him because he's the type of guy who gives everything he has and has made the most out of his abilities. He knows what it takes to be a player in the National Hockey League and fighting happens to fall into that category.

The thing about fighting Twist is that you can't win. Even if you win the fight, you can never beat him because he's going to be back and he's the kind of guy who is exactly like that away from the rink and in real life. He's tough about everything. He's paid the price and fought everyone who's tough and now he's here and, hopefully, he'll be here a long time.

Twister and I are such good friends that I find it hard to imagine myself fighting him. But if it came down to it and we had to drop the gloves, we would probably fight just because we know that we have a job to do. Twister is happy-go-lucky and I don't think it would bother him much if we fought. He's the kind of person who can go out and swing at someone and then go for a beer with him later. Other guys take it more personal. Maybe I wouldn't fight Kocur or Clark because I grew up with them in Saskatchewan and we see each other in the summer. That's a little different.

I caught a break in St. Louis because there were a lot of injuries and since the club didn't have a lot of depth, I got to play. Brian Sutter taught me that I had to practice hard and be intense every day — not just on game days.

After Brian left for Boston, Bob Berry showed me how to concentrate and work harder on what I didn't do well, and to always be good at what I did so well. If I keep concentrating and play well defensively and still get a forecheck going, I'm doing my job and I'll get more and more ice time.

Sutter was a very intense individual and it was hard to communicate with him off the ice. He intimidates guys a bit and wears the club colors on his sleeve. He didn't pull any punches. If he thought you were a dog, he'd come over and tell you so. That made me a better person on and off the ice and it made me realize lots of times that I took things for granted, like where I am today. He made you realize that you shouldn't take the NHL for granted because getting that far is a destination that not many people reach.

The 1991-92 season was my first full year in the NHL. I played 46 games, got a goal and two assists and had 264 penalty minutes. Fighting is a bit different for me than it is for the bigger guys. Being small, I'm in a win-win situation because if I win the bout, I'm the greatest guy in the world and if I lose, well, I wasn't supposed to win anyway. So, I'm fortunate and basically I have to get in tight on guys. I can't stand back and punch with a lot of them because most of the guys are tougher than I am or throw harder than me, or are bigger than I am.

I'm in a situation where I have to tie guys up and just make the most of fighting on the inside. I can't stand back and throw them on a Dave Manson or Bob Probert or guys like that. If I stand back and throw with those guys, punch for punch, I'm eventually going to lose. Either I'm not going to reach them or I'm going to lose. I have to be smart about it and pull guys in tight and hit guys on the inside. I have to switch hands and hold onto guys.

I'm confident with either hand but I have to adapt to how the other guy fights. Nine times out of 10 if I'm going to fight, I have to do something to counterattack the other guy and not go so much on the offense. Against a Probert, I have to try and tie him up the best I can and get in some shots. I have to get on the inside and make sure he doesn't push me out. If I get pushed out, I'm never going to reach him and he's going to hurt me. Those are the kind of guys I must get in tight with and come up on my punches and try to switch hands on them once in a while to keep them off-balance. Bobby's a big, tough man and everybody knows that; if you stand away from him, you are going to be in trouble.

I fought Probert a couple of times and he hit me a few and he missed me with a few big punches. That was because I was inside where I had to be. If he hit me with those big ones, then the fight could change in a hurry. I hung in there and I'm still talking today, so I guess I did alright.

I'd just as soon fight the bigger guys than smaller ones like Alan May. It's easier to tie them up and, as I said, there's that win-win situation. Some of the little guys are smarter fighters and have a tendency to tie you up more. They are smarter with both hands whereas big, tall guys try to get in that big punch and you can tie them up better.

Alan May is fiesty and he throws with both hands and he's a tough guy to fight. Win or lose you have to show up and you have to let everyone know about it.

By contrast, Craig Berube is a heavyweight. He's a strong, strong man and he's powerful and willing to fight. And that's half the battle. He's very fair and never cheap. He'll talk to you and you know he's not going to sucker you. He's a big, strong, tough individual and you have to give him respect. You have to give him credit since he's one of us guys who didn't have the unlimited talent coming in, but he caught some breaks and has made the best of them.

I'm a little concerned now that the NHL is making the game too restrictive with its new rules. The more rules they change to try to get fighting out, the more guys can hide. If you do something cheap to somebody, you should be able to face that person one-on-one. There shouldn't be the stickwork and cheap shots and other things, but it's all part of the game.

Fighting is just another part of the game. I have a role to play and fighting is just part of it. A lot of the cheap stuff should be stopped and fighting is just a reaction to the physical nature of the play.

The fans seem to love fighting. When there's a fight, you read articles saying that fighting is hurting the NHL. Yet everybody is on his feet when a fight breaks out. Fighting is part of the game and should be the player's choice. If I want to fight, I fight. Besides, it's not as if people are really getting hurt from these fights.

Some fights puzzle me. For instance, I can't see why a Tie Domi would want to aggravate a Bob Probert. Why would Domi want to incite Probert? The bottom line is that the media made a big issue about something that was not a big issue. Of course, Tie might have said something to somebody and he may not have wanted it printed. Matter of fact, I talked to him about it. It became an issue out of something that originally was not an issue.

When all is said and done, I have to say that fighting takes its toll on your hands. I've had surgery on them but overall I've been lucky. Those big guys who stand back and throw those big 200 mph haymakers are going to have a lot worse hands. Guys like Joe Kocur suffer. My hands get sore but, then again, that comes with the territory. But I'll leave you with this: there are lots of worse ways to make a living.

Chapter 13

I'LL KEEP SHOWING UP: JEFF ODGERS

"Basil McRae impressed me with his willingness to talk to me and not hold a grudge after our fights. It taught me a lesson, and now that's the way I am off the ice as well. If I fight somebody, I'm not going to hold a grudge after the game just because we traded punches. The other guy is doing his job and I'm doing mine."

There were few bright spots on the 1992-93 San Jose Sharks. One of them was Jeff Odger, a bone-crushing right wing who checked his way to the big tent. In a season during which the Sharks won 11 games, lost 71 and tied 2, Odgers emerged as a valiant performer for a severely undermanned hockey club. He became respected for his tenacity and improved play.

Odgers did his basic training between 1986-87 and 1989-90 with Brandon of the Western Hockey League before turning pro in 1990-91 with Kansas City of the International League. He played 77 games in the IHL and rang up a hefty 318 penalty minutes. If nothing else, he commanded attention. The Sharks signed him as a free agent in 1991-92.

Odgers made his NHL debut on October 29, 1991, at Nassau Coliseum against the New York Islanders. He was shipped back to The I for a dozen games with Kansas City before returning to the NHL. In 61 games as an NHL rookie, he scored seven goals and made four assists. His penalty total was 217 minutes, the second-highest on the Sharks.

Odgers is a rugged young forward trying to hang on to a big-league spot on a struggling hockey club. In an interview with Eric Servetah at the Embassy Suites Meadowlands Hotel in New Jersey, before a game against the New Jersey Devils, Odgers wove the story of his hockey life.

It's funny, but I can't remember the first time I put on a pair of skates. But I do remember my first hockey game. I was four years old. It was a Saturday morning, and I was watching cartoons when the coach called and told me I would have to get ready to play. At the time this was a big decision for a four-year-old to make, since I had to decide whether I wanted to play hockey or finish watching the cartoons.

I chose hockey, although it was almost comical the way it happened. I remember not knowing where to stand and the referee showing me where to line up for face-offs and where to go. Obviously, I had a lot to learn.

I was born in Spy Hill, Saskatchewan, and grew up on a farm two-and-a-half miles outside of town. I have a younger brother and two sisters. My kid brother, Scott, and I did a lot of things together on the farm, where you pretty much do everything with the family. Scott and I are both hotheads, so we'd get into the odd tussle every so often, although nothing very serious.

My dad spent almost his whole life in Spy Hill. He began farming when he was about 16 or 17 years old. My mother moved there when she was about 13 or 14 years old. My father played hockey until his teens but not much more after that. If anything, he instilled honesty in me and the importance of sticking up for what you believe. In terms of confrontations, he believed that if you could work out the problem, work it out, that fighting was only a last alternative. I tended to get along with people and didn't get into many scraps in my early hockey years.

After a bit more exposure to hockey, I fell in love with the game. Every spare minute I had I'd be out in the yard, shooting tennis balls around in the summer or being on ice in the winter. My parents took me to all the practices and the games, which made things a lot easier in my hockey development.

By the time I was five years old, I was playing organized hockey, and of course, I followed the pros on TV with "Hockey Night In Canada." You couldn't miss that. The next day at school all we talked about was the game we had seen on TV. Then, about Thursday, we would start talking about the game that was coming up that week.

Me, I was a Boston Bruins fan. I liked Bobby Orr and, later, Terry O'Reilly and Rick Middleton. When I was younger, I wanted to be more like Bobby Orr, who was a big goal-scorer. I loved to make the end-to-end rushes.

I started off as a defenseman, but on our team you had to be prepared to play other positions. You see, our town was small and sometimes we had only nine guys on our whole hockey team. I remember times when guys were sick and there were so few players that we played without any line changes. We'd have the coach on the bench by himself and we'd play the whole 60 minutes. I loved that. Sometimes, when we went to tournaments, we'd play two or even three games a day and I'd be playing all 60 minutes.

Despite all that ice time, I never became a great skater, although I was fairly strong and had a pretty good shot. Part of the problem was that I had a weak ankle and had to wear molded skates for six years until my ankle got strong enough for me to wear regular skates.

My first hockey fight was a strange one. I was 10 years old and the game had actually ended. A kid on the other team was skating by me and fell. As he went to grab on to something for support, he grabbed on to the back of my neck and dragged me down to the ice. We ended up having a little tussle, but that was about it.

A more serious bout took place when I went to the Saskatoon Blades' camp. I fought a left-handed guy and he just whipped me around. I got two black eyes and was cut over both eyes. He absolutely destroyed me, and part of the reason for it was that I hadn't done much fighting up until that time, whereas the other guy had done a lot of it. Mind you, I landed a few shots on him, and he ended up with a big black eye himself. But he left me beaten up and ugly.

Apart from that, I didn't get into much real fighting until I got into Junior hockey at the age of 17. I found that in minor hockey you don't do much tough stuff until you're 15 or 16. That's when the intimidation factor sets in — in the earlier years it wasn't really present.

I played a lot of hockey with Kevin Kaminski, who grew up in a town about 20 miles away. He made it up to the American League in 1992-93, and when we were playing back home in Saskatchewan, he had a bit more skill than me. He had a great set of hands and was very involved in the game. He'd do anything to win, even at that age.

The big thing for me as a teenage hockey player was to get noticed by a Junior team. When I was 15 I went to a midget camp in Yorkton, Saskatchewan, and made it through the first few cuts. But then they let me go just before the season started. I was devastated, so I went home and played there for a year. The calibre of hockey wasn't as good, but things went well generally and I wound up winning the scoring title.

My first experience with a bench-clearing brawl took place when I was 16. We were all out there fighting. I was on the ice when it started and paired off with a guy and we started throwing them. Although it wasn't my first fight, it was my first real fight in this kind of situation. I did pretty good and remember cutting my finger on the guy's teeth. That required a couple of stitches. I got ejected from the game, and the whole team was talking about it for the next three weeks. It must have affected me, because that very night after the fight I couldn't fall asleep because I was so pumped up. It wasn't until three in the morning that I finally conked out.

I still liked scoring goals, but mixing it up was something I began to enjoy. Getting involved made me feel good. I didn't mind fighting at all, although at this point I don't think I was very good at it.

You may wonder why I got into fighting. The main reason was that I wanted to show people that I wasn't scared to do it. I wanted to make myself look better for the scouts and I was conscious of having the need to fight and impress. Of course, I didn't have much of a style at the time — I'd just grab on and start throwing. The problem with that style is that you get hit a lot more than you should.

It's funny, because boxing actually had been a part of our family. My grandfather was a boxer for Canada, and he actually started training my brother, who went on to box in the Canadian Nationals. My grandfather started a boxing club in our home town, and twice a week we would box, do aerobics and hit the heavy bag. I did it for conditioning, but my brother was more serious about it.

Anyway, the big break for me came in 1986, when I went to Brandon's camp and the Wheat Kings decided to keep me for the year. I was ecstatic, because I was playing hockey and that was what I wanted to do. I would have gone anywhere in the world to play.

I had a few fights during the exhibition season but I still wasn't very good at it, although I was game. I was just showing up and doing what I could to impress the coaching staff to keep me on the team.

My first fight in the Western League was against Darin Kimble. It was in my very first game, and I didn't do too well. Kimble was a known heavyweight. After that I remember saying to myself that I had a lot to learn. Kimble likes to throw them quick and so do I. The thing that separated us then was that he was stronger than me. He got the shirt over my head and hammered me. We ended up fighting two more times that year and each time I did better against him than I had before.

I learned to keep my balance so that I didn't just go in there throwing. Instead I got set up and then started fighting. Good fighting has a lot to do with balance — once you get off-balance, you're finished. Once you get twirling around, you're finished.

Our Junior team didn't have a lot of veterans who could teach you things about fighting the way other teams could. There was myself, who was 17, and Kevin Cheveldayoff, who was 16. The way it worked out, we did most of the fighting. One thing I did was learn in a hurry. I remember having a black eye every week. My face was a mess all year. I had stitches and a black eye all year. Believe you me, it was pretty ugly.

Not that it bothered me, but it made my parents real sick. Whenever they came to see me, I'd have a new black eye or a scar somewhere. But that's the way it was on our team — you either stood up for yourself or took abuse.

There were a lot of tough Junior teams around and it was all intimidation. We didn't make the playoffs, and it was a tough year, but I got a chance to play, and that experience was invaluable.

You had to wear a visor in Junior hockey, so when a fight broke out, you usually dropped your gloves and took off the helmet. You'd go into the fight without a helmet, grab on to the opponent's shoulder pad or guy's arm and start throwing.

For a kid of 17 it was a rush, with the people in the stands going crazy, so it was something I didn't mind doing at all. The best fight I had that year was against a guy named Gord Green of Swift Current. We just stood at center ice and went toe-to-toe for a minute-and-a-half, punch for punch.

In my second year of Junior they wanted more offense out of me, since I had proven that I could fight and work hard. But it wasn't until my third year with Brandon that the goals and points started to come. I also was getting more room, because other teams knew that if they messed around, I would go, no questions asked.

Unfortunately, with all the fights, my hands started getting screwed up. I'd get into a fight, hit the other guy's visor and wind up cutting my hands and bruising the tendons. At times I wasn't even able to put my hand in my pocket or start my car because my hands were so banged up. It was tough to play like that.

Mostly everything I threw then was with my right hand. The opponents who gave me the most trouble were the ones who were really strong and who grabbed on to my right arm. If they got my right locked in, I didn't really have a left at all. At first I'd spend the whole time trying to yank my arm from out of their grip. With some guys, I wasn't able to do it, so then I started trying to throw lefts. The first few times I did that, I left myself wide open and was caught with some rights. Then I started trying to jockey for position and trying to cross-grab, hoping that the other guy would loosen his grip on me.

At that age, you want to go with guys just to see how you do against them. The feeling then was that you'd give your team a big boost if you beat their guy. It would really get your team going. I was beginning to punch pretty hard then and I could tell that I was hurting people.

I wasn't intimidated, I was more scared of losing. The fear of getting beat up scares me more than anything. Losing real bad and losing in front of your teammates scares me the most. For your own confidence, you don't want to lose. I'm not actually scared about fighting a guy — it's the fear of losing the respect of your teammates and respect for yourself.

After three years with Brandon, I had hoped to get drafted, but nobody picked me and I was devastated. I thought my hockey life was over, but then I got a break when a fellow in Brandon hooked me up with the Minnesota North Stars. I got a tryout with them and wound up at their camp. It went well. I fought Basil McRae four times in one scrimmage. It was a case of my realizing when I came to camp that nobody knew my name. Half the scouts wouldn't have a clue who I was, so I wanted to do something that would get me noticed. That's why, when I played against Basil's team, I went after him.

It wasn't much of a fight, and then we went to the penalty boxes, and when we returned he was mad at me. We ended up fighting again and it was broken up and then we fought a third time. In that one we didn't even bother to put our gloves back on — we just fought. After that, they didn't let us play against each other in the scrimmages.

I did all right against McRae. He's a smart fighter, but I hit him a couple of times — nothing major — and he hit me a couple of times and that wasn't serious either. But I did good by showing up and being there.

Afterwards, I met Basil in the dressing room and we chatted. I felt that he respected what I was trying to do, since he once was in that position himself.

Basil McRae impressed me with his willingness to talk to me and not hold a grudge after our fights. It taught me a lesson, and now that's the way I am off the ice as well. If I fight somebody, I'm not going to hold a grudge after the game just because we traded punches. The other guy is doing his job and I'm doing mine.

Interestingly enough, McRae and I have fought a couple of good fights since that talk. We both landed good shots and it showed me that Basil isn't slipping at all as a fighter.

After being at the North Stars' camp, I was assigned to Kalamazoo of the International League. I was happy about that because I knew that some other players in my shoes already had been sent home. I was 20 years old and still around.

I played two exhibition games with Kalamazoo, but then Minnesota sent more players down to The I, and suddenly I realized that I was the only guy there without a contract. I knew then and there that the handwriting was on the wall. Besides, I didn't have an agent.

I wound up being sent back to Junior, which wasn't the worst thing in the world, because I knew that I had got my foot in the door for next year. I was happy with my camp and played the 1989-90 season with Brandon. I was the veteran on the team, had a good year, got 37 goals and didn't have to fight as much — until the end.

The low point occurred while we were in a playoff run for the last spot and I got into a fight with a guy I had tussled with quite a bit. He and I hated each other and would fight just about every time we played. In this particular case the fight got out of hand a bit and I was suspended for eye-gouging. He didn't get suspended — only beat up.

So, here I was — the leading scorer on the team — and I'm suspended for the last four games. Our club went to the final game to make the playoffs but I couldn't play in that one either because of my suspension. Here I put four years into the team just to be able to go somewhere with it and now that we get the chance, I can't even help. I had a bad feeling about this.

After the season, I realized that there was some interest in me so I got an agent, Art Breeze out of Calgary, and let him work for me. We found out that Minnesota, Vancouver, Philadelphia and Toronto were all interested in me, and San Jose wanted to sign me to a personal services contract.

I decided to go with San Jose, and right away the Sharks decided that I needed to work on my skating and shooting and develop other skills. They sent me and a couple of other guys over to Finland for a month. At first I didn't know what to think — I didn't even know where Finland was — but I went and stayed for a month.

They put me on an élite team called Elva and we played in a tournament in Russia. It was a different kind of hockey for me — you played on bigger ice surfaces — and I was getting dizzy skating in circles so often.

The trip from Finland was something else. We took a flight to Moscow and from there took a 12-hour train ride to Kiev, which is like "the Train from Hell." Our room on the train was about six feet long and four feet wide. There were four bunks in this area and four of us had to share the room. The facilities were unbelievably scary. So it was myself and three other guys from the Sharks in this little compartment, and while we were sleeping somebody came along and robbed us of watches and cash. To this day, we think the culprits were the ladies who worked the train.

If nothing else, being in Russia made me appreciate life in North America. The food was awful and there never was enough of it, assuming you wanted to eat. Talk about shortages — we saw cars lined up for two miles just to get a tankful of gas.

The Finns had hoped that I would be their leading scorer and win a lot of hockey games for them, but I wasn't going to do that. They needed somebody to be an impact player and I wasn't it. Which is not to say that I didn't leave Finland with a smash.

The Big Bang happened in a game against a team from West Germany. We had a guy on our club named Teemu Peltivic who was kind of a haywire type of individual. In this particular game he got into a fight with a German at the end of the second period.

Fights in Europe don't happen with the same frequency that they do in North America, so this was a bit uncommon. Anyway, the next thing we knew the whole German team climbed over the boards and dashed to the fight. But only the four of us from the Sharks came over for the Finns.

So it's the four of us and Teemu against all the Germans. At first the Germans thought we were Finnish guys doing the fighting but they found out in a hurry that we weren't. We had a lot of fun and the few of us did very well, while the fans were going nuts. It was said that this was the biggest fight in 12 years. The people were shaking their heads as if we were crazy while the West German team was going nuts yelling at the referee. It was, in the end, hilarious, and naturally we got thrown out of the game.

That did it. They sent me back to North America and I returned to Brandon and worked out with my Junior team.

After that, the Sharks assigned me to Kansas City. It was the start of the 1990-91 season. The first year I was on my own with my own place to live. It was the first time I was in such a big city and, to be honest, I wasn't used to it. At the age of 21, I had a lot of adjusting to do.

Still, the year in Kansas City was great and I loved it. I was third-line winger and a hard worker. I had 34 fighting majors, not counting a fight in camp, where I beat a guy up pretty bad and he got 20 or 30 stitches in his face. In another exhibition a big boy of about 6-3, 220 pounds, tapped me on the shoulder and wanted to fight. I figured that if I wanted to make a name for myself, here I go. I started off taking a few and then I got inside and landed a punch. I knew I caught him solid with it because he went down with the blow and there was blood all over the place. He ended up with a flattened nose that needed reconstructive surgery. That was the hardest I've ever hit anybody.

When something like that happens, I have mixed feelings. On the one hand, I was pumped that I had won the fight, but on the other hand I didn't want to hurt anybody like that because I knew that at any given time somebody like him could land a punch like that on me.

Still, the knockdown was a big confidence-booster for me, because I had been timid going into the new league. I didn't know how strong the players were and what the league was like.

Unfortunately, our team didn't get off to a very good start. After 20 games we were something like 2 and 18 but I was just happy playing in the league and picking up a check every two weeks. I was making $30,000 that year and thought I was the richest guy on earth.

I played a total of 77 games for Kansas City and scored 12 goals and made 19 assists. In most of my fights, I would just stand in there and go, with no decisive winners. I learned how to grab a bit more and developed a left hand. I had to be smarter because the guys were bigger, so I had to get inside because I couldn't sit back and throw, since I wouldn't even reach them.

To build myself up, I hit the weights as much as possible and that helped. The fellow who gave me the most trouble, fight-wise, was Enrico Ciccone. He made it hard for me to get inside because of his long arms.

I also had a few absolute doozies with Paul Kruse, who is strong, about my size, and fights the same way I do. We had some head-slammers in two or three fights and just went without holding on. I don't know how you can determine a winner in these fights. Maybe I landed two or three more punches but I don't know how you could walk away from a fight like that and say you won — or he won. This much is certain — we have a lot of respect for each other and could still talk after the games.

Lefties don't bother me unless they are big. If he's a lefty who is my size, I try to go punch for punch. I go right and he goes left and, hopefully, I get my right arm inside his left arm so his punches go off of my elbow pad. If he's bigger than me, then I try to go inside and get a hold of his left and maybe try to cross-grab and get my left hand on his left biceps. Then, I try to throw rights from this position.

In any event, Kansas City was a good experience. I was helped by Doug Soetaert, my coach, and Kenny Morrow, the assistant coach. They gave me a chance to play. Doug liked guys who mixed it up and played hard, so I got a chance to play, which was the biggest thing for me. I needed the ice time and the chance to work hard.

After the season I took power skating lessons, and in September 1991, I was signed as a free agent by San Jose. I went to camp and we all were told that they didn't want any fighting, but we fought anyway. I had one fight with Perry Anderson, who had been with the New Jersey Devils. The funny thing is that Perry and I are really good friends now, but on that day we fought and they kicked us off the ice and wouldn't let us practice for the rest of the day.

I played a couple of rookie games for the Sharks and then was told that I was being sent back down to Kansas City. Really, I didn't expect to make the Sharks' varsity right away, but still I was disappointed in being sent down. I wanted to play at least one exhibition game with the Sharks, just to measure myself, and I told this to management. Sure enough, they called me up to play against the North Stars.

It was a good game and I wound up fighting Shane Churla twice. We just ran into each other after a whistle and I gave him a little shove and he was happy to go. Once again, I felt that I had something to prove to management. I also wanted to catch their eye.

In any event, they sent me be back to Kansas City, only this time I was named captain of the team. I'm wearing the "C." Well, we started off like gangbusters and were 10 and 0 when I got the call to go up to the Sharks. You couldn't believe how excited I was when I heard that — so thrilled I can't even describe it.

When I got to San Jose the coach, George Kingston, pulled me aside and said, "You're not here just to fight — I want you to play the game." Those were comforting words, and I knew that George meant it because he knew a bit about me from seeing my games in Brandon.

Anyway, my first NHL game was against the Islanders, whose enforcer was Mick Vukota. I was nervous before the game and wanted to get the fight out of the way. Sure enough, Mick and I came to blows. He's a strong guy and had me hanging over our team's players' bench. Still, it was good to get it over with and it relaxed me, although I will say this about Vukota — he has this technique of grabbing you around the waist during a fight and then bodyslamming you to the ice. It's a dangerous move because it can hurt a player, particularly if your helmet comes off as you're coming down. I would hate to see someone get hurt because of that.

Well, I managed to survive that first game and played 60 more for San Jose. They put me on a line with Dean Evason and Paul Fenton, two hard-working guys, and we worked well together. I finished the season with 217 penalty minutes and even had a fight with Dave Manson, and John Kordic before he died.

I fought Kordic in my third game in Quebec, after I had fought Herb Raglan. I hate saying whether I won or lost, but in the instance of the Raglan fight, I felt that I took him. Before the next face-off, Kordic came out and wanted to go. I'd known about this guy forever and now my heart was pumping about 500 miles per hour. I knew we were going to fight as soon as the puck was dropped. Bang! Just like that, we started going pretty good, punch for punch. Our styles were similar in that we threw them quick and didn't hold on a lot.

The next time Kordic came to San Jose he wanted to fight again. We ended up swinging, and I'd have to say it was one of my NHL highlight fights. We squared off and went and then switched hands. I ended up breaking my hand in that fight after my fist hit his helmet. We both went punch for punch and threw and threw until we were both dead tired and then the linesmen came in and broke it up. For me, it was the biggest fight because I had known so much about John

Kordic and his battles. The result was that I also broke my knuckle and that sidelined me for five weeks. After I came back, I knew that I had to be more careful about throwing punches. I didn't want to hit the other guy's helmet, or his head.

I always try to fight fair because the worst thing, in my estimation, is to be known as a cheap-shot artist. If I fight someone and knock him down and the fight is over, I'm not going to gouge or keep hitting. I have had guys do this to me but I, personally, don't believe in doing it to anyone. You fight, it's over and that should be the end of it.

It's no secret that our problem in San Jose is winning hockey games. Being on a loser is not easy and it weighs on you a lot. The good thing about the Sharks is that they have a lot of character guys — guys who can pick the rest of us up when we're down in the dumps.

Not surprisingly, we finished out of the playoffs in 1991-92. Once our NHL season was over, management asked me to go down to Kansas City to help them in the playoffs. I had no problem with that, since being in the playoffs was a new experience for me and we had a great team in The I. We wound up winning the championship.

After the season I signed a two-and-one-year-option deal, but going into camp in September 1992, I wasn't assured a spot on the Sharks. I knew what they expected of me and I wanted to keep working hard to increase my offensive numbers. I made the team and it all fell into place. I improved offensively, and the only hang-up was that I broke my hand in a fight with Brad May of Buffalo. I did well in the fight but the break set me back six weeks and hurt my ability to shoot the puck.

When you fight that many times in a year, you get used up. I have to learn when to do it and when not to do it. There are times when it has to be done, but if I ever get thinking that I don't have to fight and can become an offensive player, I won't be in the league much longer. I have to remember my role, and it's not just fighting — it's also playing hard every night and finishing my checks. I need to be mentally tough about that.

As for the league's new policy about fighting, I have no problem. I totally agree with the thinking that if a guy goes out just to get another player off the ice by getting into a fight, it's wrong. But I also think that when two guys who are playing hard run into each other and go . . . that's something that should not be taken out of the game. That style keeps people honest and eliminates a lot of pretenders. Just having fighting makes guys think in the back of their minds that they might have to answer for their actions. But if you know that there's no fighting and you don't have to answer for your actions, a lot of people are going to be a lot braver — especially with their sticks.

Chapter 14

THE IRONMAN OF THE NHL: KEN DANEYKO

"I've never considered myself a goon. I play a physical style of hockey, but there's a big difference between that and being a goon. Anybody who knows the game will tell you that."

If any contemporary National Hockey League player can be called a throwback to an earlier era, New Jersey Devils defenseman Ken Daneyko fills that label to the nth degree.

Daneyko's obsessive dedication to the game is best reflected in his Iron Man stats. Through the 1992-93 season, he had played in 311 consecutive games, and in seven full years had missed only seven contests. Only Steve Larmer of the Chicago Blackhawks outdistanced him in this department.

"Kenny is as dedicated as anyone you'll ever want to meet," says Ottawa Senators' goaltender Craig Billington. "He LOVES hockey."

Daneyko, born in Windsor, Ontario, but raised in Edmonton, also loves to hit. At 6 feet, 210 pounds, his center of gravity is conveniently low and he relishes body contact, often leveling the foe with shoulder and hip checks of devastating proportions.

Until the 1991-92 season, Ken also had been the Devils' penalty leader, compiling four consecutive years with more than 200 minutes, many of which were for fighting.

Short-fused through the first five years of his major league career, Daneyko had learned to restrain his temper with the result that he has become a more effective — yet still pugnacious — leader.

Daneyko's I.Q. (Intensity Quotient) remains among the highest in the league, and the respect with which he is held by teammates and opponents alike ranks among the top of all the NHL's hitters.

An amiable, long-time bachelor, Daneyko finally tied the knot with Jonnalyn in the summer of 1992. The couple and her father recently opened an Italian restaurant in New Jersey. Ken delivered insights into himself and the business of being a banger to reporter Eric Servetah after a workout at the South Mountain Arena in New Jersey.

Ever since I put on my first pair of skates at the age of four, my dream was to make it to the NHL. Growing up in Western Canada, I was obsessed with hockey like so many of my friends. If I had been born in the States, I'm sure it would have been football or baseball, but in Edmonton the game of hockey was king.

I was the baby in our family with one older brother and two older sisters. My brother, Peter, played organized hockey up to the midget level and then gave it up. I began at the age of four and never gave up. My brother and I used to fool around with hockey a lot, even in our house. We'd go down to the basement, put on hockey gloves and helmets and beat each other up. He was always a little bit bigger than me so I got the worst of it quite often. But then, when I turned 16, I shot up in size and, for the first time, I was bigger than him and I beat him up. After that, the fighting between us stopped.

My parents came from Germany and they knew nothing about hockey until they moved to Canada. They settled first in Windsor and then, when I was seven years old, they moved the family to Edmonton and that's when I began getting serious about hockey.

It was hard not to get involved. Winters were long and cold and we had outdoor rinks on almost every block, so if a kid wanted to skate it was no problem. I would go to school but all I would ever think about was coming home, lacing on the skates and playing hockey. When I was eight years old I told my mom that I wanted to be a professional hockey player, but I never thought I'd turn out to be the kind of player I am now.

In Junior High School I was more of a peacemaker than anything else. I was one of those respected kids who would stop the bullies from picking on the nerds. I could get away with that role because I was friends with everybody and I didn't get into much trouble, although I did have the odd fight.

Once, when I was in the sixth grade, I was considered the strongest guy in my school. There happened to be a rival Catholic school nearby and I and about three other kids gathered around and we got into it. I wound up being matched against the toughest kid there. I wasn't too crazy about it. Next thing you knew the principals arrived and got in to break it up. Other than that, I had very few run-ins as a kid.

It's interesting that my idols, during my teenaged years, were not the tough guys but rather skill players. I grew up liking the Toronto Maple Leafs and my favorites were Darryl Sittler and Borje Salming. I'd watch them on the "Hockey Night In Canada" telecasts every Wednesday and Saturday and I'd hate it when the Leafs lost. With me, that was the bottom line — win or lose.

I really wasn't that interested in the physical side of hockey until I was 15, playing on the Tier II Junior level in Yorkton, a small place in southern Saskatchewan. The game was rugged there and I was up against a lot of older guys, so I had to learn to handle myself if I was going to survive because it was pretty wild. Some of the harder guys who played in Yorkton were Joe Kocur and Dave Brown, which tells you a little bit about the toughness around there.

Playing for the Terriers was my first taste of big-time hockey in the sense that we were a traveling team. When the opportunity to play for them came up, it was a big decision for me and my family. I had only two days to decide whether to stay home in Edmonton or go to Saskatchewan, but I decided then and there that I would make hockey my career and I thought that this was the best step for me.

When I got to Yorkton, my game was a bit different than it is now in the NHL. Yes, I played defense and a physical game but I got a lot more points (laughs) than I do these days in the NHL. I found that it's a lot tougher being an offensive defenseman in the bigs than it is down in Tier II.

Yorktown was a farm team of the Spokane Flyers of the Western Hockey League. That was Tier I and big stuff in terms of competition. In other ways it wasn't so hot in that we didn't have a very good team and lasted only a year and a half before we folded. After a year and a half in Spokane, I was moved to the Seattle Thunderbirds, also of the WHL.

Anybody who's played in the WHL will tell you that it was a tough, fighting league. Fellas like Alan Kerr, Greg Hawgood and Doug Bodger were there at the time.

The Devils drafted me in 1982. I was their second pick, 18th overall. New Jersey brought me up in 1983-84 as an underaged 19-year-old and after 11 games I got into a fight with Ed Hospodar, who was with Hartford at the time. He grabbed me and although we never really got going, I fell back to the ice near the net with my leg getting caught underneath me and it snapped, just like that. I broke my leg and missed most of the season. Then Kamloops of the WHL traded for my rights from Seattle so I got to go back to Juniors and play for the Memorial Cup, which was very good experience for me down the line.

I thought I could come back healthy in training camp the following September and make the big club, but I didn't have a good camp and wound up playing for Tommy McVie in Maine of the American League. That turned out to be another blessing in disguise because, even though I was in the minors, I got a whole lot of tutoring from McVie and that made a huge difference in my career.

What I liked about Tommy was that he was a hard-assed guy and took absolutely no nonsense. At times I hated him and wondered why he was putting me through such a tough grind but, in the end, it all turned out for the best. Lots of times, when you're a young kid, you don't realize how important the hard work is but later on you reap the benefits and that was the case with me and Tom McVie. I needed a push back then and he was more than willing to give it to me.

My philosophy, then as it is now, is to be a team guy; stick up for your teammates. Some rugged players make a big deal out of having bouts with others and beating up on other guys. It's important to a lot of them but has never been very important to me. I can recall instances where I beat up a guy who was supposed to be tough and, yeah, it gave me a lot of confidence but the thing is, I never made a whole lot out of the incident. And the reason I didn't is that I never considered standing up to someone anything more than just part of my job as showing up. In Ken Daneyko's scheme of things, the most important thing when it comes to hockey is showing up.

We played a game in Buffalo and on this night Rob Ray, one of the Sabres' tougher players, was running guys on our club. Well, if a guy like Ray gets out of hand, I have to settle him down and if fisticuffs come, they come. It's a natural part of the game. In that case, I had to resort to them to keep Ray honest.

But I'm not one of those guys who get 25 to 30 fighting majors a year. I prefer playing consistent, solid hockey. Remember, I've been in the NHL since 1983 and after a while you get a reputation for being able to stand up for yourself and, after that happens, you get more room, which is what's happened with me.

It happens with others around the circuit. Take a guy like Dave Brown; not too many guys want to go with him because they know his rep as a fighter. Dave has been the cream of the crop for a lot of years and unless you really have to do it, you stay away from him. He's a tough guy who can fight and he gets a lot of respect out there.

I remember my first bout with Brownie. I had hit Tim Kerr, who then was the Flyers' leading scorer, in front of our net. At that split second, Brownie came rushing in and we started to scuffle. I had known Brownie from the WHL but that didn't matter. He had a job to do and I did likewise. He threw a bunch of punches at me and I hung in there, which is all I can say. Dave got the better of me in that one.

Hockey fights are hard to figure sometimes because every so often a fellow will come along who you know nothing about and he'll give you a good pasting. My biggest surprise came in a game against the Minnesota North Stars and, if nothing else, it proved that you can't underestimate anybody when it comes to throwing them.

This fellow, Bill Stewart, didn't fight a lot but when he did — look out! He gave me a pretty good spanking, caught me with the first few and I couldn't re-group. I underestimated him and learned my lesson. You win some and you lose some and I've lost my share, but that's fine with me as long as I can keep coming back.

Fortunately, I haven't been injured in a hockey fight ever since the Hospodar incident. Over a period of about seven years I've only missed about seven games. Once I hurt my wrist and missed a game but other than that, I've had some cuts and bruises and sore hands but I battle through that stuff. Unless it's an out-and-out break, I'll be suiting up for the next game. To my way of thinking, you have to go out there and play.

In addition to the fighting itself, you get a lot of verbal battling going on all the time. A lot of intimidation is tried and a lot of it comes from the talking, chirping here and there with some funny one-liners thrown in. Once, Perry Anderson and Tim Hunter were going at it and the humor was so rich, I nearly fell over backwards in the penalty box laughing. In the end, all the verbal stuff is just another attempt to throw off the opposition and help your team win.

A lot of people have complained about fighting in hockey over the years and lately the league has taken action to curb the big brawls, and there's no question that fighting is down a lot. I don't believe that fighting can ever be completely taken out of the game since it's been a part of hockey's fabric ever since it was first played in the 19th century.

Another consideration is that — believe it or not — fans actually like fighting on the ice because they know that hockey has always been and always will be a very physical game. That means there's hitting all the time and a reaction to the hitting which, occasionally, results in a fight. By totally eliminating fisticuffs, it's more likely than not that the best [skill] players will become open to more attacks rather than as now when the enforcers protect them.

Take away fighting and you'll find a lot more guys running around trying to hurt the star players because they'll feel they're free from getting hurt in a fight. You can't have that situation. The way the NHL is handling the situation now is more than adequate; that is, the game is still physical, fighting is down, but it still is there. What's happened is that by emphasizing the instigator rule, the nonsense fights have been curbed.

If someone on the opposition tries to take out one of our skill players, it's incumbent on me to step in and stick up for my man. I see nothing wrong with two guys going at it when it's necessary like that and if it's a good, clean fight. People understand that, and if you take that element of fighting out, it will take something away from the game.

I understand the league's position. They want to get away from that stereotype line, "I went to a fight and a hockey game broke out." That kind of image is bad for all of us and it's made worse by some of the TV newscasts. A terrific hockey game could be played that night but what the news people will do is take the one lousy fight and use a news clip of that as if the fight was the most important part of the game, which it wasn't.

As far as I'm concerned, hockey is the best spectator sport going — assuming you watch it live. It's got more speed than basketball, hitting like in football, and the odd fight which creates even more excitement.

What makes it so great is that you can't get away from the physical aspect. The trick is not to have people think that hockey is just fighting. People in the know understand that it is more than that; a good hard game with lots of great hits. There is nothing better than a good, open-ice hit, even if you happen to be the guy getting hit. It's important to remember that the league has curbed a lot of the nonsense fights where a coach sends a guy over the boards to go pound on another player.

There still are plenty of good one-on-one fights. The Bob Probert-Tie Domi fight [1992-93] was one of the best I've ever seen and how the hell the two of them managed to stay upright, going toe-to-toe, for so long, I'll never know.

Probert-Domi reminded me of a great one from the past — Ron Delorme, who was with Vancouver, and Jamie Macoun of Calgary. Macoun wasn't known as a fighter at the time but he gave Delorme, a great fighter, a real test that night. It proved my point that you can't underestimate anybody on any given night.

People have interesting reactions to fights. Some fans get out of hand just because a player suffers stitches or even a broken nose as a result of a bout, but I don't consider that drastic stuff. Stitches or a broken nose are nothing to me, and if that's the worst thing that I suffer from a toe-to-toe fight, then that's great. The fact is, you rarely see anybody seriously hurt as a result of a hockey fight. Not that it can't happen. Joey Kocur broke Brad Dalgarno's cheekbone pretty bad when Joey was with the Red Wings. Joey has beaten a few guys very badly and you have to be careful of him.

If you fight smart, you should be able to handle punches like that, but there also have been a lot of kayos. Troy Crowder, when he was with the Devils, beat a lot of guys and so have Dave Brown and Bob Probert, both big boys. When they catch you flush, they're going to hurt you a little bit.

I've seen guys get knocked down or even knocked out, but they eventually got up without a mark on their face. Funny things happen. I've seen average guys beat tough guys and that can happen on any given night, like Mike Eagles pounding Mike Peluso. Things like that happen but people don't realize the circumstances behind a fight like that. A champ could be hurt or sick on that particular night but the fans may not know it, or a guy might have a bad hand or he might slip and you hear people booing.

The other factor is that hockey fights end quickly. Bing-bing and it's over. One fella gets in a punch and he might catch the other off-balance, because when you're on skates, it's tough to keep your balance. In a regular ring, it's easier to regroup. One night I fought Kris King and I was sick from the flu; that diminished my strength and I was tired from playing two games in a row. But I go back to what I said earlier — the key is showing up.

Some players have a fighting style but I'm not one of them. All I aim to do is get in the first punch. Do that and you have a good chance of winning the fight; otherwise, you have a good chance of losing. I'm a lefty and for some reason being a lefty has always been an advantage although to this day I don't know why opponents seem to have a tougher time with lefties.

I never modeled my fighting style after any other player. As I mentioned, my favorite defenseman, when I was a kid, was Borje Salming and he was known for his clean play. If anything, I learned how to fight the hard way — by fighting. I didn't look to do this or that because it all comes down to being spontaneous and working by instinct. And it helps that I have one of the harder heads around, so I can take a punch pretty good. You either have a good head or you don't. People tell me that I can take one pretty good. It all comes natural to me. There really is no big deal about the whole thing and I think you'll find that in the NHL, even the guys who don't fight can handle themselves, and that's why it isn't smart to underestimate anyone's fighting ability.

Every one of us experiences the feeling of fear at one time or another. Everybody gets scared. In the back of your mind you know that some guys are tougher than others, but my thinking is that if I lose, I lose. When I was younger, I was more nervous about fighting. Today, I don't get nervous about that stuff anymore. I figure that if it's going to happen, it will happen. I know enough about the business not to worry.

One advantage I've found is tying down my jersey so that the opponent can't lift my sweater over my head and then pound me. I'd feel helpless with the sweater over my head and I couldn't see. It's a big disadvantage to fight a guy whose sweater is off because you have nothing to grab on to for leverage. Bob Probert is very dangerous without his jersey on but everybody's different. If a guy

hits you in the right spot — I don't care who you are, even Bob
Probert — you're going to go down.

Over the years, I've heard talk about specific coaches telling
specific players to "go after this guy" and I know coaches have done
that, sure. But I've never in my whole career ever been told to go out
and start a fight, and if it had ever happened I would hate it. I don't
think any player should ever be told to go out and fight. If it had
ever happened to me, I'd probably hit the coach myself.

I've never considered myself a goon. I play a physical style of
hockey, but there's a big difference between that and being a goon.
Anybody who knows the game will tell you that.

There are players who have been characterized as goons who have
turned into very useful performers. One who I respect a lot is Craig
Berube who is a very smart fighter and improved his game by a lot
when he was in Philadelphia. He knew early on that he wasn't going
to stay in the NHL just by fighting so he addressed his skills and has
since turned into a good, solid winger. That's the type of player I
really respect. He's a gamer and ready for anybody. He'll do the job
but he knew he had to improve his game along the way and that's
what he's done. He got his foot in the door by playing tough and
then honed his skills as best he could.

Tie Domi is what I call a character guy. Everyone is different from
everyone else and some guys are more character players than others.
Tie gets people going and has the hardest head in the league. The
funny thing about him is that even though he's an opponent, I
actually get a kick out of his style and I see a good side to it because
he has the fans roaring — at least the ones on his side. Believe it or
not, people love to see that stuff once in a while.

You'll find that even though the media might deplore fighting they
also go ape over potential fights. I saw that when Troy Crowder was
with us in New Jersey and he belted Probert the first time they met
at Byrne Arena. Well, the next time they were scheduled to meet in
Detroit, the papers went crazy over it with "Tales of the Tape" and
that sort of stuff. The papers devoted almost nothing to the game
and everything to "The Fight," and the people loved it; 20,000 fans
jammed the arena even for the pre-game warm-up.

On the other hand, a lot of players around the league respect
Probert not only for his fighting but for all the tough stuff he's had
to battle through in the last couple of years. The thing with Bob is
that he's also a good player as well as tough. I mean the guy can
play. He's one of the premier physical forwards who can get you
some goals with the hits, and he can do things with the puck. He's
got good hands for a big man and you love to have guys on your team
like him.

Me, I want to continue playing my game until they have to rip my
skates off my body. I don't fight as much because I'm smarter than

I was when I broke in with New Jersey. It has nothing to do with my wanting to shy away from the rough stuff or that I'm not as hyper as I used to be. Actually, I've learned that being too hyper detracted from the good and welfare of my overall game and that it's better for me to be the way I am now — just a little cooler on the ice. Otherwise, I don't feel any different than I did at, say, age 22.

The game has changed and I've adjusted, changing with it. So naturally I'm going to get into fewer fights. In the "old days," all you needed was for one guy on the opposition to shove me and all of a sudden I was throwing them. Now I have to be careful, especially with power plays and special teams becoming so important. I can't afford to take bad penalties at the wrong time. I'd rather take fewer penalties and have fewer fights than be on a loser and fight all the time.

My enthusiasm for the game hasn't waned. I want to win as badly as I ever did as a kid, only now I control myself. Not that I haven't snapped. Once during the 1991-92 season we lost a big game to Washington, 3-1, and I snapped in our dressing room because we lost due to a lack of effort. Things like that really tick me off and I let my teammates know about it.

As I've said, the bottom line for me is winning. Period.

Adam Graves (left) played in the shadows as a Red Wing. Since his trade to New York, the Toronto native has emerged as a key forward. Here he battles Claude Lemieux. (Bruce Bennett Studios)

Dave Manson was notorious — more for his temper than his ability. But after moving from Chicago to Edmonton, the defenseman received more respect for his talents. (Bruce Bennett Studios)

A full-blooded Algonquin Indian, Gino Odjick has been Vancouver's premier ice cop and number-one pal of Paval Bure. (Bruce Bennett Studios)

Mike Peluso, a little worse for wear after a duke-out. Battlin' Mike went from the top (Chicago) to the bottom (Ottawa) in a year. (Bruce Bennett Studios)

Shane Churla (left) and Todd Ewen are among the "Kings of Swing." Here they're separated by linesmen. (Bruce Bennett Studios)

Kelly Chase of the Blues (left) has his hands up in the traditional pose as a linesman stretches to keep him apart from New Jersey's Tom Chorske. (Bruce Bennett Studios)

Jeff Odgers (right) is proof positive that perseverance pays off. After a long struggle, he earned an NHL berth with the Sharks. (Bruce Bennett Studios)

Ken Daneyko (left), the Devils ironman, lays a hit on Rangers forward Jan Erixon in front of the New York bench. (Bruce Bennett Studios)

The aftermath of Dale Hunter's behind-the-back assault on Islanders ace Pierre Turgeon in the 1993 playoffs. Turgeon (left) crumpled to the ice in pain. (Bruce Bennett Studios)

Rob Ray's (right) bark is as big as his bite. Here he battles Terry Carkner of Philadelphia. (Bruce Bennett Studios)

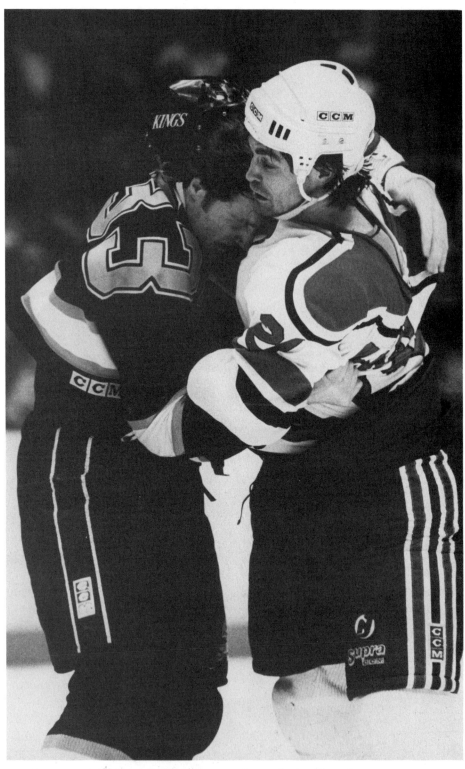

Randy McKay (right) succeeded Troy Crowder as the Devils enforcer. A strong, silent type, McKay also has proven that he can score. (Bruce Bennett Studios)

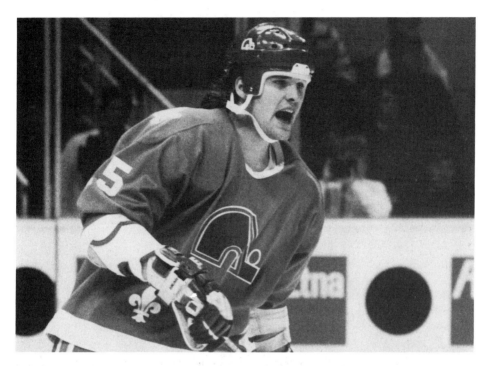

Tony Twist added sock to a Quebec team long in need of a physical presence. (Bruce Bennett Studios)

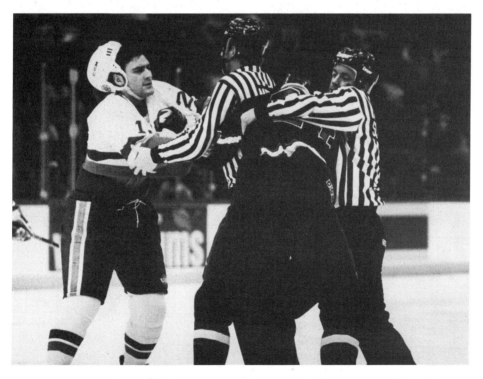

Mick Vukota (left) was a Washington Capitals reject who became an Islanders hero. Mike's specialty, the body slam, has been a controversial battling technique. (Bruce Bennett Studios)

Rick Tocchet (right) was captain of the Flyers before he was dealt to Pittsburgh. Toch won his first Stanley Cup in 1992. (Bruce Bennett Studios)

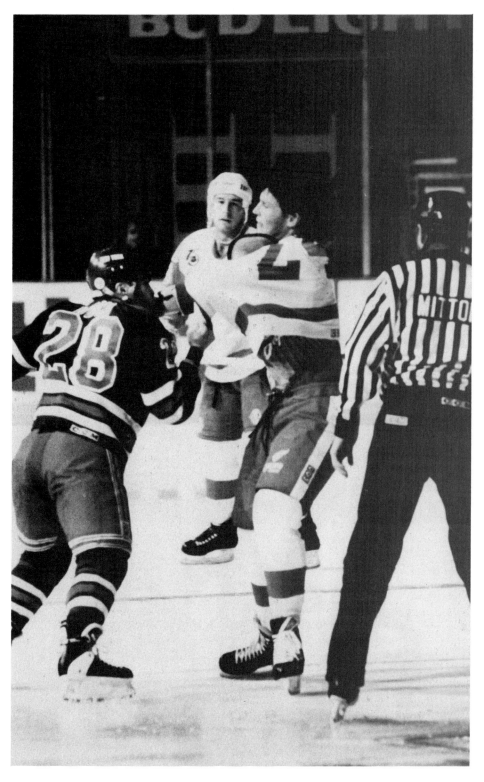

One of the most pre-ballyhooed fights in NHL history — Tie Domi (left) vs. Bob Probert. (Bruce Bennett Studios)

A rather typical post-fight Tie Domi pose. Enemies say his head is impervious to pain. (Bruce Bennett Studios)

Bob Probert (right), the NHL's reigning heavyweight champion, rubs elbows with a long-time pretender to the throne, Greg Smyth. (Bruce Bennett Studios)

IV

THE AGITATORS

Chapter 15

CENTER OF CONTROVERSY: DALE HUNTER

"I want to go after the better players
to slow them down, so I'm always
thinking, 'I've got to finish my check.'
If I have a chance, I'm always going
to lay them out."

In some ways Dale Hunter is one of the most versatile hard guys to come down the NHL pike since Stan Mikita.

He hits. He disturbs. He plays defense and he can score.

During the 1993 playoff between the Washington Capitals and New York Islanders, Hunter scored a pair of goals — including the winner — in Game One and then followed with a hat trick in Game Two. Not many pains-in-the-neck can make that statement.

"Dale gets on your nerves," said Dean Evason of the San Jose Sharks. "He gets you off your game, makes you forget what you're supposed to be doing."

Sometimes Hunter oversteps the lines of propriety. In the third period of the sixth and final game of the Islanders-Capitals series, Dale pursued New York's Pierre Turgeon well after his opponent had scored a series-clinching goal and peeled off to his exuberant teammates at Nassau Coliseum.

Hunter rammed the unsuspecting Turgeon from behind separating the Islander player's shoulder and causing him to miss most of the Patrick Division final against Pittsburgh.

Never before had media wrath so severely scathed the irascible Capital. "Throw the Book at Cheap-shot Artist" demanded the New York Post.

New York Daily News *columnist Mike Lupica labelled Hunter a "cheap hockey hoodlum." Even Don Cherry, an advocate of tough hockey, said "Dale was wrong. He should have never done that."*

NHL commissioner Gary Bettman's response was a 21-game suspension for Hunter during the 1993-94 season.

Precisely what effect it will have on Hunter's future deportment is debatable although Dale-watchers believe that he will continue to play gritty hockey, but in a more discreet manner.

At 5-10, 198 pounds, Hunter is less than an imposing figure unless you're an opponent who happens to run into his stick, a not infrequent occurrence. There simply is not a more determined in-your-face foe anywhere in hockey, but also one who continually surprises with his offense.

"When we got him, I knew that Dale would be involved physically," says Capitals' general manager David Poile. "What I didn't realize was what a good finesse guy he is with the puck. He makes great passes. He's a very complementary player who makes those around him play better."

The proof is in the stats. During the 1992-93 season Hunter became the 72nd leading scorer in NHL history with his 800th point. By some point in 1994 Hunter and Hall of Famer Gordie Howe will be the only players with 900 points and 1,600 penalty minutes.

Not that everyone loves the native of Petrolia, Ontario. During the 1990 Bruins-Capitals playoff, Hunter massaged Boston's Craig Janney so vigorously that then-Bruins' coach Mike Milbury opined, "If Dale Hunter was the last player on Earth, I wouldn't want him on my team."

Gentlemanly and soft-spoken away from the ice, Hunter blunts all barbs with a grin and the conviction that he is playing hockey the most practical way he knows how and may the devil take the hindpost.

Washington reporter Mary McCarthy, who has carefully studied Dale for the past six years, offers this analysis of Dale: "Hunter is very smart on the ice. He is a brilliant tactician and a very good executor, combining hockey and human skills. That is, he can make those perfect little passes into the slot at the same time that he's totally ticking off — thus distracting — one or more defenders. Watch him sometime when the Caps make a goalie change. He can think of a zillion ways to slow down the play for a while to let the new goaltender gather his wits and warm up his muscles a bit.

"Once in a while, but not often, he does something that seems a bit — can we say it? — dirty. Those times are rare these days, though.

"Off the ice, there's not a nicer guy around. Very unassuming and modest. He goes out of his way to help his teammates, he's always accommodating to fans, he puts up with the press (I don't know anyone who Dale Hunter has ever snapped at). The same can be said for his whole family, including wife Karynka. Nice people.

"Illustration: One day during training camp in 1992, the Caps had a buffet lunch set up. Pizza and such. Players were coming directly off the ice and kind of poking at the food, piling up their plates. In comes Dale's brother, Mark Hunter. He fills his plate up, then turns around and says to public relations aide Julie Hensley, 'Thank you.' I raise an eyebrow at this incongruous behavior. 'He's a Hunter,' says Julie. 'It's upbringing. It's all upbringing.'"

In some quarters, Hunter is described as "Jack Nicholson on skates" because, like Nicholson, Dale always wears that characteristic devilish grin. He also is a prideful athlete but one who is reticent to blow his own horn, unless vigorously pushed.

"I'm proud of my career," says Dale. "I've been consistent through the years and I've stayed in good shape. When I was a rookie, like everyone, I thought I would play 10 years. Now I'm past 13 and I haven't thought about how long I'll keep playing. I'll know when I'm no longer able to help the team."

For more than a dozen years Dale Hunter has been one of the most consistent — and irascible — of professionals; a Peck's Bad Boy of the pond. Mary McCarthy interviewed Dale after a practice at the Caps' Piney Orchard scrimmage rink in Odenton, Maryland.

My parents were both raised in the area of Petrolia, Ontario, where I was born. I guess it was natural that I was a feisty kid what with brothers like Mark and Dave around. I had to fight for every inch, just like on the ice.

I started playing hockey when I was about five years old. Bobby Orr was my idol and Boston my favorite team. When I played kids hockey the rules were pretty lenient and I didn't get thrown out of games. You could pretty much do what you wanted. Oh, maybe you'd get a slap on the wrist if you knocked somebody's teeth out.

Obviously, it's different in the NHL. I've had my share of controversy and, of course, people bring up Mike Milbury accusing me of things. Well, Mike Milbury saw stuff on the ice he didn't agree with.

Have I ever regretted later anything I've done on the ice? Yeah, sometimes. I think later, "I shouldn't have done that." But it's too late to worry about that now. I don't stop and think, "Well, I'm not going to do that again," because the events on the ice happen too fast.

There have been series where I hit an opponent and the press said that it made a difference in winning or losing. They said it about the 1990 playoff series with the Devils. What happened was that we wanted to go out in that game and get a lot of left-handed shots and close down the defense.

I remember the play [with Devils defenseman Viacheslav Fetisov]. A guy was forechecking ahead of me and he kind of set things up. Fetisov has a habit of turning back, instead of going behind the net. He turned back and I had a good idea that he was going to do it, so I just got him.

It wasn't as if I had planned to get him before the game but I always want to finish my checks on the D. I want to go after the better players to slow them down, so I'm always thinking, "I've got to finish my check." If I have a chance, I'm always going to lay them out. Of course, when you do that, you never know how the opposition is going to react. Some don't react very well while others react really well and they just go on getting better.

I was criticized during the Bruins series for the conference championship when I had a confrontation with Glen Wesley. Well, he was cross-checking from behind and that started it right there. He used to take two or three chops [with his stick] but this time he was taking 10, so I was pretty pissed off and I let him have it. (Laughs) And I didn't get caught, either!

Every game I'm responsible for certain players on the other team, but what I try to do is take the better players off their game. As it happens, lots of times I'm matched up with one guy all night. I get them off their game by talking to them; a little hit here and a little hit there. Little bumps. Maybe, after a while, they get pissed off and they retaliate; they go to the penalty box, too. It's a little cat-and-mouse game.

When I talk to them, I don't get into anything personal because everyone has troubles. I call them an "effin" this but I don't get personal. I do hear things on the ice that I don't agree with. Players do say some stuff. Like when Big Al [Iafrate] was having troubles. . . . Well, I don't agree with that [kind of talk].

My game has changed a bit lately, ever since the NHL altered the game. Personally, I kind of liked it the way it always was but the change was made by the decision-makers up top and if they're going to change it, then I guess it's for the best. After all, they're the brains behind the league.

Since the changes, I've had to watch my penalties a little more. I'm trying to cut down a little. Like, I don't want to get four minutes for roughing. I can get two minutes but I don't want to take that extra little shot and get the four because I could lose a game for us by doing that. It has changed everybody's game. When my dad came to Washington and saw the "new" game, he said that hockey was turning into a "girls" game. That's because he likes to see his boys mixing it up.

When it comes to fighting, as far as the heavyweights go, there's a knack to it. The best fighters are Bob Probert and Dave Brown. They grab on — they're big and strong — and strength means a lot. A fellow like Bob Probert is so tall and strong. His reach comes way out. A fellow like Tie Domi likes to take a lot of punches in the head just to get in. That's because he's short like me. If you're a small guy like me and you're fighting someone big, you know that you'll have to take a few in the head just to get inside.

Me, I don't go looking for fights. Fights are just an immediate reaction. Besides, I'm not a heavyweight, I'm a welterweight. I'm down the list and I believe that you have to fight within your weight group. (Laughs)

If I were to give advice to young players it would be to work hard. A rookie should not expect any team to hand him a spot on the roster. And when he does earn a spot, he has to work hard every day.

My dad always emphasized that. He wouldn't bring us to the rink if we weren't going to work hard. What he said was, "You don't work, you stay home and work on the farm." Naturally, we wanted to get out of working on the farm. So, we had to work hard on the ice. If a youngster isn't going to work hard, he's not going to last long in the NHL.

Every once in a while the younger players don't follow through on our system and they have to be told. It's not always up to the coach to tell them; sometimes it has to be one of us [veterans]. I don't talk too much; they know from my "look" that I'm mad at them.

I talk to the linesmen and referees a little bit. Since I take a lot of face-offs, I've gotten to know them pretty well. Fellows like Gord Broseker and his colleagues. They're told before a game to watch certain players, so their attention is sometimes on me. I think they know my name. (Laughs)

I take my hockey seriously and that's why, a few years ago, I went on a diet. When I was younger, I didn't used to worry about what I ate but I was too heavy. I was 205 and now I play at 192 or 195. And I work harder. When you're young, you really don't have to do it but when you get older, you have to work harder at it, off-ice. I watch what I eat and have tried to cut down my body fat. The younger guys may be quicker, but I'll be in better shape than them, so that will make us almost equal. At least, that's my philosophy. Where in the past I might have eaten chicken wings late at night, I don't do that anymore and I've cut out gallons of ice cream although I have to admit that it was hard to do.

What I've learned about the league lately is that the kids coming in are a lot smarter than they were when I broke into the NHL. Ten years ago, guys blew their money a lot. Nowadays, the college kids are all reading the stock pages and they make everyone a lot more aware of it. In the old days, when a guy finished his playing career, he had to go to work, so it's good that the younger guys take more interest. They know that they have to take care of themselves now because hockey has become a big-money sport.

Chapter 16

"THE RAZOR'S EDGE": ROB RAY

*"I'm always talking out there,
even when I'm sitting on the bench
yelling at them, getting them going. I
think sometimes players are
intimidated by me."*

Before the 1991-92 National Hockey League season
began, the Buffalo News ran a headline proclaiming,
*"RAY BECOMING A REAL PAIN FOR SABRES'
OPPONENTS."*

The subject was Rob Ray, a rather nettlesome warrior
reminiscent of Dale Hunter, Ken Linseman and other
disturbers.

"Rob is the hardest guy in the NHL to play against,"
said Rick Dudley, the Sabres' coach at the time. "His
whole function is to be a pain in the butt and he does it
very well."

Words couldn't be more well said. As we have found
out from many of his fighting peers, Rob is viewed
unanimously as one of the most hated players in the
league.

A native of Belleville, Ontario, Ray began excelling in
organized hockey with Cornwall of the Ontario Hockey
League before turning pro with Rochester of the American
League. During three years of Junior hockey, he averaged
more than 190 penalty minutes per season.

"I get a lot of penalties because of the way I play," said
Ray. "I've got to take shots here and there and talk a lot;
just try to get guys off their games, get them thinking
about more than what they should be doing. You're going

*to get a lot of penalty minutes just because you're
drawing other guys into penalty minutes."*

*In 1988-89, Ray played 74 games for Rochester and
reached the 446-minute mark. A year later he was called
up to Buffalo for 27 games and tallied two goals and an
assist as well as 99 penalty minutes. Incredibly, his PIM
figure was 335 for only 43 American League games that
year.*

*Ray was up and down with Rochester and Buffalo until
1991-92, when he spent an entire season with the Sabres.
He played 63 games, scored five times, made three assists
and reached the 354-minute mark.*

*Explaining his technique, Ray told Milt Northrup of the
Buffalo News, "You can hit a guy hard. Sometimes when
the ref's not looking, you give him a jab. You're saying
something to him, you're doing something dirty to him
and you're not going to get caught, and this guy's ticked
off because the ref's not calling it or he's mad at you
because he knows what you're like and it eventually
works on him. You've just got to hope when he takes a
shot, the ref's looking."*

*According to Northrup, Ray became an almost instant
hero in Buffalo. On the smaller rink at Buffalo's
Auditorium, it was more difficult for foes to get out of
Rob's way. And his energy quotient endeared him to the
blue-collar fans.*

*"Fans relate to people who work hard," Ray explains.
"I got the work ethic from my father. He has his own farm
machinery dealership. He's there every day, working on
the machines, fixing tractors. He's not a guy who stands
around and tells everybody what to do."*

*Rob worked hard enough to remain a big-leaguer while
living by the checker's credo. "I might not get a goal or a
point but if I make a big hit, I've done my job." In an
interview with Keith Drabik at the Memorial Auditorium
in Buffalo and in the locker room at the Meadowlands
Arena in New Jersey with Eric Servetah, Ray offered
insights into his rugged profession.*

Growing up, my idol was Gordie Howe. He was a guy who played
the game with skill, but he was also tough. He played both roles well
and that was something I respected. A guy like Bob Probert also
plays the game both ways and does it pretty well. It's better to be
well-rounded like that.

Fighting styles change. I try to take my elbow pad off before I
actually get going with somebody. I used to get pumped up too much

and my arms would get constricted. I wasn't getting enough circulation in my right arm, so the key was to either get the elbow pad off, or slip it up higher on my arm.

Now I feel less constricted and it's easier for me to throw a punch. Plus, it makes me feel more comfortable. That's something I didn't have for my first three years in the league. Now, I'm much more at ease when a fight is about to start or when the fight is actually going on.

To me, Dave Brown is a legitimate heavyweight. He, in my mind, was the best in the league, in that he hurt people. He doesn't just fight; he only fights the guys he has to fight. He doesn't go out looking for it or anything like that. He just fights when it happens. He's the kind of guy who simply hurts people.

When I fought Dave Brown I was really nervous about it. I always thought of him as the Heavyweight Champion and I was almost in awe of fighting him. This was the first time and I thought I did really well. I have a lot of respect for Brownie since he's done it for so many years and now he no longer needs to instigate fights or go looking for them. That's why I was kind of surprised that he gave me a few bumps and sort of called me on.

It was a good fight. We dropped the gloves and he started to move toward me. As he moved in, I said to myself, "Holy f—! What am I going to do?" Brownie has that big reach and that hard left, and I was worried about it.

So, we started throwing them and I was doing good. We each landed our good share of shots, and then I caught him near the end with a booming right.

That fight was a big confidence-booster for me in that I stood up to Brownie and gave him all he could handle. It made me feel real good and the team was psyched up. But, then again, Brownie is not the same as he used to be.

After Brownie, I got on a roll and my confidence boomed. I had a fight with Darin Kimble in Boston and did real well against him. I began getting much more room out on the ice and was creating more room for my teammates. Guys aren't taking cheap shots anymore at me or my teammates.

It's funny but in my first three years in the league I don't know if I won a single fight but now I want to win consistently and now I'm doing well. I'm much calmer and when I drop the gloves, I set up and get ready to throw bombs with these guys. Now I have more of a chance of winning than before. Besides, I don't need to fight every night the way I once felt that I did. I can go out there and hit and bang and hit and I would have served my purpose. Not every part of my game has to involve fighting. In the eyes of some opponents, I'm an agitator and, because of it, I draw a lot of penalties. Lately, I've been getting more ice time in key situations and I have a reason to be out there every time I'm on the ice. I'm there to hit, create turnovers and get the other team off its game.

John Muckler, our coach, feels more confident in me and has me playing against some of the bigger scoring lines in the league. I even skated during an overtime for the first time in my career. That made me feel good.

I play a good defensive role and, right now, my best asset is skating. I'm pretty fast and solid on my skates, so I'm able to forecheck well. I'm fast enough to get back into the play even if I get caught down low trying to hit someone. My speed creates offensive breakouts.

My fighting style has changed with experience. For one thing, I don't panic anymore like I used to when I was younger. I try to pick my spots more and am willing to take a couple of shots to get one good one in against my opponent.

In the past I would just throw them wildly and wind up being all off-balance and out of control. In a lot of my fights, I used to be tossed around like a rag doll. Now, before I throw a couple, I get set and I think that helps determine the outcome of the fight.

In the case of Dave Brown — and others I've fought — I have a great deal of respect. Then there are others. I had a fight with Tie Domi but, in my mind, he's not really a hockey player. He's an act and doesn't know how to play the game. I say to him, "Yeah, yeah, yeah," when he's mouthing off, but he can't play the game and you have to play the game. Take, for instance, the entire Domi versus Probert fight. It was so much hype that Domi built up. He builds that kind of stuff up just to get publicity, because that's all he can do.

When I fought Domi, the fight broke out on our first shift. He bumped into me and I said, "Don't screw around." He kept bumping me and saying, "Let's go!" Things like that.

I just told him to shut up and try playing the game. Finally, he pushed me and I just backed off and we dropped the gloves. I jerked down my right elbow pad and got ready to fight him. We grabbed each other and started exchanging punches. I was throwing a lot of rights, and for a while the fight was even.

Finally I landed a big right and pulled his jersey over his head and started to light him up. I nailed him with a lot of good shots and then the officials broke it up. It was a good fight and got our bench going wild.

We fought again in Buffalo a few weeks later. Tie probably got the better of me there. But then I read his comments after the fight and you could see why the stuff started with Probert — Tie talks way too much. I did pretty good against him in Winnipeg and I just wanted to be ready for this fight. If he'd just go out and do his job and shut up and play, everything would be okay. Guys don't like guys who go around yapping.

It may surprise some people, but when I was younger I always played as a goal-scorer. The change came when I reached the age of 15 and started playing Junior B hockey. Everyone I played against was so much older and so much better that I had to do something to stay on the team and I fell into the [fighting] role.

My first fight took place in Junior B training camp. The guy just slapped the piss out of me because I'd never been in a fight before. He knocked me down and I'm down on all fours and then the guy picked me up and just threw me head-first into the boards. And that was it; it was over.

In the NHL one of my worst fights was with Tim Hunter. My arms got caught in my jersey and he had a hold of me and kept hitting me. It was a good thing that he stopped, because I was tied up inside and the refs were getting in and he just stopped hitting because he realized that I was tied up. That was probably my worst.

I would be kidding you if I said I didn't hear the fans, particularly when they chant, "We want Ray." The fans are good and they make me feel good. I might be sitting on the bench for the whole game and people will still realize that I'm out there and realize what I can do for the team. It's nice that way.

Another good fight I had was in Game Six, our last game of the 1990-91 playoffs, against Donald Dufresne of Montreal. I had my shirt and shoulder pads completely off in the fight. I took a lot of flack over that because of getting into the fight at the end of the game and the end of the series. People didn't take too kindly to that, but it happens.

Every so often the fights create a stir in the newspapers. I remember when I was in the minors playing against Jimmy Roberts' team. It was New Year's Eve in Rochester and I had a fight with their captain in front of the bench. I really hammered him, knocked him down right in front of Roberts. Jimmy was standing there yelling and I shouted right back at him. I said, "You're next!" I was just goofing off, like that.

Well, in the next *Hockey News* there was a headline that Roberts had put a two-hundred-dollar bounty or something like that on me. So the very next time we play them, this Dean Ewen guy comes up to me and says, "I'm here for the bounty."

And he did the exact same thing during the pre-season in 1992. He said, "I can still collect on this bounty." I said, "This is so stupid."

The NHL's crackdown on fighting has some merit, but the referees have to use a little more discretion when they call the instigator penalties. Too often it seems that they penalize players by reputation. It seems to be a question of who you are and that's when they call it. If I go at somebody who doesn't really fight all the time, it's like they give me the instigator because I fight. They automatically assume I started it when maybe I didn't.

Actually, the new rule changes are better for me. Now I can go out and play my role, get people riled up, and I know that nobody's going to come after me. If they do come after me, they're going to get a penalty. It makes my job easier.

I never shut up. I'm always talking out there, even when I'm sitting on the bench — yelling at them, getting them going. I think sometimes players are intimidated by me. They're not sure whether I'm going to hit them or not. I've got a lot of people thinking, wondering if I'm going to fight — wondering what I'm going to do because I just don't always do the same thing.

Chapter 17

THE LARRUPIN' LITHUANIAN: DARIUS KASPARAITIS

"If you want attention, hit
Mario Lemieux, Wayne Gretzky
and Mark Messier."

When the New York Islanders drafted Lithuanian-born
Darius Kasparaitis in June 1992, there were murmurings
among several NHL scouts that the Isles had obtained a
throwback to an earlier NHL era.

They were right. In no time at all, the muscular, blond
defenseman demonstrated that he was unafraid of
delivering open-ice body checks that were reminiscent of
the 1940s and early 1950s but had become virtually
extinct.

"Darius hits like Leo Boivin used to hit when he played
defense for the Bruins," said Islanders' television analyst
Ed Westfall. "He uses his hips in the old style and never
picks his spots."

And that may be an understatement.

From the very beginning, the rookie blueliner showed absolutely no
preference for his victims. During a collision with the Rangers'
center Mark Messier in a corner of the Nassau Coliseum rink,
captain Messier unceremoniously tossed a right cross at Darius.
Most NHL opponents would be willing to leave it at that, but
Kasparaitis counterattacked with such vigor that even the normally
implacable Messier was taken aback.

"Darius has kicked Philadelphia's Kevin Dineen during a fight,"
noted *Hartford Courant* reporter Jeff Jacobs, "and hit the Bruins'

Steve Heinze in the face with the butt end of his stick. In the Patrick Division finals, he dropped Lemieux and Jaromir Jagr as if they were a couple of nobodies."

Early in the 1992-93 season — when it had become apparent that Darius was a terror on skates — many observers believed that Kasparaitis would be fortunate to finish the campaign in one piece. He not only did that, but also had put the fear of god into many of the foe.

While his Russian compatriots expressed a fear of television interviews, "Casper the Friendly Ghost," as he was nicknamed on Long Island, showed absolutely no concern about appearing in front of the camera.

During an interview with SportsChannel's Jiggs McDonald, Kasparaitis was asked if he was the hardest-hitting player in the NHL. "No, I don't think so," he replied, "but I like my game. It's my game. I give clean hits. I like my hits. But I know a lot of guys from other teams don't like me because I hit stars like Lemieux and Messier. I'm friendly, but on ice it's hockey. It's a job. It's my money. I hit because people like hits. When I play the Devils, I know before the game they'll hate me. I go into the game ready. I don't want to hit Randy McKay, but this time I hit McKay and the players from the Devils go hit me, fight me, but I'm not scared. That's my game."

Ever since Kasparaitis nailed McKay with a hip check early in the 1992-93 season — and sidelined the Devil for a considerable period — Darius has been a marked man in Byrne Arena.

"He hurts people," said McKay. "He got me good. He saw his opportunity and he gave me a big hit. I definitely don't like the way he plays, but that's why he's effective."

Many opponents have acknowledged their dislike for "Casper the Ghost," but allowed that they would love to have him on their side.

"The kid runs around like a nut," said Devils' defenseman Ken Daneyko. "He's got a lot of spunk and plays hard, but we can do without the cheap shots. He's going to have to expect the same back. He's going to learn the hard way. It's going to be a long career and it's going to catch up to him. You live by the sword, you die by it."

Those who listen to Kasparaitis during interviews are touched by his candor. For example, he was asked about his mother's first visit to the United States. He told me (Stan Fischler) on SportsChannel: "It's her first time outside Lithuania. She come to America and feel like she's in a dream. She go shopping, watch glass. I say, 'Mom, you can touch. You can buy this.' She says, 'I feel like I'm in a museum.'"

Another time I (Fischler) asked him whether he's bothered about getting the opposition angry.

"Yeah," he replied. "Sometimes I feel bad. I make clean hits, but guys don't like them. I hit a guy in the first period and the whole game I must turn around always because one guy might come and fight with me, give me an injury. But that's my game."

Veteran teammates such as Ray Ferraro are often awed by "Casper's" ingenuousness.

"Sometimes he says things and he has no idea why the guys are laughing," said Ferraro. "Before game seven of the playoffs in Pittsburgh [May 1993], the anthem singer was practicing. Kas comes in the room, singing 'The Star Spangled Banner.' But the words were all in the wrong order. It was hilarious. He knocked the guys right off their seats before our biggest game of the season. At least he had the tune right."

Out of the arena Kasparaitis is often just as hilarious. He bought an $80,000 BMW, drove it to Manhattan and twice in the same day it was towed away for parking violations. During the playoffs, he backed his expensive auto out of the Nassau Coliseum parking lot but, in the process, knocked over a light stanchion. The repair bill was $500.

His teammates often have fun at Darius' expense.

"The guys teach me everything," he recalled, "bad words and good words. When I talk with the guys, I get good practice for my English and they teach me how to get the other team angry. They taught me to tell them, 'How is your wife and my kids?' Funny, huh?"

Obviously, the enemy doesn't consider "Casper the Friendly Ghost" very funny. But Islanders' fans adore the young blond, and his teammates second the motion.

"Just what we need," concluded captain Patrick Flatley, "a Russian with an attitude!"

V

THIRD DEGREE

Chapter 18

THE HEAVYWEIGHTS

SILENT BUT DEADLY: RANDY McKAY

"It's the most important thing to keep your balance, so even if you get hit real hard you have your balance and you have your feet underneath you and you're able to protect yourself."

When Devils' favorite Troy Crowder was plucked by the Detroit Red Wings during the summer of 1991, New Jersey hockey fans mourned the loss of their enforcer. However, the Devils received Dave Barr and Randy McKay as compensation.

To the delight of Byrne Arena denizens, McKay not only emerged as an effective enforcer, but also displayed a scoring talent that far exceeded Crowder's. While Troy quietly faded into obscurity, McKay emerged as the archetypal slugger-checker who also could put points on the board.

McKay tells it like it is in an interview with reporter Eric Servetah during a game between the New Jersey Devils and the New York Islanders at the Byrne Meadowlands Arena in New Jersey, in which McKay sat out due to a face injury.

ES: You're respected as a hard-nosed player and for your tenacity.

RM:If talent was the only reason for people being in the league, I don't think I'd be here. I have talent, but everything that I've accomplished has been because of my persistence. When I fight it's the same thing. If I take a couple of shots, I'm not happy tying up the guy and losing the fight by a little. Taking a couple of shots makes me even madder and hungrier to come back and turn the fight around.

ES: Do you watch fight tapes?

RM:Not really, although I watched one in the locker room once in 1992-93. I'm not one of those guys who sits around and studies other player's fighting. I watch my own fights to study what I do right and what I do wrong. This much is certain — any time a fight happens during a game you see people on their feet, screaming and banging. Fans like fights. They're paying to get in, so we should let them have that fun.

ES: You always have a stoic look on your face when you're on the ice.

RM:When I'm out there, I'm trying to do the best I can and I work hard. I take the game seriously. For example, doing this interview is unusual for me, because I don't often like to talk about this part of the game.

ES: What's the strong point of Randy McKay's game?

RM:My work in the corners and my forechecking. I have to get in there crashing and banging to get the puck loose. I like to go to the net. That's where I've scored most of my goals. A lot are scored from within three feet of the net. I'll go in deep and work for the puck and go after rebounds. That's what I have to keep doing. I was a bit disappointed with my point production in 1992-93. The knee injury set me back a bit and I struggled to get back in shape.

ES: Is Randy Mckay going to get over 40 points one season?

RM:I would love to score 40 points. A lot depends on how I'm going to be used. But whichever way I'm used, I have to work hard and do the best I can. If I'm used in a fourth-line situation to get things going and change the tempo, it's going to be tough.

ES: Why haven't you fought Tie Domi?

RM.In 1991-92 I almost fought him at home. I've always wanted to fight Tie. I was going to fight him early in the game, but it didn't happen. I remember wanting to get back on the ice at the end of the game to fight him. Robbie Ftorek gave me shit for wanting to fight him. He told me, it's not going to prove anything. At that point in the 1991-92 season, I had 15 goals and I was playing regularly on the top three lines. Things were going real well and I realized that I wasn't going to prove anything by fighting him late in the game. It wasn't going to change the score in the game, and the only thing that I was going to do was either hurt myself or look bad. Either way I wasn't going to gain anything. When you fight a guy like Domi, if you lose, you look dumb because he's so small and stuff — and if you win, well, you were supposed to win. So it's a lose-lose situation.

ES: What do you think about Tie's antics and the Probert incident?

RM: It was hyped by Domi himself and blown out of proportion. He promoted the whole thing. He was talking to the papers all the time and saying stuff about Probie and himself. He got himself the publicity and he paid for it. He got beat up and he looked stupid in the papers. With as many punches as Probie hit him — somebody said 46 times — he still didn't hurt him. It was a lose-lose situation for Bob. As good as he did — and he beat Domi bad — Tie didn't have a cut on his face. Probie won the fight, but Domi looked good.

ES: Talk about your wars with Mike Peluso.

RM: We had our first two fights in exhibition a few years ago. I didn't know too much about him other than he came up through the minors. The year before I had only played three games for the Wings and I was going into training camp with coach Bryan Murray. Before you knew it, we fought twice in that first exhibition game and since then it's worked out that in every game we play against each other, we fight. We have a little thing with each other and it continued into 1992-93. I have more respect for him after last season. He's a lot like me in that he can play the game also. It was his shot last year and two years ago was my shot to prove myself as a player. I think last year was his chance to prove himself and he did well and showed people that he can play. He shows up every night and works hard at his game.

ES: How did your first two fights go?

RM: In the first one I would have to say that I won that fight outright. I was very motivated, since I missed some of the first exhibition games from being hurt, so I was all wound up inside. We were fighting right in front of our bench and I came out the winner in that one. The next fight wasn't much. It happened behind the net. I was tired and I grabbed on and we started wrestling more or less. From then on, we fought quite a bit.

ES: Do you think Mike is a better fighter since he's done some things to improve his balance, like taking the tape off his skates?

RM: His balance was a big problem for him. He fought and showed up all of the time, but it seemed like he would lose his balance. I think he still can learn a little bit, since he's a good fighter, but he tends to lose his balance. I was watching a fight tape the other day with a bunch of the guys and in every fight you could see him lose his balance. He does well in the fights until he starts to stumble. He's got to learn to get his gravity and center himself over his feet and get himself comfortable.

ES: How important is balance for you?

RM: It's real important and one of my biggest assets. I get myself a good base and I grab on and I'm on a solid base to stand and fight from there. It's the most important thing to keep your balance, so even if you get hit real hard you have your balance and you have your feet underneath you and you're able to protect yourself.

ES: A good example of this was in your fight with Brad May. You were in trouble, but you stood up and you were able to win the fight.

RM: I came up from behind him and I didn't think he was going to be ready and he turned around and dropped his gloves and hit me right away. I grabbed on and he has the big jersey and he kept throwing them. He did real well and he surprised me in that he was a little better than I thought. I had hurt my wrist and I couldn't hold on and it seemed as if I had a good grip on his jersey, but I couldn't hold him off. My wrist was bending too much in his jersey and I couldn't hold on, so I had to take some punches. I took about four or five good punches and there was nothing I could do, so I pulled my head up and I stood in there and tried to swing back. We were going toe-to-toe and he hit me and I would hit him. Then I switched hands and then I went back to my right. It was the kind of fight where I had to stay in and go with the flow. I had to hang in there and wait for my opportunity, but I was taking some punches. There was nothing I could do about it. That was a good fight and I came back strong. I've watched it on video maybe four or five times since then.

ES: Do you like watching your fights?

RM: Yeah. I like to go home and watch them and see what I did and what I could have done.

ES: What have you learned from this? What was the best thing you got out of watching all these fights?

RM: I learned that when I throw, to keep my head up to make my punches count rather than just throwing them. I make sure I keep my head up and keep the fights from getting away from my style.

ES: A player like Marty McSorley wears a big jersey. What do you think about that in terms of fighting?

RM: It's great to wear a little nothing jersey, but it can hurt you if a guy get's a hold on your sleeve. My jersey's a little tight so we tried to order a new one, but it never worked out. But definitely I'll wear a bigger jersey. The problem is, if a guy gets a good grip on your right hand with a tight jersey, there's nothing you can do. You can fight all that you can, but you're just tiring yourself out trying to get loose and trying to punch. It can help a little bit wearing that oversized jersey like Marty does because you go to grab him and you come up with a fist full of sleeve. So with a bigger jersey, it definitely helps as long as they don't grab your arm itself.

ES: Do you tie down?

RM: Yes. It's something that I've always done and if you look at a lot of guys who don't tie down anymore, they get that jersey caught over their heads and wind up taking some shots. Ken Daneyko and I were watching some fighting tapes and saw that more and more guys weren't tying down. I could see the bonus of it if the jersey comes completely over your head and you're free, but it hurt Dave Brown when I fought him. I saw Wendel Clark fighting Probert and Bobby didn't have the jersey tied down and it hurt him. The jersey came up over his head and Wendel landed a bunch of punches. If you get out of your jersey, it's a bonus, but then again you could get your jersey caught up on you. So, I think I'll always tie down and go to a bigger-sleeved jersey. I'm happy enough just staying in there during a fight and throwing them. I've had enough success throwing them just the way that I've done it.

ES: Are you good with the left?

RM: I use it once in a while and I started using it a couple of years ago, and in 1991-92 I used it. It depends on how the fight is going and who I'm fighting and what I'm doing. I'm aware of it and have started to use it more and I've been pretty successful at it. I hit Brad May with a couple of good lefts and at the end when he stopped and I actually hit him with a real good left. I just find that I don't keep my balance as well when I throw a left. I could throw them pretty hard, but I find that it throws me more off-balance and I don't like being off-balance. I like to be in control during my fights.

ES: You mentioned that in your first fight with Mike you were really wound up. How much motivation is there when you fight?

RM: I was wound up in that fight because I was trying to prove myself to a new coach and trying to prove myself to a team that didn't know me well. So I got pumped up, and as long as I go out and enjoy it and as long as I want to be successful in this league, I have to do it.

ES: Early in the 1992-93 preseason, Dave Brown took his jersey completely off before his fights. What do you think about this?

RM: Then it's more of a bar-room brawl then a regular fight. It would throw me off a little bit. I don't think it makes much sense, and if it happens during a fight, then it happens. But I like to stand back and fight with the jersey on. If I'm ready to go, then I go and I drop the gloves and that's it. If you have to stand back and drop your gloves, and then first take your shirt off and then say "Let's go," it loses the spirit of the moment.

ES: What do you do before a fight?

RM: Every time I fight, I adjust my elbow pad and push them up and make sure that everything is set in place.

ES: Tell me about the fight you had with Darin Kimble in the playoffs two years ago between the Wings and the Blues.

RM: That was a good fight, but I felt that he beat me and I was a little bummed out because he hit me more than I hit him. I was throwing a lot of them, but most of my punches were missing. That was my third fight of the game and I was just coming back from an injury. I was trying to motivate the team and it was a quick little fight in which we were throwing some bombs. This was the first and only time I fought Kimble and he didn't beat me by a lot, but he connected more than I did. Once a guy starts connecting it throws your momentum off, and once you get your momentum off, you're trying to battle back and it's hard to win a fight when you're not in the groove.

ES: What was your role with Detroit when you weren't fighting a lot?

RM: At first I didn't fight much, but then I started to fight and that made Joey Kocur available in a trade. He knew it and I knew it, and because I was fighting more, he was the big name and they could afford to get rid of him. They had me as the new guy and decided to keep me and Probie there to do the rough work. That's why I couldn't believe that they picked Troy Crowder up and left me available. I couldn't believe that because I thought they were real happy with me, but it probably was the best thing that could have ever happened to me. I came to New Jersey and I wasn't in the shadow of Probert or Kocur and it was just me and Ken Daneyko. We knew that we had to do the fighting and that I could be the lone physical forward on the team. So I started to fight more with the Devils and I started to get real good at it.

ES: Tell me about coming to New Jersey and replacing Troy Crowder, especially since not much was known about you.

RM: I was aware of it from a fan's point of view and I was told by the brass and the coaches that I wasn't expected to replace Troy. The papers were saying that, but they told me to feel no pressure and that I didn't have to fight. Tom McVie knew what kind of player I was from the minors since I played against him and he told me to just play my game. He said, "You're not here to replace Crowder as a fighter." He never made me do anything. Tom played me as a fourth-liner or a third-liner and I worked hard and did everything and started to work my way up. Fighting was a part that I took on myself. I fought nine times in the exhibition games and that's when they told me that it's not something that I have to do to prove myself.

ES: How did those fights in exhibition go?

RM:I fought everybody (laughing). I was doing real well in every fight and I started to get into a groove. My last year in Detroit I was starting to get good, but it was in the exhibition games during my first season in New Jersey when I was really good at fighting. I started to realize then that I was fighting heavy-weights every night, I was successful, and I realized I could do it. I became more and more confident last year and I kept on doing well all year.

ES: How much did Joe Kocur and Bob Probert help you in regards to fighting?

RM:They didn't help me in teaching me how to fight. But in Detroit, Joey would make sure that I didn't have to fight the heavy-weights. I remember one night in Edmonton when Dave Brown was chasing me, Joey had the coach not let me to go on the ice and fight him. Back then I was just breaking in and it wasn't the time for me to be fighting a big heavyweight. They were two different guys. When Probie fought, he had the reach and the strength and you never knew what he was going to do. There was no rhyme or reason for anything he did. He just did it and went crazy and would beat up his opponents. Joey was a great fighter, basically because of his right hand. One thing I learned from Probie was that you should let the guy tire out as much as you could. Probie would take a lot of punches when he fought and then allow the guys to tire out before fighting back. So Bob would drop the gloves and hold on, take a couple and wait, take a couple more, and wait for his opening. Learning that has helped me more than anything. I have people in Detroit telling me that I fight like Probert. I would grab on and wait and after 10 or 15 seconds the opponent would start to get frustrated, and then I would start to throw them. That's one thing that I learned from Probie.

ES: If it came down to it, would you ever fight Bob Probert?

RM:I don't think we ever would, unless something really happened. With me, any time I'm a good friend with someone I'll play hard against him and hit him, but to stand back and fight him is different. I have to be mad at someone or I have to be doing it for a purpose, and I couldn't fight a friend unless something arose that made me real pissed off. It's the same thing with Joe Kocur, since I was his roommate for a year-and-a-half in Detroit. We have too much respect and we're too good as friends to fight. We got along real well in Detroit, and unless something bad happened I don't think we would fight.

ES: I'm going to be critical of you and your non-involvement in that big 1992 brawl with the Rangers. Take me through the incident and your reason for not getting involved.

RM: When it first broke out, it was calm and cool. Joey Kocur came over and when I tried to get in somewhere, he grabbed me. We sort of danced around a little bit and watched what was going on. When I tried to go after someone else, Joey just held me and wouldn't let me go. He said, "Randy, stay back." I believe Adam Graves was hitting Claude Lemieux from behind and then Tie Domi jumped over the boards with Scott Stevens, and then I broke away from Joey. I went over to Graves and I got hold of him, but that was at the end of it. It was tough, because Joey grabbed me and I grabbed him and I wasn't going to let him go anywhere and he wasn't going to let me go anywhere. We pretty much neutralized each other and we were still doing our jobs, without standing back and throwing them. I remember the whole incident. Claude Lemieux, who was my roommate, asked me where I was during the whole incident, when he was getting banged around from all different sides. I was watching the incident the whole time and if something happened I'd remember it, because when Graves did something I got away. I pushed Kocur out of the way and I grabbed onto Adam. I was trying to make sure that nobody was going to get cheap-shotted and, if they were, I was going to jump in. I was waiting to jump in and it turned out that Joey and I neutralized each other.

ES: What are your thoughts on that incident looking back at it now?

RM: It was stupid. We were winning the game and they got frustrated and wanted to do something. That was really cheap. I like to play physical and do this during the game, but at the end of the game like that, it doesn't prove anything to anybody.

ES: That season Tom McVie said, "Randy's been chopping down all of the trees this season." This was in reference to your fighting all of the heavyweights. What did this mean to you?

RM: It meant a lot to me. You love to have a coach respect you as a player. It's just like a coach who respects a Mario Lemieux or any great goal scorer like an Alexander Semak or a Claude Lemieux on our team. It's what they do for a team and it's similar to what I do for a team, but it's not with the goal scoring. Tommy respected me for what I did and that was showing up and playing hard; because of that, I admire him as a coach.

ES: You said that you were full of confidence with your fighting. So was it your intention to go out and chop down all of the heavyweights?

RM: It wasn't my intention to just go out and do that. If you look back to the exhibition games, people knew that I was a gamer and I fought, but they came to fight me. Sure in the exhibition games, I accepted their challenges and at the start of the season I did it. I think that I must have had 20 of my majors by the 50-game mark, and after that I may have had only seven or eight in the last 30 games. This wasn't a lot of fights. I had established a reputation as not just a fighter. The better you start doing and the more you are wining the fewer guys out there who want to fight. Fights won't happen so spontaneously anymore.

ES: How do you handle the adjustment of fighting and playing it tough and yet maintaining a skill level of hockey on the ice?

RM: It's tough. The tougher I play, the more I play. Guys start to shy away and back off and it gives me a little bit more room to develop and show my skills. Any time you get an extra step on someone, you're that much better of a player. That's what happened and because of it my point total started to go up.

ES: Talk about your big game-winning goal against Montreal in the 1991-92 season. Was that the start of your offensive success?

RM: I had two against Montreal, one of which was a game winner. It definitely was the start of my offensive confidence. I had five goals going into the game and then I scored my sixth and seventh against Montreal. It was my home town and I was the first star of the game. It was almost a dream come true. From there on I had a little more confidence and things started to go for me the more I played.

ES: Tell me about your fight with Robert Dirk of the Canucks.

RM: It was in New Jersey and I did well against him. Dirk is a big kid and I had the right hands going and landed most of the shots. I also fought Gino Odjick that year, and fought over 25 guys.

ES: Talk about Gino Odjick. Do you respect him as a fighter, since a lot of guys seem not to respect him as much as they do others?

RM: It's hard to say since I only see him a couple of times a year. I fought him twice in 1991-92 and he was more of a wrestler. He just wanted to tie me up and not throw many punches. I don't really know him and I can't really say, since I don't play him enough to know whether he's dirty or not. Our fights were more of a wrestling match than anything. We tied up and wrestled. We didn't sit back and throw them.

ES: How do you feel about wrestling in a fight? Is this something you want to do?

RM: No. I'd rather just stand back and throw them. I want to throw as many punches as I can. I don't like tying up and throwing one, tying up and throwing one. If we're going to throw them, I'd rather just stand back and throw as much as I can. That's what's fighting is about and that's what's best for me.

ES: Who else did you fight?

RM: I fought Dan Kordic, the big Philadelphia Flyers' defenseman. That was one of my earlier fights and I did real well against him.

He's a big kid and young. I threw everything but the kitchen sink at him. It was an unbelievable fight and my hand was killing me after it. I don't think he did so good, because he's usually a righty and I think I grabbed onto his right and he de- cided to go left against me. That was not his strong point. So he had his left against my right and I managed to get the better of him.

ES: How about Alan May?

RM: When I fight Alan, he tries to do a lot of cross-gripping. He's a lefty, so he tries to reach across with his right and grab onto your right and tie you up and throw. I fought him and I did well against him a couple of times. He's hung in there and I respect him for what he does. I fought him again and did well against him. We fight when we run into each other, so you could expect a few more tussles in our days.

ES: Which type of fighter gives you the most trouble — a bigger guy or a smaller guy?

RM: The bigger guy. It's not that it's more trouble, it just that I'm more aware of him. I have to make sure that I'm thinking and I know what I'm doing and reacting. I have to be aware of a big guy's strength.

ES: Tell me about your fight with Stu Grimson.

RM: It went well. I fought him a couple of years ago and he tied my right hand up real well and I went left against him. I wound up doing okay in the fight, but Stu's a gamer. I've seen Stu stand in there in a lot of fights and throw them. I only fought him that one time and I'm happy the way I did against him.

ES: In your fight with Doody Wood of the Sharks, the referees jumped in really quick. Talk about the fight and your thoughts on the linesmen's quick entry.

RM: They jumped in fast because they wanted to protect him. Doody's a young kid, so I think they felt it was a good time to jump in before we started throwing them. I was tying him up and I was waiting to see what he was going to do, so I didn't jump right at him. But just as I got ready to start throwing lefts — I thought it was a good opportunity to surprise him and land some lefts — the linesman jumped in and broke it up. The majority of the linesmen do a good job, and it is their responsibility to jump in and break a fight up before it starts. It's always a tough situation, because that night when they jumped in, I could have hit him. I had thrown about three punches. I guess they thought we were just going to wrestle and they would jump in and break it up.

ES: What are your thoughts on the direction of the league in regard to fighting?

RM: The rules are fair. The instigator rule is good, because it stops guys from running around and starting fights. If you fight three times in a game and you get thrown out, that's a good rule too. It's not taking fighting out of the game, but it's cleaning the game up a little bit. It gets rid of the guy who just goes out and starts a fight, and that's his only purpose. There's no need for a guy who takes three shifts and then wants to fight. But if the league tries to do more than this, a lot of guys are going to be skating around brave and start wielding their sticks. Guys are going to start doing chippy things that they would not normally do. Players don't really get hurt from fighting, so I think that there's still room for it and a need for it. If there's no fighting, guys who don't fight after a whistle will stick you or give you an extra cross-check or a face rub. With fighting, you keep the game more honest and respectful in terms of less dirty stick work.

ES: Which young fellow on your team can you help out with advice regarding fisticuffs?

RM: Billy Guerin would be the guy. I don't think he'll ever have the need to fight as often as I did, but I've spoken to him about it. There's room for fighting in his game and I've told him that any time players know that he's willing and ready to go, he is going to get an extra foot. Any time you get that extra inch or foot it's going to help. You also won't get as pushed around as much after the whistle. Guys will start to respect you. I told Billy that every once in a while, when the need arises, and if he feels it's a good situation to fight, he should fight. He's a big kid and knows his role and this opens up his mind more and his game.

ES: What can you offer Bill Guerin regarding the style of fighting?

RM: He needs to work on his balance and get stable before he throws. Right now he's young and he gets a little excited and he goes in too quick and starts to throw them. He's got to learn how to be patient and grab on and hold and hold until he's stable and sees an opening. He's learning that and he's going to get better.

ES: What's the worst that you have done to a guy in a fight and the worst that has happened to you?

RM: I've broken a couple of guys' noses and I've given a couple of guys stitches. The worst that has happened to me was getting a few stitches and nothing real major that has caused me to miss a game. Sometimes it's the funniest things that cause you to get stitches. When I fought Alan May he hit me four or five times as hard as I could be hit and nothing happened, and then another time I got hit once and got cut. It really depends upon how you get hit and where you get hit. Once, when I fought Link Gaetz, he hit me and cut me on the chin with one punch.

ES: Was this your first fight with Gaetz or the second fight with him?

RM: This was my second one. The first fight I had with him was when I was with the Red Wings. He hit me with a hard punch and there's not much difference in his fighting ability from the first time I fought him a couple of years ago to the one I had with him more recently.

ES: Tell me about your fight with Cam Russell.

RM:That was early in the year in Chicago and it was a good fight. He hit me in the throat and I wound up with a hoarse voice. I did well in the fight, but he caught me with a good punch in the throat. It really hurt at the time and the doctors don't know if it's going to go away. It's a lot better than it used to be.

ES: What were your thoughts going into your second season [1992-93] with the Devils?

RM:I wanted to come back and have another good solid year. The toughest thing is not to sit back and be satisfied with what you have done. I always have to keep pushing to keep the pace with what you have done or even take my game to another level. That's what I tried to do and I thought I had a real good camp and started off real well. I wasn't fighting as much, but it wasn't because I didn't want to, it was that things weren't arising as much. Then I got hurt and that set me back a little bit.

ES: Tell me about your injury in a game against the Islanders.

RM:Darius Kasparaitus hit me low with a hip check and it caught my right knee. I came back after four weeks and when I first came back, I wasn't 100 percent. It took me a good seven games to get going. I had to wear a brace but I wasn't comfortable with it.

ES: Was it a dirty hit?

RM:It was not a penalty because hip checks are allowed in the league, but I think it was a cheap shot. I was coming across the middle and he didn't step up on me, he came across on the side and it was cheap. He does it every game and it makes him a marked man. When I play against him, he better keep his head up and remember, because it's not just me who will be after him. There are a lot of guys who want him. Craig Berube went after him in Nassau Coliseum and at that point in the game, with the Islanders losing 7-2, it's not the time to start making enemies. Darius has to learn when to do things and when not to do things. I'm sure he'd do it again on me and that's fine, but he better remember to keep his head up and watch where I am on the ice.

ES: Now that you've had success with fighting, do you come to training camp thinking that you're not going to have to go through the fighting of previous camps?

RM:After you establish a reputation like I did, guys aren't really going to come after you as much. Guys aren't looking to prove themselves against you. They are looking to fight guys who they think they could take in a fight. It's the kind of thing that happens and I just went into camp and made sure that I was in good shape and ready.

ES: Was your fight with Dave Brown in 1992-93 your first one?

RM: No. I had previously fought him in an exhibition and he probably beat me, but I think I did well against him. I popped him really good and I stood in there and I threw some at him and he threw the big left at me. But I was very happy. When I fought Brown, I wasn't preparing for it at all, but I knew it was going to happen and I got ready. I wanted to get a good start on him and I pulled his jersey over his head and then I started throwing them. I got lucky when he got tied up in his jersey and he wasn't able to punch back. I got worried when he started to come out of his jersey, but I just kept throwing them.

ES: Do you keep a mental book on different fighters in the league?

RM: I keep a little bit of one. I think Ken Daneyko keeps a big book on the guys in the league. He knows the styles of every fighter in the league and how they fight. If I have an idea that I'm going to fight somebody, I'll ask Dano if he's a righty or a lefty or what he does. Dano knows pretty much about every fighter in the league and what to do against them.

ES: Talk about Danekyo and the fact that he never really loses a fight.

RM: The thing is that he's so strong; he stands in there and he grabs and throws and grabs and throws. I fought him when I was in Detroit and now he's one of my closest friends on the team. It's something that happens and when you look back, it was probably a dead-even fight. He hit me with the first three or four and then we exchanged punches for three or four and then I hit him with the last three or four. It was a great fight.

ES: How is it having fighters like Danekyo and Scott Stevens on your team. Does it make your job easier?

RM: I don't know that's it's easier. Kenny plays so much now that it's not really wise for him to fight. He's expected to do it when he has to do it and he'll jump in for his teammates when he has to, but it's hard for him to do it when he's playing 20 to 25 minutes per game. He will play strong and fight the odd time and will be there with his physical presence. Stevens hits a lot and plays physical, but when he's playing 30 minutes a game there's no need for him to go off for five minutes to fight. Scott doesn't have to prove himself anymore. If somebody gets carried away, Scott will jump in and do it, but it's more my job than anybody else's on the team. It's up to me to straighten anybody out that needs some straightening.

ES: Do you take pride in your job?

RM: Yes. That's part of my job and I have to know that and be aware of that all of the time.

ES: Do you like to fight and do you think that this will be something that will slip away from over the years?

RM: It's hard to say. I can't see myself fighting any less than I have this year. I want to do it sometimes and there will always be a need in my game to do it. That's one of my roles and I have no problem doing it.

ES: Explain the change in your fighting style.

RM: I try to throw more punches now and I'm not scared to take one. If I don't have a great grip on a guy, I continue to throw them. If I take a couple that's good, because I'm looking more for the bigger punches and the harder punches, than to just look good and come out of the fight with a draw like I used to. I still try to get a good grip with my left and get a good solid base under me and then start throwing. That's always been the same, but now I just throw a little bit more and a little bit harder. In order to do that you have to take a couple of chances and sometimes you're going to get hit.

ES: Did you ever take boxing lessons?

RM: No, not at all. I don't think there's a need for it with me.

ES: Where you ever scared of fighting a guy before you fought?

RM: There's always a little bit of nerves any time you get into a fight. Before I fought Brown in 1992-93, going up the ice I knew that I was going to fight him and it was just a matter of time. When it happens you are a little bit nervous about what you are going to do and how you are going to react when the fight starts. But that happens a lot and it's very seldom that I go out and fight with a cocky attitude that I'm going to go out and rip his head off. I'm always aware and a little nervous. I was a lot more nervous earlier in my career. When you are a young fighter, you get more nervous.

ES: Do you consider yourself a dirty player?

RM: Not at all.

ES: What do you think of Rob Ray?

RM: Personally, I think he's a piece of meat. He doesn't know how to play the game and all he does is run around on the ice and yap off. I played against him in the minors and he never fought, but he had over 400 penalty minutes. I never saw him fight and he was the kind of guy who after the whistle, would cross-check you and make a big scene and yap at the referees or players and get thrown out of the game. It just wouldn't stop and he would pick up the 10-minute misconducts, but I never saw him fight, not once. Then, all of a sudden he comes up to the NHL, and people start calling him a tough guy. To stay in the NHL, he had to start fighting a bit. I don't respect this guy at all as a player. He can get his 400 penalty minutes and be happy about it. In 1991-92 I had 230 minutes and I was 20th in the league, but I was third in majors for fighting. I had over 27 fights. I don't pride myself over getting 10-minute misconducts and game misconducts, like Ray does. I care about how many majors I have for fighting and whether I'm there or not.

ES: Who are some of the guys you respect and would consider heavyweights?

RM: Joey Kocur, Bob Probert and Mike Peluso. There's also Dave Brown and Marty McSorley. I respect Brown for what he does. He's in a tough situation with not getting much ice time and he does his job. He doesn't yap and he's not dirty and he's a clean-cut guy. The time I fought him in 1992-93, he wanted to fight me again. I had been happy with how I did the first time and I didn't feel there was a need to fight again that late in the game. He said, "Do you want to go?", and I said, "No", and he skated away. He didn't stick me. He's a very clean player. He doesn't yell or cheap-shot you and he goes about his business really well.

ES: Talk about your fights with Louie DeBrusk.

RM: Louie DeBrusk is a really good fighter. I fought him more than three times already in my career. He fights a lot like me. He's a strong kid and he grabs on and he has a long reach. He uses his balance well and he throws pretty well. He hit me a couple of good ones in Edmonton when I fought him and he had a great grip on me and I couldn't get loose with my right hand.

ES: How much talking is done on the ice before a fight, like with Brownie?

RM: I don't talk much and I don't ask guys to go. It's really my physical play that does it. If a guy wants to go, I'll grab on and look at him and then go. I'm just not much of a talker to the other team and I keep pretty quiet and go about my business. There's always some talking with certain guys before a fight, but nothing major. I like to let my physical play do the talking.

ES: Talk about your fight with Jim McKenzie.

RM: I fought him in Hartford. He's a really big, strong, tough guy. He's probably one of the toughest big guys in the league, and underrated. The reason why he's underrated is that he doesn't fight that much. I don't know if he likes to do it but he doesn't fight very often. I stood back with him when we fought. He's a righty who went lefty against me, and when I lost my grip on his right, he got the best of me. He hit me with a couple and they just kept coming and I was trying to throw back and every time I threw one he'd hit me again. I hung in there and I was losing and losing, but with my persistence I came back and hit him again with a few and started to do well. So he grabbed on to me and wrestled me down to the ice. He's a really tough guy — big and strong. He got the best of me. I lost the fight.

ES: How important is it for you to win the fights?

RM: I don't ever go into a fight to lose. If you just show up to a fight — especially if you're trying to motivate your team and you lose — there's no sense in doing it. I was happy with my persistence against McKenzie. Our team was more motivated watching me standing there, taking a couple of punches and then coming back at him. I kept on coming back and hitting him and he had to wrestle me down to the boards. I never want to lose, so that's why I will always hang in there and do the best that I can.

ES: How good are you at fighting?

RM: I'm a lot better than I was, but it depends on a lot of things. Anybody can beat anybody, so you just have to go into the fight wanting to win.

ES: Talk about Nick Kypreos.

RM: I never fought him, but I respect him. He is a hard worker and a pretty good hockey player. He can throw them.

ES: What did Barry Melrose do for you when you where with the Adirondack Wings?

RM: He made me realize my potential. I had it, but he forced me to keep going after it. I think Bill Dineen had the most effect on me. He knew I could play and he just let me play in all different types of situations. Barry Melrose more or less expected this of me and made me realize that hard work is the key. He put me on lines with guys who weren't so good. Bill Dineen was my first coach in Adirondack and my first coach to talk to me about fighting. He told me that I have to stay away from some punches and that I can't always lead with my face. Melrose was different in that he taught me when to do the right thing on the ice. Barry wanted me to play more and be more of a hockey player. We had a few good guys on the team, but Melrose didn't put myself and these guys on the same line. He separated us and made each line deeper, so I didn't score as much in the beginning. He wanted me to prove myself as a player by playing with guys who weren't so good. Melrose showed me when to fight and when not to fight and how to pick and choose. This was very important. Now I don't have to fight as often and most of my fights are on my terms. For me it's important not having to fight every guy or big heavyweight who goes looking for me. Melrose never told me to go out and fight a guy. It was a case of knowing when to do it at the proper times. I picked my spots and did it on my terms.

ES: How have your hands handled fighting?

RM: My hands are fine. I never really broke anything. I've had a cut or two from some fights, but nothing broken. I don't condition my knuckles like the Twister. He must be a little bit crazy and I'm not much into that.

ES: Tell me about some of your earlier NHL fights.

RM: I fought Link Gaetz in one of my first two NHL fights. I knew Link Gaetz was a good fighter. He was too strong for me then and he won the fight. The same thing happened when I fought Mark Tinordi. He won, but I was learning then. I learned how to wait and be patient, and try to hold guys off. Right now, I'm pretty close to my prime in terms of fighting and I'm much better at it now. If I fought Link Gaetz now things would be much different than they were back then. I'm smarter and I know when to tie somebody up and how to be more patient. I'm able to stay away and tire a guy out and I know how to take a big punch. Back then, when I would get hit, I would be off-balance. Now I'm able to maintain my balance after getting hit and fight back. I don't like throwing the left, but I'm getting better at it. Throwing the left is different because you have to know when to throw it and at which particular players. I'm not as confident with the left. A reason I started fighting was because of my size. I said, "I'm going to stay in this league because of my size and ability to fight."

ES: How important is fair fighting?

RM: Fighting fair is important for me. Look at my record; I've only instigated maybe two fights.

Chapter 19

THE HEAVYWEIGHTS

THE TWISTER: TONY TWIST

"I get pissed off when I hear people criticize fighting. You never see a fan go for popcorn in the middle of a fight. Imagine somebody goes for a snack in the middle of a fight. C'mon, the fans stand up and they think it's fun."

The Saskatoon Blades of the Western Hockey League have, for better or worse, produced some of the NHL's most notorious penalty collectors. One of them is hard-throwing Tony Twist, a native of Sherwood Park, Alberta. Originally signed by the St. Louis Blues, Twist was traded to Quebec in February, 1991.

A student of hockey fights, Tony produced his own video, "The Twister," a cavalcade of Tony's bouts from his days in Junior hockey to the NHL present.

As is the case with so many enforcers, Twist is the height of gentility away from the fray. Tony knows his role. He spelled it out in detail to Eric Servetah during an interview at Nassau Coliseum, during a game between Quebec and the Islanders.

ES: Tell me about how you got started in pro hockey.

TT: I never thought I would play pro hockey until I got drafted. It's not that I didn't have aspirations to play the game — it's that I never thought that I'd be there. When I was drafted by St. Louis in the ninth round, I couldn't believe it, since I was all set to go to Vancouver's camp as a walk-on. After St. Louis drafted me I went to training camp with only one thing on my mind and that was to go out there and fight. The next thing you know, they gave me a contract.

ES: When did you first put on skates and play hockey?

TT: When I was in bantam and midget. I was captain of our team. Glen Wesley was on the second-team All-Stars and I was on the first-team All-Stars. I was playing a lot of hockey as a defenseman and doing pretty well. I started playing Junior in Prince George and found out that I could fight pretty well. I did well in my fights and started to work from there.

ES: Is this where you got into your first fights?

TT: The first fight I had was in the Juniors, not in midgets or anywhere else I played. My first fight on the ice was in the Juniors against this kid Gary Grant, who was a tough kid, tough as nails. I don't know what ever happened to him. Goddamn, he could throw a hard punch! So we'd fight every game. He got thrown out in our first fight. The last 10 minutes of the game we'd fight and they would be some real doozies. I thought that my first experience in fighting was fun, and I did well. I really had no clue about how to fight — I just started throwing and ended up with a black eye every goddamn time. But I won the fights. I caught four or five but I got in my one or two and I won the fights. They were good.

ES: What about your father?

TT: He wasn't into hockey too much, but he was a boxer. My grandfather was a very good boxer, a heavyweight and very good at it. My dad followed in his footsteps and my dad was good, too.

ES: Did they ever show you how to fight?

TT: Oh yeah! Grandad and I used to box all the time. My father would show me, too, but Grandad was the guy who I worked with the most. He used to hit me in the arms so damn hard and I wouldn't want to cry in front of him, so I would walk away and have bruises covering my whole arm.

ES: How tough were you off the ice? Tell me about some fights.

TT: I had a few off the ice. (Laughs) I had my share of street fights.

ES: Who did you fight in Juniors?

TT: I was with the Saskatoon Blades. Marcel Comeau was the coach and I fought Darin Kimble about 20 times over my two years in the WHL. Game in and game out it was Darin Kimble versus Tony Twist. The second fight I ever had in the WHL was with

Darin Kimble, and I just destroyed him. It was a good fight, but I broke his nose. He was the heavyweight in the league at the time. He didn't know who I was, or what I was about, and he took me real light. I thumped him real good, and every game after that we had some good ones. All of our fights were always good ones, but for that fight, he took me too lightly and got a licking.

ES: Did he ever return that licking?

TT: No, he never returned that licking. But we always had some good fights.

ES: What was your style of fighting then?

TT: The same as now. Darin would hit me 10 times to my two or three. He was a quick puncher, but I would hit him with two or three and it always evened out in the end. It was very entertaining for the fans.

ES: Did you have a hockey idol when you were growing up?

TT: I always loved Dave Semenko. For whatever reason, I don't know, but I always was Dave Semenko when we played street hockey. He was just a big guy who kicked ass.

ES: Tell me about getting into the NHL.

TT: When I got drafted I said, "Hey, I got a chance at this shit." I went after it. Then when I got picked up out of Saskatoon by St. Louis, I knew what I had to do. I went out there and wanted to earn a job by fighting. I fought everybody in that camp.

ES: Did you ever have any injuries from fighting?

TT: Not really, although I hyperextended my elbow a few times. That was from throwing a big punch and missing. You usually throw your elbow out from that. I've also broken a couple of knuckles and a couple of fingers. If you look at my hands, you'll see they're all cut up, but they're still working. What I did was start working with a man who was a kick boxer and he showed me how to condition my hands. So I started to condition my hands.

ES: How did you do this?

TT: I would bang them on the floor when I was watching TV. When I would tell this to people, they would say to me that I must be a stupid person. But I'm not a stupid person — I was conditioning my knuckles. When I played Junior, I was fighting a lot. My knuckles would swell up and my punching hand would swell up for a couple of days. Then I'd end up fighting again and my hand would get bigger. During the off-season, the guy who was teaching me kick boxing said he would condition the damn thing. He said that when I was watching TV, to just sit there and bang my hands on the floor for five or six minutes, take a rest and let them swell up the next day. The swelling didn't hurt me, because it made my hands get stronger. Your tendons get stronger and your knuckles get stronger, so the swelling goes away quicker. All it does is condition your hand and make it stronger.

ES: How often do you work out?

TT: I work out during the summer seven days a week, going pretty heavy between the weights and the bike. I also kick box about twice a week. Everything I do is skating oriented so I can pick up my speed.

ES: Did you ever take power-skating lessons?

TT: Many times. You have to learn how to skate better, because the game is changing to a no-fight situation. They are wrong for taking this fighting part of the game away from hockey. I'm all for a good, fast-paced game of hockey, where the guys who can play that fast game play, but the majority of the guys who do fight, damn right they could play that way also. These guys could play the game, but they get pushed into a mold. Guys like myself have to hit and grind and if you have to fight, you fight.

ES: Do you think you can play a checking role for a team?

TT: Sure I can. Craig Berube is a classic example of a player who did that. Here's a guy that can kick some ass and made his way into the league that way, but he can skate, check and shoot and he's a damn good hockey player. Craig's been given a chance and there he is, playing! Joey Kocur is as tough as can be and he's been given a chance and he can play the game. Same with Bob Probert. But I laugh at a guy like Tie Domi because of the act he puts on. I do give the kid all of the credit in the world, because he's a short guy who has built a market for himself from fighting. Watch the guy. Domi can shoot, skate and score. But, he said, "I'm Tie Domi, and I'm going to promote myself." Sure enough, he did and he has gotten himself a lot of attention. I throw my hat off to the kid and yet everybody tries to cut him down and make him out to be a goon with no talent.

ES: Talk about your fights with Gino Odjick.

TT: The first time I fought Gino, he jumped me as he came off the bench and hit me with about 13 or 14 punches. I said, "Here it comes!" Then I threw one and he flipped and turtled to the ice on me. I was pissed off, especially after they threw us out of the game. I chased Gino outside to the bus and he ran in and I never got a chance to get my hands on him.

When I fought Gino in Vancouver, it was just after I had been traded to Quebec, and it was on the first shift of the game. I hit him with one and then he grabbed my right arm, so I started to get my left loose and he grabbed onto that. It ended up being nothing at all. Later in the same game we lined up at the face-off and I had my right sleeve pulled all the way up my arm. He said to the linesman that I had to pull my sleeve down. I refused to, and then referee Paul Stewart came over and said that I had to pull it down. I said, "Stew, he's going to jump me and grab my right arm and start hitting me." The ref said that I had to pull my sleeve down. It was a close game and I was going to let Gino take a two-minute instigation penalty, so I pulled my sleeve down. Next thing you know, the puck is dropped, Gino jumps me and I look at Stewart. He saw what happened and then I dropped my gloves. Gino got my right all tied up and he threw a bunch of them but none was really hitting me. He threw a couple and then I threw them and he wound up turtling. To me that was bullshit.

Anyhow, we played them again, this time in Quebec, near Gino's hometown. This time I knew we were going to square off. I said, "Gino, let's square off and get this over with." And he said he was not going to square off with me. So I said, "Why not?" He said, "Because you have a knockout punch." Finally I coaxed him into a fight, because I really wanted to go again with this guy. After we got in the corner, and I said, "That's it, let's dance." He said, "No." So I said, "I'll fight your fight," and I grabbed onto him and as soon as I started to throw a punch he ducked and turtled to the ice. He went right down to my legs as soon as I got my right hand loose. To this day, he still hasn't had a good fight with me.

ES: Tell me about your fights with Link Gaetz.

TT: We fought once in Spokane and it was a good fight. He got the better of me. The second time, it was in Saskatoon. I was pumped and ready for the fight but I didn't even throw a punch. He destroyed me. We had squared off, but I never got off a punch. I had bumps all over my forehead and I was embarrassed in my own city. I said to him that the next time I see you, we are going to go. I told him as we were going off of the ice, that we'll fight again.

ES: What was your reputation like in the International League?

TT: I was a heavyweight in the league and Link was a heavyweight on the other side. We knew that we were going to go, since he had kicked my butt in Juniors. He knew I was going to try to redeem myself. We squared off and then he pulled my shirt over my head and knocked my helmet off and hit me with three solid ones. I saw only the white of my jersey and I said "Geez, this isn't going to happen again!" There was 6,000 or 7,000 people in my own building, and I couldn't allow this to happen again. I managed to get my head out of my sweater and hit him with three good rights, one right after the other on the side of his head. His knees buckled and he fell down and he sat on his helmet and then he got up and started to go toward my penalty box and I said, "Hey, Linker, the other one." He sat and looked at me and says, "Nice one, You got me back." I said, "Hey, I finally got you back." He smiled and I smiled and we have never fought since.

I have all of the respect in the world for the guy. Link is an honest kid and a hell of a fighter. If Link could only get his shit together . . . he's a good defensemen and a solid hockey player. He's strong and tough and he has all of the tools to be a great hockey player. He just has to put it all together and put his head on straight.

ES: Tell me about some of the better fights you have seen.

TT: I once saw Link and Joey Kocur go, when Link was just called up by Minnesota a few years ago. Link was doing okay, but then he put his head down and Kocur caught him above the eye. Link didn't go down or anything; he just got caught with a good punch.

ES: Tell me what you think wins a fight.

TT: I don't think that blood and cuts win a fight. You, yourself, know when you have won or lost a fight. It's not by what the crowd thinks, or when the crowd cheers, or what the other team thinks — it's what you know. When you are finished with that fight, you know whether you won or lost that fight. And the guy you fought knows whether he won or lost that fight.

Lots of aspects of fighting are so full of bullshit. Like when you get off the guy, you might say to somebody, "Hey, I kicked the shit out of him," mostly because you may not want to admit that you lost. But that person knows inside if he won or lost. I know when I won or lost. If I lose one, I'm the first to say that I lost. I'm not ashamed that I lost a fight. But when I know that I lose, I'm always the first one to come back and try to redeem myself. I'll always redeem myself, although it's no big deal when you lose a fight. Anybody can win on any night. It only takes a couple of punches to get a victory. You can get the shirt pulled up over your head and get cranked one. It's a matter of who shows up game in and game out that really counts.

ES: Tell me about getting drafted.

TT: I got drafted by St. Louis in the ninth round and wasn't even expecting it. So I went to camp and decided to fight everybody on the roster. I knew that Todd Ewen was the Blues' heavyweight. For the first few intersquad games, they kept us apart and then we had one game together when we were on opposite sides and I went after him. He had tape on his hands and everything else and I was thumping him and thumping him and then I slipped on a stick and I got back up. Then he hit me and cut me on the top of my forehead — because he had tape on his hands. I was laying into him and he cut me on the forehead with an uppercut, when I was getting back up. After that, everybody stepped in and broke it up.

I went to the locker room to get stitched up and he went to get his hand checked because it was hurting him. I told them I didn't want stitches, but rather sutures, because I wanted to go back out there and go again with him. Todd said, "No, we're not going again." He needed to get his hand X-rayed, because it was sore.

The next day we lined up against each other. I wanted to fight him again but he didn't want to fight. Kelly Chase was on my team and Todd and I were lined up together. I gave Todd a whack and said, "We are going." He said, "F—— off." I said, "Let's go!" I gave him another whack before we faced off. He swung his stick and I ducked. If he ever hit me, he would have knocked my head clear off my shoulders. Chaser came over from the other side and cracked Ewen over the head with his stick. Next thing you know, all of the gloves go. Nobody ended up fighting, but there was some serious stick-swinging going on.

ES: Did you fight anybody else in that camp?

TT: Yeah, I fought Herb Raglan, although it didn't amount to much, because he jumped me from behind. When I turned around he lost his balance. I had him down, pinned him on the ice with my knees over his arms. I could have hit him, but it wouldn't have served any purpose to hit a guy who was on his back.

In that first year in St. Louis, all I did was fight. I was establishing myself and got a good reputation. This was what I wanted to do and this was what I wanted to get and I got more room to play because of it.

ES: This was after you had established yourself in Peoria?

TT: I had established myself as a heavyweight. I was weighing around 227 pounds and was six feet at the time and I was fighting everybody. I was a big boy. By no means could I skate or anything, but I could knock the shit out of people.

ES: Tell me some of the guys who you were fighting.

TT: I fought everybody. I didn't miss a heavyweight. This is a classic: it was my opening game against Indianapolis. Archie Henderson was coaching and they were called Archie's Army. In the previous game they had a kid named Geoff Benic, who was the big fighter in the OHL. He came after me and I knocked him out clean. Henderson was screaming at me "This is going to be a long season, Twist." I said, "For me or your f . . . ing players!" He shot back, "Wait till you come to our barn for the next game."

We came to Indianapolis and it's opening day and Archie has his tuxedo on and his lizard skin that comes out in the fog and it's the opening celebration. Right away I went after Marty McSorley's brother, Chris, and then Darwin McCutcheon stepped in and we squared off. Three punches later, I knocked him out and he was on the ice for about 45 seconds. He still couldn't get up. He had two guys under each arm pick him up and carry him off of the ice. I had kayoed him. Meanwhile Archie was screaming over at me. But after the game Archie told me that was the reason why he quit playing hockey, right there. Archie was a good guy. I liked him.

ES: Did any coaches ever tell you to go out and fight?

TT: It never happened. I understood my role. I knew damn well what my role was going to be. I'll tell you though, Bob Plager was a coach who wanted to develop my skills. He taught me how to work on things while maintaining my role as a tough guy.

ES: Talk about being traded to Quebec.

TT: My first game was at home in Quebec, against Montreal. We had that big Quebec-Montreal rivalry going. When I finally got out on the ice I began hitting everybody. I asked Shayne Corson to fight but he didn't want to so I continued hitting everyone. Then Ewen and I were in front of the net and I said to Todd, "Let's go." I gave him a hard cross-check but he didn't want to fight. Once again, I said, "Let's go." I gave him another cross-check but he still didn't want to go. I was coming near the end of my shift and I was about to change up when Ewen dropped his gloves. He was behind me and sucker-punched me, hitting me right on the top of the helmet. Now, I'm about to get on the bench at the end of my shift. I dropped my gloves, turned around and thumped him. I kicked his ass, big time.

ES: How do you feel about guys who sucker-punch people?

TT: I never do that and never in my career have I done that. My theory is that if you're going to fight a guy, you turn and say to him, "Do you want to fight?" There's no use sucker-punching, since you get no respect from anybody and you get no respect from the guy you're fighting. If you go to the guy and say, "Let's go," and you beat him, then you got his respect. He respects you and he says you beat me straight up.

ES: Talk about a guy like Jim McKenzie.

TT: He's an honest guy who doesn't go out looking for it, and that's the way it should be. The first time we fought, I hit him a few times and he grabbed me and it wasn't much. The second time, in Hartford, it was a really good fight. We went back and forth, and back and forth — a good, even fight.

ES: How much talking goes on before a fight?

TT: You know when a fight is going to happen. Here's a good example: We were in Quebec, beating the Islanders 7-2, and

Mick Vukota lined up next to me and said, "Let's get it over with." I said, "All right," and the puck dropped. We squared off and then started to fight. That's respect. He doesn't jump me and I don't jump him. He wanted to motivate his team and I'm out there to motivate mine. Sure I'll fight.

I've only turned down one fight in my entire life, and that was because we were playing the Whalers in Hartford and we were winning 5-2 and it was going to be our first road win. This was when Quebec was on that major league slide of not winning on the road. So we were winning, and Pierre Pagé said no fighting. So Jim McKenzie was trying to get me to go and said, "C'mon Twister, I'm trying to get the team going." I told him that I couldn't. I said, "I'll fight you the next game, but I can't fight tonight." He was being honest and upfront, but I couldn't fight. So he tried to sucker me and I wasn't going to fight. He wound up taking two minutes. We won the game. We were on such a major-league road slide, I didn't want to jeopardize our winning the game. He might have caught me with a hard one and knocked me out. That would have motivated their team. That was the only time that I turned down a fight.

ES: What do you think about players who jump others from behind?

TT: I have no respect for that. I have no respect for a guy who jumps another player. To me that is not being a tough guy. A tough guy is someone who comes out and says, "Hey, do you want to go?" You go, win or lose, then go to the box. Jumping a guy is bullshit and dumb.

ES: How do you feel about a guy like Vukota, who body-slams his opponents to the ice when the fight isn't going so well?

TT: If that's his way of fighting, that's his way of fighting. That's his prerogative, but that's not my way of fighting. My fight is grab on and throw them, win or lose. That's the way it is. Grab on and throw them and see what happens.

ES: Tell me more about your style.

TT: I never hold on. I don't like to hold on and wrestle with the guys. I want to fight and throw big, hard punches. I'll take two or three to get one in. I'll take a couple, but why hold on? What's the purpose of fighting if you are going to wrestle? There really is no purpose to wrestling. You're not proving anything and you're not showing that you want to fight. You are not impressing the kids by having a wrestling match. You should drop the gloves and let the punches fly. If you get tagged with a couple and get cut or whatever, hey, it's part of the game. You fight to win, not to tie. I don't fight to tie.

ES: What are your thoughts on the league trying to eliminate fighting today?

TT: I get pissed off when I hear people criticize fighting. You never see a fan go for popcorn in the middle of a fight. Imagine somebody goes for a snack in the middle of a fight. C'mon, the fans stand up and they think it's fun. I've never had a fan come up to me and tell me that my job is bullshit because I fight. I haven't ever had a fan come up to me and say that. All I hear from fans is, "We like the way you play. You play hard, play aggressive, you bump and grind and have a fight here or there." I've never had anybody tell me off about being a fighter. Fighting is a good element of the game.

ES: What do you think about the NHL suggestion that eliminating fighting will bring in a national American TV contract?

TT: There's no way that the elimination of fighting will bring the league a national U.S. TV contract. We have a good, hard, fast-paced, aggressive game. We have grown men out there and they are going to fight. If your team's down 5-1 and you need a motivator, you get out there and give a couple of good hits. The winning team doesn't like that guy there doing that because he's motivating his team. Next thing you know, someone from the other team comes out there and fights him. It's clean. There is no jumping and suckering. It's a good fight — two guys go to the penalty box and the crowd is excited. It's a 5-1 game, and the crowd was getting a little bored. Now the crowd is excited and the teams are motivated.

ES: How do you feel about the instigator rule?

TT: It's great, because I don't want a guy jumping me thinking he's not going to get punished. I don't want that. I want a guy coming up to me, saying, "Let's fight." Then off we go. I don't need to be jumped, I'll go with anybody. The only time I'm going to instigate a fight is if a guy jumped one of my guys or ran one of our defenseman from behind. Getting run from behind like that is brutal. If you're a defenseman and you're skating back for the puck and some guy is skating full tilt and he hits you in the back, Christ that hurts!

ES: Tell me your thoughts on the suspension rule and the fact that the league may be taking money out of your pocket so that you can protect a teammate.

TT: You have to do your job. Say Tony Twist hits Denis Savard. He hits him fairly, but he hits him hard. The Canadiens won't like seeing someone hitting their goal scorer, so Todd Ewen will come out for them and want to fight me. I'll fight him, what the hell. He's not going to get suspended. You have to be smart. You see somebody get hit but you don't go out and whack him behind the shins and be an instigator and make a big commotion. Say Todd Ewen hits Joe Sakic unfairly. Do you know what

I'm going to do on the next shift? The first thing I'm going to do is run the next Montreal guy that I see. I'm going to run anybody and run them hard. It will be fair, but I'm going to run them hard. You know what? The crowd is going to go,"Wow!"

ES: How do you get back at a guy like Ulf Samuelsson, who is not going to fight?

TT: You don't fight him — you run him. You hit him fair, and anybody else fair. The next opponent who comes along, you hit him hard. I always try to line somebody up out on the ice and make an opportunity to get my point known. You don't have to be an idiot and you don't have to take two minutes or five minutes. You can make your point clear, just by giving a couple of good hits. Get the puck, dump it in and give a guy a good smash.

ES: Get back to Ulfie?

TT: If the hits that he put on guys like Cam Neely or Brian Skrudland aren't fair hits, then that is bullshit. That is bullshit, putting out a great player like Neely with unfair hits. I'm all for a hard-hitting, aggressive hockey game. But I'm totally against a guy who tries to take another guy's knee out. That's bullshit and that ain't hockey — going after somebody else's paycheck. He's taking away from that guy's family and that's bullshit. He's taking away a guy's lifestyle, his career and there's no room for that in the game of hockey. But there is room for two guys who want to fight. As for the guys who do want to go, I say, let them go!

ES: Do you think the NHL will eliminate fighting?

TT: No. You can't take fighting out of the game. It's a part of hockey. It's action and fun. I love a good hockey game and a good fight.

ES: Tell me your thoughts on bench-clearing brawls.

TT: I've been in a couple of good bench-clearers myself but I really don't like bench-clearing brawls. There's no room for a bench-clearing brawl and no sense in it. You know why? Because somebody is going to get hurt and hurt bad in it. You might have some guy who is half off of his rocker decide to take another player out. There are only three officials out there, with 40 guys who are fighting. One player might be helplessly pinned on the ice, catching a beating. There's no way to break this up. I've been in a couple of bench-clearers where everybody got on the ice. I'm thinking, "I don't want to end up on the bottom of this, because there's no way to rescue me."

ES: What was the best fight you ever saw?

TT: Bobby Nystrom against Glen Cochrane when Cochrane was on the Philadelphia Flyers. Those two guys didn't know how to hold on. All they knew how to do was throw punches — back and forth. Nystrom got floored, but he got back up and then he floored Cochrane and then Cochrane got back up and floored Nystrom. That was an all-time favorite of mine. I've got that in slo-mo.

ES: How much have your skills improved?

TT: My skill level has gone way up. I've been working the shit out of myself. My bread and butter has always been my toughness. My bread and butter still is my toughness, but I'm getting better and I'm trying my damnedest to be a better player. I work an hour before practice and half an hour after practice just to get better.

ES: Talk about Kelly Chase?

TT: I played many years with Kelly, in Saskatoon and in Peoria. Chaser was never afraid of anything. He's not afraid of screwing up. He goes out and does his stuff on the ice and he's not a big guy. He's a smart fighter. I've seen him take on the biggest of guys and do real well.

ES: Did you ever fight Alan May?

TT: I fought Alan, but I didn't think Alan was really that tough. I fought him and said, "Who *is* this guy?" He's a nobody when it comes to toughness. He jumped me, first of all, and second of all he grabbed my right arm. I started throwing lefts. I was throwing a barrage of lefts and then he dumped me on the ice. He didn't want to fight.

ES: How is your balance?

TT: I have very good balance. I'm able to load my punch back the first chance I get and change my movements and still come back with punches.

ES: Who hit you the hardest?

TT: Link Gaetz. That was that fight we had in the minors, when I came back and then dusted him. It wasn't the one when he cut me open. Darin Kimble also hits hard. It's really sad that he messed his hand up in that car accident. He's a good guy and the type who doesn't hang on when he fights. When we fought, we exchanged punches until we were too tired to throw them.

ES: Is it Kimble's style to throw as many as he can?

TT: All he wants to do is throw punches and that's great. The best fighter wins. It's fair and the most perfect fighting situation.

ES: Rate some of the better fighters in the league.

TT: There is no "best." I could beat anybody in the league and conversely, anybody could beat me. You do have guys who win on a regular basis, like nine out of 10 fights they would win. I give the most respect to the guys who fight to win. You have to fight to win. Craig Berube fights to win, Tie fights to win.

ES: Talk about your fights with Berube.

TT: We fought twice. We fought the first time in Philly and I got the best of him there. It was a good fight, and then the next time we fought in St. Louis. Chief likes to throw them fast, really likes throwing them fast, and that was his fight, and it works good for me. The fight was even.

ES: Talk about McSorley.

TT: Has he ever changed his fighting style! He hangs on and throws a couple, hangs on and throws another couple. I never thought he was that tough. I never fought him, but he didn't impress me in the ones I've seen him.

Chapter 20

THE HEAVYWEIGHTS

MICK THE QUICK: MICK VUKOTA

"I'll fight anybody for the right reason, but just to go out there and throw 'em, I don't think that's smart. There are enough guys around the league who I dislike and want to fight."

If ever a tough guy could be called likeable, Mick Vukota is just that personality. Witty, affable and articulate, Vukota is the personification of Mr. Personality off the ice.

On the ice, Vukota's deportment is something less than exemplary. In his first full season, 1988-89, he totalled 237 penalty minutes in only 48 games. He accumulated 290 penalty minutes in 76 games in 1989-90, 238 penalty minutes in 60 games in 1990-91, and 293 penalty minutes in 1991-92 playing in 74 games. In the 1992-93 season, Mick had 216 penalty minutes in 74 games.

Not surprisingly, Mick has become one of the most popular of the New York Islanders and the club's resident enforcer. At one time the club had visions of his becoming a latter-day Bobby Nystrom, but Vukota never attained Nystrom's level of scoring proficiency. In an interview after a practice at Nassau Veterans Memorial Coliseum, Mick held court with reporter Eric Servetah.

ES: When did you start playing hockey?

MV: I was born in Saskatchewan where there's not much else to do but play hockey. The winters were pretty long and cold and that's what everybody did — just play hockey.

ES: Did you have any brothers or sisters?

MV: Nope, I was spoiled rotten. I was an only child. My dad would kick me out of the house and tell me to go down to the rink and play with the other kids. That's all we did was play in the driveway, on the roads, on the ponds and on the lakes. It was the only game that we were good enough to play.

ES: Were you a tough kid?

MV: I was a candy-ass, but I was really under control. I played a lot of senior football as a kid. I was a big kid and my leg calcified from the hits. I wasn't able to skate for three months, so I became tall but scrawny. I couldn't do cardiovascular work and I couldn't ride my bike, so all I could do was work out with the weights. I would bench-press all the time. Every single night I'd go downstairs and do benching. I was on crutches, so all I could do was just lie there and bench. I did this even though it's not supposed to be good for you to do every day. I'd do about 23 sets or at least 20 every night. My bench went up almost 60 pounds over those three months. I went from lifting 145 pounds to 220 pounds. I was still scrawny, though, and I remember being in shop class at school and getting roused by some tough guys. They were the headbangers of the school who would wear leather jackets and smoke cigarettes. They were the cool kids of the school. This one kid in particular was all over me. He was a big guy. I snapped and cracked my crutch over his head and then after that everybody left me alone. That's pretty much why I started fighting in hockey.

ES: So this was your first real fight as a kid?

MV: I fought in hockey a couple of times. I started fighting in the midgets, although I wasn't a tough guy. I would fight once in a while, but the midget league had some tough guys in it. Dave Manson was there and so was Wendel Clark. This was before the WHL. I played against those guys a lot. I fought Manson in midget when he was 15. I was 16. Because we wore face cages, we'd keep our right gloves on and then drop our left and just pound each other and try to get the guy's helmet off. Once his helmet and cage came off, I would drop the other glove. It was a pretty fair fight.

ES: Before leaving midget level, what did you do? Was hockey the sport that you always wanted?

MV: It was the only sport where I couldn't wait for it to start. I went to summer camps for the entire summer and hockey schools.

I'd skate for three weeks out of the summer, which was a lot. My dad would put me in the camps and leave me there all week. It was good for me.

ES: Did you ever consider football?

MV: I liked football, but it's nothing like hockey. Hockey is our national pastime. I grew up watching it. Dave Brown played for South West City and Joey Kocur played for the Blades. Those guys were mean and nasty. Brownie was the king, at least in our eyes at home. Dave was the toughest guy out there and there were some big guys running around. Brownie was the first one to come out of Saskatoon and he came from the West Side. I looked up to him. There's an East Side and a West Side of Saskatoon. Brownie came from the West Side and I came from the West Side. We're kind of the only two hockey players to come from the West Side of the city who made it in the NHL.

ES: Did you want to fight Brownie?

MV: I've fought him two or three times. I wanted to fight him, but I didn't want to just go up and jump him, because I knew if I was going to fight Dave Brown, it was going to be because he did something to one of my teammates, or I had done something to one of his. I wanted it to be a fair fight. I had one fight with Brown when he was with Edmonton. That was the first time we fought and it was a fun fight. He gave it to me pretty good. It was okay to take a loss, but I showed up.

ES: Did you tie up his left?

MV: I don't think I've ever seen him use the right. I don't think he has to, though. He's got such strong arms, and he's a strong man. The time I fought him I tried to tie up his left, but he just ripped it away from my grasp and pulled it right out of my hands. I've got a pretty good grip and he just ripped it right out of my grasp.

ES: Is fighting what you were known for in your teens?

MV: Not particularly. I went to this new team and they didn't even know who I was. My invitation said, "Dear Bill." But they crossed out "Bill" and wrote in "Mick." The coach was sitting in the press box. He called everybody over before the scrimmage started, and said, "I just want everybody to know that I plan on having the toughest team in the SAJHL." So, I knew that if I wanted to make this team I would have to fight. I fought three shifts in a row and did okay in a couple. I got pounded by some big Native American guy, about 6-4. He pounded the piss out of me and I went back at him again the next shift and he pounded the piss out of me again. But I kept going back after him the next couple of times through camp and the coach just liked that I was young and I wasn't afraid.

Making the team boiled down to me and a couple of other guys. We went to a town called Swift Current and the coach paired me with the captain who was a little Indian, who kind of stirred up the pot. He'd keep fighting and was always spearing the big guys, and my coach told me that if anyone touches him, I was to get in there and be the first guy off the bench. So my captain spears the biggest guy on the other team and I got in there. If you fought twice, then you were thrown out, so I got in my two fights and was tossed. I was just about finishing undoing my laces when I heard the fans cheering. I looked up to see if somebody scored and our coach and a couple of players were going into the stands. I jumped over the glass, ran across the ice and jumped over the glass again to go in the stands. I started tossing a few people around, telling them to stay away from my teammates and coach. Later, on the bus ride home, the coach said, "What number do you want? You fought for your team, didn't worry about yourself." To me, that was the ultimate, to say that I was doing the job for my team. That was the best thing I could hear.

ES: How were your skills?

MV: I could play the game, but I knew my game was hitting and fighting and I was afraid that I'd get away from it, because I've seen guys who got to be 19 and 20 stop fighting. These guys just didn't want to fight anymore. They wanted to play more. I would tell myself to stick to my game and not worry about the points and stuff like that. I needed to keep on fighting and playing it tough and I wouldn't allow myself to forget it.

ES: Tell me about some of your fights in the WHL, playing for Saskatoon.

MV: I remember in my last game against the Prince Albert Raiders, I got into two fights. I got the shit beat out of me by a little guy and I one-punched another guy named Curt Fraser. Ken Baumgartner, who played for the Raiders, was running around in that game. He wound up getting kicked out with a game misconduct early in the game for jumping someone. We would have fought for sure that game because I was going to go after anybody I could. Bomber terrorized guys in that league, and if he had played in the same division as us, I'm sure we would have met each other a lot.

ES: How were your fighting skills at the time?

MV: Near the end of the season I started to do well. In the first 30 games I took a lot of beatings. I was fighting a lot of 20-year-old guys and I was only 17. I would do well against anybody my age, but the older guys got the better of me.

ES: Did you have a fighting style as a Junior?

MV: No, I just grabbed on with my left and threw with my right. I never cared what hand the other guy threw with. So I finished out the season and then I got a trial with Kelowna of the WHL.

I went to their camp but I got in a street fight right before the training camp. Eight guys jumped and beat up me and a friend of mine. That's where I got all the scar tissue from. I took 22 stitches in the lip. So I remember driving to Kelowna all by myself with the stitches and looking in the mirror and going, "What are you doing with your life? You're going all the way to Kelowna to get to training camp and you've got stitches." So I didn't fight the first couple of days of camp because I wanted to wait until the stitches came out. I waited for the pre-season games and my first fight was with Rudy Poeschek and I hammered him. In training camp, if you have one fight, then you're gone; so I went back to the locker room. I didn't know who he was, but I remember seeing this guy stare at me on the face-off. He was just staring at me, so I skated right up to him and when the puck dropped, we dropped our gloves and I hammered him. I remember going to the dressing room and some of the older guys came in because fights broke out. It was a big rivalry — Kamloops and Kelowna. The older guys were like, "That was Rudy Poeschek, you hammered him." I said, "Who's he?" and they said, "He's one of the toughest guys in this league." I figured that I'd be okay with the fighting since I took Rudy. I threw rights and he threw rights against me, but I came out the winner. So the coaches kept me around that year and I helped out with some tough fights over the year. Rudy came back and beat me the first game of the year. I had jumped on him and he came back and threw me a couple.

ES: In those kind of fights, you're leaving yourself open, you're just going punch for punch?

MV: We were just going punch for punch. Especially when I was 17, 18 and 19. I didn't care about stitches or black eyes. We just grabbed on and threw. I didn't look to tie the other guy's arm up. I tried to grab them at the elbow and start throwing. I had some good fights that year.

ES: How good was Craig "Chief" Berube back then?

MV: He was good. Guys were pretty scared of him. He's like a serious type of player. He doesn't yap a lot. He just played hard and he's the staying-back type. He and Todd Ewen were on the same team, so I had some good fights with them. I fought him a lot that year.

ES: Did any of your coaches ever tell you to go out and fight?

MV: One time a coach sent me after Cliff Ronning. That was the first and only time in my career that a coach ever told me to go after a player. I hated doing that. It was my first year in the WHL and the idea was for one of the guys on my line to start a fight with Craig Berube. Then I was supposed to go after Ronning, get his gloves off and get him out of the game. We would lose a player, but the coach thought it would be a good trade off. He told the whole team this plan before the game and the guys were like, "Yeah, that's a good idea." So a fight broke out at one end of the ice and, by the time I got in it, Cliff Ronning was almost on the bench. So I threw him down and tried to pull his gloves off but he was turtling. I started to panic and started shaking him up and down and dragging him around the ice. Then Todd Ewen came off the bench and basically gave me a beating. The next game our tough older guys were hurt and I remember the coach telling me that I have to replace these guys. So I'm sitting there and I didn't want to do it. If I was going to fight, I didn't want to beat up the little guys like Ronning. That was a big character game for me, because I went in and I fought Ewen and Berube. I never felt more alone on the bench, but I did well in those fights. Guys on the team were saying things like, "It's okay to be alone and do it for the team. It doesn't matter what the coach says." From that point on, I became a big part of the team and I moved up to the second line.

ES: How tough was the WHL?

MV: There were so many mental games. For example there was "cruising the red line." If another guy skated over the red line in warm-up, there was a good chance that we would have a brawl. Everything was premeditated. You knew right before the game started who you were going to fight and I really enjoyed fighting. I loved to fight. There was nothing like dropping the gloves when I was a kid.

ES: Tell me about another good bench-clearing brawl.

MV: When I was playing for the Springfield Indians of the AHL, I fought Scott Shaughnessy of Fredericton with about five minutes left in the game. As I went off the ice, the late Ron Lapointe, who was then coaching Fredericton and who had me later when I was with Washington in training camp, screamed at me because I had the better of his guy in the fight. "You're a bruiser and you're never going to make it in the NHL, be happy you're here and you're horse shit." So I walked off the ice and my coach Gordie Lane went after Ron Lapointe. He said, "Don't talk to my players. If you have something to say, say it to me." So I came back to the bench and our players were on their bench and everybody on the ice was fighting. Shaughnessy was still on the ice, because he never made it to the locker room and Gordie Lane grabbed hold of my jersey and wouldn't let me on the ice, because I'd be suspended. We were one guy short in the brawl and Shaughnessy was skating around and popping guys, so I said to Gordie, "If you don't let me go, I'm going to kick you." I had my skates on, so Gordie said, "Do what you have to do." So he let me go and I went out and beat on Shaughnessy and it was a huge brawl. Dale Henry head-butted a guy named Jacques Malicot and I have the tape at home. The announcer said, "It looked like Malicot got cut by a skate." There was blood everywhere, but what happened was that Malicot tried to head-butt Henry, but Dale blocked it. Henry was known for his head-butting and he just landed a head-butt on him. He drilled Malicot with it and it broke his nose and made his eyes swollen shut. Malicot couldn't get off the ice. He was unconscious, then on one knee and one hand and then he fell down. He was knocked out cold. Rod Dallman was in the penalty box and they wouldn't let him out, so he scaled the penalty box and jumped over to start beating on some Fredericton guys. The Springfield fans were going crazy.

ES: Who helped you the most in your fighting at this time?

MV: It had to be Rod Dallman. When we played at Springfield, we also lived together. Dallman was the kind of guy that on the nights when my hands were sore and we'd go into Hershey, I'd tell him that I didn't want to fight, but I'd be there if he needed me. He would go out and run the goalie, spear their goal scorer and trip at their bench in a matter of 30 seconds. Now I'd have to fight and play tough. Dallman would never give me a break and always kept me going. Ken Baumgartner and I talked about Dallman and we figured if he was a little bigger, he would be one of the best fighters in the league. His shoulders and knees were always bad and he was only about 5-11, 195 pounds, but he would fight with everybody. He fought Dave Brown in preseason games, and got beat up real bad. But he never gave up and the next game he went out and took a beating from the late John Kordic.

ES: How were your hands back then?

MV: My right hand was always in bad shape. I used it most of the time, so it always took the punishment, and even today it still gives me trouble.

ES: Did you ever try boxing?

MV: I did one summer in Edmonton, with Craig Berube. I liked it and was pretty good at it, but I needed to concentrate more time on power skating.

ES: Explain how you can hang out and box with Craig Berube, even though you two fight each other during the season.

MV: We weren't buddies or anything off the ice. It's just that we've grown up knowing each other. I mean guys like Berube and John Kordic, who I played against my first year in Juniors and his last year, we grew up and watched each other improve as players. We'd see each other every year and you're almost happy to see each other, but you're still going to go out there and knock each other's brains out. You still have to go out on the ice and do your job. It's never anything personal. I remember when I saw him in the gym, we talked and we knew that we'd probably be fighting each other in training camp. As it turned out, we did fight a couple of times that year. The thing is, it's nice to see that you know what you're training for and that you're trying to improve your game.

ES: How did you get to the NHL?

MV: I was part of the Capitals' organization, and I was a bouncer in a nightclub back home in Saskatoon. Joey Kocur used to come in a lot and he was a bouncer in that same nightclub a couple of years before me. I remember talking to Joey one night and asked him, "Joey, listen. I'm going to Washington Capitals' camp. Is there any advice you can give me?" He thought real quick and said, "Washington, Washington. Okay, Dwight Schofield. Fight him! Soon as you get the first chance, fight him. Fight Dwight Schofield and if you lose, fight him again." So I went to the Capitals' camp and I saw Schofield and he was at the end of his career. He was hurting and the fight never happened. But I still got into a lot of fights in camp. I fought Jamie Huscroft, Perry Anderson and Dave Marcinyshyn.

ES: What happened after Washington's training camp?

MV: They sent me down to Binghamton to play in the American League games. I played two of them but I didn't know what was going on. They didn't give me a contract, so I said, "You've got to do something." In my last game I had two fights. I did well, but they said they had enough tough guys and that I should go back to Junior and work hard. So I went back to Junior, my overage year. I played a lot. I worked on my skills and racked up like 337 minutes, a lot of majors. I had 25 goals, 25 assists, 30 assists, whatever. I had a real good year in Junior.

ES: Were you the heavyweight on the team?

MV: Yes. It was me and Dean Ewen at the time. I would say that Rudy Poeschek and I were the heavyweights of the league. That year Link Gaetz broke in and I had a couple of good toe-to-toe battles with him. He was a couple of years younger than me, but when you're 20 years old and you're still playing in Juniors, you have to win your fights. It's a big lift for the team if you win all of them. The first time I fought Link, I scored my 20th goal of the season. I remember saying that this guy was going to be tough. He wasn't very built then, but he could throw them. It was a good toe-to-toe fight and I would have to call it a draw. In our second fight, I would have to say that he got the better of me.

ES: What are your thoughts on losing a fight, if you did lose one?

MV: Early on in Junior I'd just go right back. You lose, you go back. That was all. It was automatic. If you lose you go back when you get a chance — just keep fighting the guy until you win.

First shift of the next game, you got to go back at the guy. But fighting will hurt your hands. Once I broke my hand and I played with a cast on, so my hand healed kind of funny. Everybody plays with it. I'm not the only guy with a bad hand. Every guy has a bad hand. You never heard of a tough guy sitting out with a sore hand. I will never complain about my hand as long as Joey Kocur is playing hockey. I see what that guy has done to his body and I don't see him complaining. Nobody in this league has the right to say, "Oh, my hand hurts," when a guy like Kocur can still fight. His hands are unbelievable.

ES: Have you fought Kocur?

MV: Never. I'll fight anybody for the right reason, but just to go out there and throw 'em, I don't think that's smart. There are enough guys around the league whom I dislike and want to fight.

ES: I know that you and Ken Baumgartner are good friends. Would you fight Kenny?

MV: "Bomber" and I are best friends and we both know it's a job. If there's a turning point in the game that means the difference in your team winning the game, we'd fight each other. I know he would do the same. It's not even a thing you discuss. It's something that we know. The guys around the league know this. Whether you're friends or not, you know when it has to be done and you do it. Otherwise, we leave it alone and don't talk about it.

ES: How did you end up with the Islanders?

MV: After my season in the WHL, I wanted to go to the AHL and pick up with a team at the end of the season. My agent, Bob Strumm, told me that not only was Washington interested in me, but also the Philadelphia Flyers, New York Islanders, Hartford Whalers and the Vancouver Canucks. When Washington decided not to sign me, it boiled down to a choice between the Islanders and the Flyers. Both of their American League teams were supposed to make the playoffs, so it was a good opportunity. I looked at Philly's roster with Berube, Brownie and Darryl Stanley being there at the time, so I thought that I might have a better shot with the Islanders.

ES: How was your first camp with the Islanders?

MV: I had a couple of good battles in the Rangers pre-season games. Bobby Nystrom was our assistant coach and I fought Mark Tinordi twice in one game. There were eight consecutive fights, one after the other in that game. Rod Dallman fought Jimmy Latos, Dean Ewen fought Rudy Poesheck and Kerry Clark fought somebody. So we had all of those fights and Bobby Nystrom loved it. I fought John Kordic in one of those exhibition games, when he was with Montreal. I cut him over the eye and he was bitter. He was screaming at me down the hallway. So the next shift of the period, he gets on the ice and I'm coming off at the end of my shift. When the guys on the bench yelled, "Heads up!" I turned and looked and Kordic's flying. He came from the other side of the penalty box and I moved. He went flying into our bench! He stands up in our bench and I'm on the ice and we start throwing punches. This is no good: he's got way better footing. So I pull him back out on the ice and throw him down. But I fall down with him. Everybody was like, "You've got to be strong to throw a guy around like that."

ES: Who was coaching the Islanders then?

MV: Terry Simpson was the Islanders' coach. He said, "You know what you've got to do. You know what kind of player you are. Just make sure you work on your game." So I'm grateful. I want a chance to make the American League team. They've got a lot of guys. I've got a two-way contract. I could go to wherever, East Coast League or something like that. I just remember going down and Gordie Lane was coaching Springfield. We get off the bus and the TV cameras are there and they called Rod Dallman and me over. And they say, "So what are you guys going to do to stop Ken Baumgartner?" "Bomber" is in New Haven and I guess he terrorized the Indians at the end of the season. I remember going "What?", not knowing what they were talking about. Rod Dallman had played with Bomber, but he says, "If Bomber comes near me, I'm going to beat the shit out of him." He said it just like that on TV.

ES: Tell me about some of your fights in Springfield.

MV: I fought Greg Smyth, who was playing for the Hershey Bears. I gave it good to Bruce Shoebottom, who was with Maine. Every team had two or three guys who could throw. There was one guy named John English who I had some fights with. He was a big guy who could throw some bombs. I finished that year with 396 penalty minutes in 58 games and I fought every tough guy on the other teams.

ES: Do bigger players give you more trouble in a fight than the smaller guys?

MV: Big guys give me more trouble because I don't have the longest reach. I'm not one of the guys who likes to get hit. I'd rather be giving it out than taking it. The guys with longer reach give me more problems, since I'm going to take more punches when I fight those guys.

ES: Did you fight "Bomber" at all?

MV: Nope. He got called up to L.A. Then I got called up to the Islanders to play one game. It was in Hartford and my parents just happened to be down in Springfield. So my parents got to see my first NHL game because it was in Hartford. Terry Simpson calls me in his office, said, "You're going to play." There were some injuries on the right side and they lacked toughness. I remember Terry saying, "Just work hard." I started the game on a line with Brent Sutter and Greg Gilbert. I thought I was going to puke during the national anthem. I've never been that nervous in my life, ever. I played a lot on that line with Sutter and Gilbert. Near the third period, I lined up and Tiger Williams comes out for Hartford. And I line up beside him and he goes, "So you want to go, kid?" And I look at him and say, "Yeah, I want to go." But I was real apprehensive about it. Then he says, "When the puck drops, we're going to go." It seemed like forever before the linesman dropped the puck. As soon as the puck drops, I drop my gloves and Tiger skates away and they feed him a pass in the slot and he scores. I'm picking up my gloves and Tiger scores. I remember skating back to the bench and Terry Simpson was just burning a hole in me. I got sent back to Springy that night. I remember thinking, "That's it. I don't care. I played one NHL game. I don't care if I f . . . ed up or not." I don't know if we lost the game or we tied or whatever; I just remember f . . . ing up.

They sent me back down and I played a couple more games. Then they called me up at the deadline. They sent Brad Dalgarno down, and called me up for the rest of the year. When Terry called me in his office, he said, "Do you know why you're here?" and I said, "Yeah." He said, "I don't know if you do know, but let me explain it to you. I told your linemates not to pass the puck to you because you can't handle the thing. You've got a great shot, but you'll never get it away at this level. Your skating has to improve, but you're working at it, so stick with that. I tell you what, you give me a reason to keep you here and I'll do my best to keep you here." I respected his honesty. My first whole game here, I fought Tim Hunter that night and did pretty good. That was my first NHL fight. I threw him against the boards and tied his right up. I was pretty defensive.

ES: Who did you fight the rest of the year?

MV: I fought Craig Berube in Philly. We both were squaring off and dancing for a good minute, and then we both grabbed each other's rights. It was okay. We both tried to throw a couple. I think it was just mutual respect. I liked to tie the guy up and get my shots in, but I wasn't able to get them in on Craig.

ES: Did you win any that year?

MV: It was a bit of a learning experience. I fought Garth Butcher that year and I hate him. He wasn't a very good fighter. I also dropped Larry Melnyk. He dropped his gloves with me, came after me, and I dropped him. I didn't have very good fights my first year because I was pretty defensive. I was just very defensive. The next year I started to relax. I had a better season and

I had a lot of big fights. At the end of my second season, I had a good toe-to-toe bout with Kevin Maguire. I signed a new contract after that season and that fight, I think, had a big part to do with it. It was our last home game of the year, and I skated from my right side all the way over to Maguire, dropped the gloves, and we both threw, maybe like 25 each, 20 punches each, just toe-to-toe, punch-for-punch. The last one I hit him and he fell down on his stomach. The coaches liked the fact that I came over for another guy that fast. I didn't think about it. It was instinct and they liked that. That's when they signed me to my second contract.

ES: What are your thoughts on fighting and the rule changes?

MV: I think they're shooting themselves in the foot. I remember when Claude Lemieux jumped Hubie McDonough, giving it to Hubie. I honestly believe that that would never have happened if Claude Lemieux knew the next time that he played us, he was going to get the shit beat out of him. I know he's a ballsy player, but I just don't think he'd have done that. But that's the way the game is going. You're going to see guys take liberties because of the narrowing of the intimidation factor. The thing that people don't understand about hockey is that it's by far the most intimidating sport next to boxing. You can't catch a pass and run out of bounds. You have to take the pass and you're going to get hit no matter what. You don't have 6-6, 300-pound linemen hitting 6-6 300-pound linemen. You have 6-3, Bob Probert hitting 5-11, Steve Thomas. When two guys like that go into the corner, the bigger guy is going to win the physical battle, but not necessarily come out with the puck. That's the art of the intimidation factor. Guys like Bob Probert, Cam Neely and Rick Tocchet can play hockey. They are very talented players, but they use their size to their advantage to intimidate the players because they can. Size and strength are two of their assets. If you eliminate the intimidation factor, you lose the heart and soul of hockey.

Why do you think everybody loves it when Pat LaFontaine drives around the defensemen as he's getting chopped and hooked and winds up still scoring a goal? It's because he's overcoming that intimidation. He's giving a second effort and that's what hockey's all about — second and third efforts. I don't think it's about the pretty power play. Now, it's heading in that direction. Your specialty teams are putting teams in the playoffs, winning championships. But you're never going to replace the grinders. I won't call us goons because I don't goon people. But I don't think you can replace the grinders with another group of players who will give as much for their team. I'd say that 90 percent of the players who fight in hockey are the guys who work extra in practice and work extra in the summer as far as trying to be better players. They are the same guys who think about winning games more than anybody else. They'll sit there for four or five shifts, not get a shift, and go out there and work their balls off and be happy if their team is winning. It takes a lot for people to respect that. Everybody's got a job, no matter how big or how small. Gretzky, Turgeon — those superstars sell hockey. They make the game much more exciting. But we keep the game that much more honest. We make sure they work hard.

ES: Why do you sometimes grab your opponent by the waist and body slam him to the ice?

MV: I never liked to be on the bottom. It was one way I could always make sure I was on top at the end of the fight. When I did it in Junior a few times — and even the first times when I was up here — I'd end up smashing the guy's head into the ice and he'd be cut. I don't know a harder way to hit a guy than hit his face into the ice. Then you pick the guy up, get the elbow across the head and slam him into the ice. His head bounces on the ice. I remember hitting Neil Sheehy a couple of times, dropping him like that. It's nuts. I've had my head drilled into the ice a couple of times and it hurts. A pretty strong upper body I think has a lot do with it.

ES: Are you still benching at all and hitting the weights?

MV: Yeah, but nothing like the strength. . . . I'm not half as strong as I was in my first couple of years. I used to throw around 305-310 on the bench and work out with that. When I was in the Capitals camp, I weighed around 228 pounds. I was lifting heavy weights then for only eight reps on two or three sets. Now, I go three or four sets and I'm up to 12 to 15 reps. I'm looking for stamina and flexibility now. I can't have too much bulk, because I lose my flexibility. The game is all about power and speed and my weight training is geared towards making me faster in my fights and on the ice.

ES: I saw you drop Al Secord once.

MV: That's when Ken Baumgartner first got here to the Islanders There was a big buzz about how we were going to be a tough team. The puck was dropped and it went over the glass or something. He kept skating over to our side of where the face-off was, so I went over and just bumped him. He said, "You want to go?" I said, "Yeah, I want to go." I knew he was a lefty so I threw and I caught him right in the temple and dropped him. I just started fighting lefties by throwing left because I thought I could tie them up better than they could tie me. That way I would get more shots in. I haven't switched [hands] that many times, only a couple of times. Against Mike Hartman once, I threw both. Against Tie Domi, I threw them both a couple times, starting with the right and switching to the left.

ES: You said you don't like fighting with bigger guys, but guys like Hartman and Tie are smaller, more compact guys.

MV: Tie has a huge head that's as hard as a rock. He puts his head down and all you're going to hit is the top of his head, because he's so little and compact and he's powerful. He's like a little bulldog. All you're going to do is bounce them off his head.

Chapter 21

TOUGH GUYS WITH SKILL

IN YOUR FACE:
RICK TOCCHET

*"I knew then and there that if I didn't
fight and play aggressively, I wouldn't
be in the NHL. And I can tell you that
there's no way I would have reached
the point I'm at today. In the early days
I couldn't rely on my scoring and
passing. I needed the other element."*

*During his early years with the Philadelphia Flyers,
Rich Tocchet was one of the most reviled forwards in the
National Hockey League. A skating bulldozer, the
Toronto native did what he had to in order to win and,
sometimes, the results were bloody.*

*During one gory episode involving Islanders
defenseman Dean Chynoweth, Tocchet was accused of
gouging Chynoweth's eye. On other occasions he wasted
not a second before dropping his gloves and pummeling
the foe.*

*Only a precious few scouts believed that Rick would be
anything more than a hard-driving, brawling forward, but
his metamorphosis into one of the NHL's premier scorers
has truly been remarkable.*

*He became a scoring star with the Flyers and even
captain of the Broad Street sextet. Following a shake up*

*of the Philadelphia roster, Tocchet was dealt to the
Pittsburgh Penguins, performing nobly during their run to
a second straight Stanley Cup in 1992.*

*Of Italian descent, Tocchet still is prone to the on-ice
explosion. Late in the 1992-93 season he erupted after
New Jersey Devils defenseman Scott Niedermayer
allegedly jabbed Rick with his stick. Tocchet's response
was a head-butt that earned the Penguin an early exit
from the game.*

*Later, in the dressing room, reporter Eric Servetah
confronted Tocchet. "Rick, what happened?" Servetah
inquired.*

*"He speared me with the stick," Tocchet replied.
"Really, it was no excuse for me to head-butt him."*

To which Servetah added, "But Toc, that's your game."

*Tocchet mulled over the thought and then nodded, "I
guess it is."*

*In person, Tocchet is a pleasant, witty individual,
delighted to do interviews and forthright to a fault. When
Stan Fischler originally interviewed Tocchet, he was
lounging on a sofa at Meadowlands Arena in East
Rutherford, New Jersey, wearing a black jacket that
seemed better suited to an Atlantic City croupier than a
hockey player. Tocchet was also interviewed in the spring
of 1993 during the playoffs.*

*The following is the question-and-answer interview
with Tocchet conducted by Stan Fischler.*

SF: How did your parents wind up in Toronto from their native
Italy?

RT: They were born just outside of Venice, and my dad came over
when he was 15. He wound up in Toronto and got a job as a
mechanic. Then he sent for my mother a couple of years later
after he earned enough money to pay for her trip and buy a
house in Scarborough, just outside of the city.

SF: Did you speak Italian at home?

RT: My parents spoke Italian among their friends and my two older
brothers and I spoke a little, but mostly we tried to speak
English.

SF: Were you a fighter as a kid, the way you became one on ice?

RT: The first fight I remember was when I was eight years old, in
grade school. We were in the lunchroom and a kid threw an
orange at me. I went after the guy, then his friend got into it and
a friend of mine joined the battle, so it wound up four eight-
year-olds swinging away. It was a long fight with the teachers

jumping in like linesmen and a couple of us, me included, ended up with bloody noses.

SF: You were a competitor even then?

RT: I had to be because of having two older brothers in the house. Right from the start I was playing hockey and football with guys five or 10 years older than me. I had to have a lot of aggressiveness in me just to keep up. Even then, I never wanted to lose; never wanted to back down from anybody. I had a few fights with my brother Dan, who's three years older than me, but the funny thing is that me and Andy — he's eight years older — fought more often. I remember him knocking me cold a couple of times. (Laughs) I never got even, either, because once I grew up, I grew out of the idea of going back at him.

SF: When was there early evidence of the Rich Tocchet we're seeing today?

RT: When I began playing for [Toronto] St. Michael's midgets. In 40 games, I scored 28 goals and 20 assists, so I had my point-a-game average and was at the top of penalty minutes. Then and there I was a two-way aggressive hockey player. Like today, I liked to do something and get my nose dirty.

SF: So, how come you were drafted so poorly? The 125th pick in the sixth round? That's about as low as you can get.

RT: They thought I couldn't skate well and the truth is my skating didn't get better until my second year of Juniors at Sault Ste. Marie. I should have been picked higher because I had a great season in my third year of Juniors, but Buffalo and Calgary, who could have taken me, went for Swedish and Finnish players ahead of me; something I'll never forget.

SF: What prompted Philadelphia to take you?

RT: Terry Crisp, who coached me in The Soo. He played for the Flyers and knew guys in Philly. He begged them to draft me. The way it turned out, the Flyers had the last pick in the sixth round before the long break. Crisp had them take a chance on me.

SF: How much were you hampered by the skating problem?

RT: First of all, it wasn't as bad as my detractors thought it was. Secondly, I could get to the puck just as fast as anyone but I did feel I needed help so I started taking power-skating lessons from Cindy Bower, the daughter of [Hall of Fame goaltender] Johnny Bower. That helped me a lot.

SF: You managed to move into the NHL without any minor league experience. How come?

RT: Bob Clarke had retired to become Flyers' GM, and two other good ones, Bill Barber and Rick MacLeish, also were gone, which meant that a lot of spots were open in Philly. Me, Peter Zezel, Derrick Smith, Murray Craven and Ronnie Sutter all got chances. Clarke did a house-cleaning and [coach] Mike Keenan wanted young players. We were lucky; on another club we'd have wound up in the minors.

SF: How good did you think you'd be in the NHL? A 45-goal scorer?

RT: No. In my first couple of years I was fighting all the time and I scored 14 goals as a rookie and in my second season. What I knew I had was the heart, drive and capabilities to stay. There are a lot of variables and ultimately I controlled some of them. With hard work and getting the chance to play with offensive types, things began to change for the better.

SF: What did Mike Keenan do for you?

RT: He got that something extra out of me. I might have thought that I had had enough and couldn't go on any more, but Mike convinced me that I had that little reserve tank in me that got some more mileage. Keenan got the most of out most players and he was at his best with players like me and Ronnie Sutter; guys who aren't the most talented but have some talent and work hard. He made us better players than we were. On top of that Mike taught me how to become a leader, how to forecheck and become a mentally-tougher person.

SF: What was the down side of Keenan?

RT: Sometimes he went too far, and I think he realizes that now. In his younger days, he figured he couldn't be your friend and he didn't think you could be friends with him. He felt he had to distance himself so much from the players.

SF: Compare Keenan to Scotty Bowman.

RT: Since Scotty has been in the NHL so long, he doesn't care about the bullshit. We really didn't see Scotty too much; only behind the bench. Keenan and Bowman have similarities but Scotty is not as outgoing as Mike. Scotty keeps to himself whereas Mike will joke with you and have fun. But the next day after Keenan's jokes, you'd better be prepared to work or you won't play.

SF: What did Scotty do for you?

RT: He realized when I came to Pittsburgh that I had already been in the NHL for nine years and that he should just play me. He put me on a line with Mario Lemieux and said, "Just play!" He didn't say too much to me and I can't recall when he ever sat me down and told me to do this or do that. He let me go out and do what I wanted to do, which was good. But sometimes I need to be told if I have made a mistake. Maybe not all the time, but once in a while. Like, "Rick, I'd like to see you do this more." Or, "I want you to play more aggressively."

SF: How important was fighting in your development as a hockey player?

RT: It was a major, *MAJOR* part of my game and our Flyers' team. I knew then and there that if I didn't fight and play aggressively

I wouldn't be in the NHL. And I can tell you that there's no way I would have reached the point I'm at today. In the early days I couldn't rely on my scoring and passing. I needed the other element.

SF: What important early fights do you remember?

RT: I recall a big fight with [Buffalo defenseman] Larry Playfair in my rookie year. At that point in my career I really didn't care if I got punched out or not; all I wanted to do was survive. With that in mind, I stood up to all of the tough guys, but I remember Playfair in particular because he was so big and so tough. Another memorable event was merely going into Boston Garden when the Bruins had heavyweights like Terry O'Reilly, Brian Curran and Gord Kluzak.

SF: Did you enjoy fighting in those early NHL days?

RT: I enjoyed what it did for our team. I enjoyed sticking up for my teammates and after the fight, having the guys on the bench and in the locker room coming up to me and saying, "Thanks a lot, good job!" That, I liked. On the other hand, the tough part was knowing I was going into Boston Garden, realizing that there would be fights and that I was going to be involved in one of them.

Those were the days when Jay Miller was fighting for Boston and I went in there knowing that I was going to fight him. As a result, my heart was pumping all day. It's a tough kind of fear. In my position, I was torn; I couldn't be too keyed-up, but I also couldn't be too low. I had to find the median level and, believe me, that's tough.

SF: When did you start putting the brakes on your temper?

RT: After my fourth year in Philly, Bobby Clarke pulled me aside and said, "I don't want you fighting so much; I know you have to get in your eight or nine fights a year, but I don't want you fighting 20 times." He said I was too valuable to the team and he didn't want me getting involved with guys like Miller and Ken Baumgartner. "If you want to fight," he said, "fight guys like Cam Neely, Wendel Clark or Mark Messier — tough guys who play a lot." So, I took his words to heart, and also those of Mike Keenan who basically said the same thing.

SF: That put you in an awkward position one night when Baumgartner jumped you at Nassau Coliseum. Remember?

RT: Do I ever! It started with me checking somebody on the Islanders. Then Baumgartner came at me from the side and his stick hit me first and then he started throwing punches. I got cut from his stick which gave us a five-minute power play. We ended up scoring three power-play goals and won the game, 5-1. In that situation, I had to stick my ego in my back pocket but the equation was terrific. I got a few stitches but in return we won the game, so it proves that sometimes it pays to sacrifice your ego for the good of the team. As for Baumgartner, I never really got the chance to get him back and I might never have the opportunity. Then, again, there might be a chance that I will.

SF: Did you enjoy the transition from fighter to player?

RT: Sure. When I cut my fighting in half, it meant that I could concentrate on offense and not have to worry about the other stuff. When Baumgartner or Miller took a run at somebody on our club, it was another Flyer who had to take care of that business. But the good thing for us was, at the time, we had the luxury of having a very tough team in Philly. For three or four years, we had the toughest team in hockey.

SF: How come you couldn't beat Edmonton in the two times you met them in the Stanley Cup finals?

RT: The first time [1985] we were too young and they were too experienced and too good. The second time [1987] we had them on their heels. I remember this very well. We played them at the Spectrum on a Thursday and beat the Oilers. Normally, the next game [seventh in the series] would be on Saturday night but they postponed it for a concert or circus in town. That extra day gave Messier and Gretzky more rest. If we had played them on the Saturday, we would have beaten them. As it was, we were ahead 1-0 in the seventh game before they pulled even and finally went ahead.

SF: What was it like to get so close to the Cup and then be denied?

RT: We were devastated at the moment, but we didn't have a feeling of hopelessness in terms of the future. With the team we had in Philadelphia at that time, we took it for granted that we would be in the finals again the following year. But then things took a turn for the worse and during the next couple of seasons I began to think I'd never be in the finals again and would never taste Stanley Cup champagne.

SF: What went wrong in Philadelphia?

RT: A lot of things happened, starting with Keenan getting fired, trading players. The trade of [defenseman] Brad McCrimmon was the start of the downslide. It left all the players with a bad feeling because Brad was an important part of our team, and we all knew that he had a lot of good years left. Not only Brad but also Mark Howe. Together, they made up the best defensive pairing in the league for at least two or three years. Next, Bobby Clarke became unhappy with management and he and [president] Jay Snider had problems which began snowballing.

SF: In the meantime you became captain. Was that good or bad?

RT: At first it was good. It put pressure on me and I like pressure. But when we started losing, they blamed the captaincy, claiming it was too much pressure for me. That was bullshit. It had nothing to do with it.

SF: What was the problem?

RT: Two years ago we were one or two points out of first place going into March but we didn't make a trade. Our guys worked hard and I remember [general manager] Russ Farwell saying we were not working hard. He gave it to our team which was unjust. Every guy tried but we didn't have the horses. I never really wanted out of Philly. I loved it there. The fans are great but finally I realized that it was inevitable that I would go because I couldn't communicate with Farwell. I was working hard but I didn't believe that the Flyers believed in me anymore. And I didn't believe in them, so it was a two-way street type of thing. I knew that they had made a decision to go with younger players and that they would make a trade. I knew they weren't going to get rid of Rod Brind'Amour so there was just a handful of guys that they could get a return on and I was one of them. I knew I was gone.

SF: What did you do about it?

RT: I went to [agent] Steve Mountain and told him I was very frustrated. I talked to him every single night for a whole month and every time, he told me, "Hang in there!" Meanwhile, my ice time was reduced and I was getting heat because the team was losing. I thought I was going to the Red Wings; I would have put money on that but the deal didn't go down because the Flyers wanted too much; they were asking for everybody. At least five GMs were trying to get me, including Mike Keenan. Then, it happened.

SF: How?

RT: I had been out with five of the Flyers at a little tavern having a couple of beers. The guys kept telling me that something was up on account of [coach] Bill Dineen had said he wanted to see me the next morning at 9:30. Being captain, I thought he wanted to talk to me about the team, so I didn't think much of it, but my teammates were sure a trade was going on.

I should have caught the hint earlier. We had played the Devils in Jersey and tied them. After the game, we were in the bowels of the Byrne Arena waiting to get on our bus for the trip back to Philly. That's when I noticed Farwell and Jay Snider talking in the corner. Obviously something was up because, normally, the bus doesn't wait that long after the game. So, anyway, I say good-night to the guys after the beers and headed home. No sooner do I get in the house when the phone rings. It's my old pal, Paul Coffey, calling me at three in the morning.

He told me he was going to Los Angeles and I was going to the Penguins. I couldn't believe it because Pittsburgh was one of the last places I thought I'd wind up, especially since they're in the same division as the Flyers.

SF: How did you feel about it?

RT: Ecstatic. I was going to be playing with some of the greatest players in the world: Mario, Kevin Stevens, who is the best left winger in the game, Jaromir Jagr, Ronnie Francis and Ulf Samuelsson. It was an unbelievable list and I was going to be with these guys.

SF: What was the reality like?

RT: Nothing like what I expected. I couldn't believe how loose they were. Yeah, certain guys are serious but the Penguins had the feeling that reminded me more of a baseball team than a hockey club. You play so many games and if you lose, you lose; that's the way it felt. But once the games started meaning something in the playoffs, it was just like you could see Mario's eyes get wider and it seemed that everyone turned it up a notch. Not too many teams or people can turn it off and on when they want, but we have some guys who are able to do that.

SF: You came to a team that had been unimpressive for a good part of the season. What did you think about the chances of winning the Stanley Cup?

RT: To go the route, we had to beat Washington and the Rangers. That seemed impossible. You get by one team and then you've got the same type of style with the next one. First we went up against Washington who I figured had the most depth of any team, and with lots of grinders as well.

SF: With that in mind, and the fact that Pittsburgh was down three games to one to Washington, how did you beat them?

RT: Not too many people outside our dressing room know the answer, but I'll tell you. After they took the three-to-one lead, I was sitting on the train with Mario, Ronnie Francis and [assistant coach] Barry Smith. We were trying to figure a way out of the dilemma when Mario came up with an idea. He suggested that we go to the "one-four" forecheck system; send one man in and have four guys back. Mario went and told Scotty and that's what we did. We allowed their defensemen, especially Al Iafrate and Kevin Hatcher — they were killing us — to come out. Before that we had sent two guys in and they beat us back and it allowed their third and fourth guys to get goals. So what we did was clog up the middle and they didn't know what to do. We felt that if we gave them 10 chances and we got 10 chances, that we would win the hockey game because we have better offensive players. But if we gave them 16 or 17 chances, it would have been harder for us to come back. And that's how we won the series.

SF: Against the Rangers, it was even tougher, with Mario, yourself, Bob Errey, Kjell Samuelsson and Joey Mullen all hurt and your club down two games to one. Explain that win.

RT: Discipline. The Rangers had more talent than Washington and with all our guys hurt, to get out of that series was incredible. The answer was discipline. In today's hockey, more than ever, you have to have discipline.

Eight years ago, if the same series were played, the Rangers probably would have beaten us because not as many penalties would have been called. But you can't play the aggressive way the Rangers played that year and try to beat us. They played stupid and I know for a fact that Mark Messier was mad about the way they played. You cannot kill penalties and you cannot play stupid hockey in the NHL right now and win. The rules won't allow it. If you don't change with the times, you are going to be out. I've tried to change with the times. Everybody has to change with the times and you need discipline. That's the reason we won; that and Ronnie Francis. Ronnie stepped up for Mario and scored and played unbelievably. On that series alone, you could see that the trade for Ronnie and Ulf Samuelsson was well worth it, let alone all the other stuff they've done. People don't realize that Ronnie is a two-way player and not just a scorer.

SF: It must have been excrutiating for you to be sidelined during parts of the first two rounds when the club was in trouble.

RT: I tried to come back against Washington in the fourth game, but it was stupid of me because if I had stayed out of that series altogether I would have been ready for the first game of the Ranger series. But I tried to play and I aggravated the shoulder more than I hurt it in the second game. I had come back from what they called a "second-degree separation" and that was my fault — too soon. Sometimes you just have to wait and there's nothing you can do about it. Hopefully the club can get by without you and win, but I wanted desperately to come back and play the Rangers.

SF: What stopped you?

RT: Craig Patrick [Penguins' GM]. He knew I wanted to play badly but he kept telling me, "There's no pressure on you to come back." After we lost the second game to the Rangers and were tied one-to-one on the series, he took me aside and said, "Look, Rick, even if we lose the next game, we're okay. We don't need you for Game Three." So, we lost that game and were down two-to-one. This time, he tells me, "I know you want to play but I got a feeling we're gonna win tonight! You just sit a couple of more days." If you remember, we won that game after Francis scored a long [65-foot] shot against Mike Richter and Ronnie got the winner in OT.

SF: But you were still hurting when you came back. Right?

RT: To compensate for the pain, I tried to hit with my other shoulder and, of course, I tried to watch to see if someone was going to hit me. At that point, the adrenaline takes over and I didn't really care about anything. Sure, I was hit in that game but I was so excited and doing everything I could and we wound up winning. So I had two more days to rest. To tell you the truth, in retrospect, I feel lucky that I even survived that game. Then, we came back and beat them in Game Six and the series was ours. Amazing!

SF: Explain.

RT: We were more excited beating the Rangers than we were about beating Boston and going to the finals. You have to understand that everyone was saying New York had the best team in the league, and every paper was picking the Rangers to win the Cup. They had Mark Messier and he was going to lead them all the way, and everything was supposedly falling into place for them. We snatched it away from them and it was something to feel in that last game because the fans in Pittsburgh during that last game were on their feet from beginning to end. Even then I wasn't able to play my best.

SF: When did you hit your peak?

RT: In the finals against Chicago. I was at the top of my game more than I had ever been before. That was the best hockey I've played in my entire career. I felt every time that I was up there, that I could do something right and help the team. In the last game — the fourth of the finals — I had a goal and two or three assists. I scored the tying goal and sunk the game-winner. I intercepted a couple of passes and sent Mario out on a few breakaways. Everything was coming together just right.

SF: What made the difference in the finals?

RT: The thing with our team is that when we get down by two or three we don't panic, and that was evident in the opening game of the finals which I like to call "The Tommy Barrasso Show." Tommy was the guy who kept us in until we got our act together. We don't panic because we know we have a chance to come back. If there's a power play, we can score. If it takes a Jaromir Jagr individual effort, he can do it. We have that luxury whereas in Philly we always had a team effort. Here we have a team effort and individual efforts.

We have guys who can take the puck, beat three guys and score. You saw that when Jags got that incredible goal against the Blackhawks; one of the greatest goals ever. Remember, he had to beat a guy like Brent Sutter, one of the best two-way players in the league, and then he had to beat Dirk Graham, another good one, plus yet another defenseman and then get a great shot off and score.

SF: Compare Jagr and Lemieux in terms of skills.

RT: There's a big difference. Mario is a more complete player. Jagr is a one-on-one player. Jagr will take the puck and go one-on-one as good as anybody. Mario has vision all over the place and can see everything around him. He's the best. There aren't many guys who can play 35 minutes every night, get a three-point game, kill penalties and just dominate games like he can. That's why Mario has to pace himself; he can't go crazy all the time.

SF: What's your role with the Penguins?

RT: For me scoring 50 goals doesn't make a difference on this team. It doesn't matter if I score a lot with all the talent we have. I'll probably score my 35 or 40 goals and maybe I have an outside chance at 50 this year, but I have to play aggressively. I have to get to the net since I'm playing on Mario's line and obviously my job is to protect Mario, too. I can't allow anybody to take liberties with him, and I understand that.

SF: At what point do you step in for him?

RT: I have to be smart about that. In training camp I had five fights and Mario kept telling me not to fight. He is one guy who doesn't want me to fight. If there's a pile-up with him involved and I'm trying to get in there, he'll look at me and say, "Don't worry; I'm just getting pushed." If a guy jumps Mario, I have to get in there, but if somebody hits Mario hard, I can't go after him because that's part of hockey. Mario doesn't expect me in there in that circumstance, but if a guy takes a cheap shot at him, that's where I have to step in.

SF: You've played for Mike Keenan, Scotty Bowman, Bill Dineen and Paul Holmgren. You haven't mentioned Holmgren.

RT: He's a player's coach; kind of like Keenan only friendlier. He gave me free rein, but he would tell me if I played badly and I'd feel bad. When Paul told you that you didn't play well that night, you felt bad for him. Other coaches will tell you the same thing and you'll just blow it off, like you didn't care. With Holmgren, I cared.

SF: Should the Flyers have fired him?

RT: No way. The team wasn't good enough. They never gave him the players he needed. They told him to be patient. He tried to play guys like Kimbi Daniels, Dan Kordic, guys who might be good players someday, but this was the regular season and we were losing games. Holmgren was the scapegoat.

SF: Is there anybody in the league you wouldn't fight now?

RT: No. I would fight anybody for the right reason. I wouldn't fight a guy for no reason, especially now.

SF: Who was the toughest guy you ever fought?

RT: Gord Kluzak of the Bruins hit me in the helmet and it popped off and I remember feeling his punch. He was a big, intimidating guy.

SF: You once said, "Once I get hit hard, for the first three seconds, all I want to do is kill the guy." How much truth is in that?

RT: I said that after I fought Dean Chynoweth of the Islanders and hurt him. I remember him elbowing me in the face and I was stunned and I was just fighting out of instinct. People don't realize that when you're in a fight, you're just trying to survive.

SF: Is the game too soft now compared to when you broke in with Philly?

RT: It is. What happened is that every year they put three or four rule changes in and it reached a point where they're rewriting the rulebook so much that the game has changed dramatically and the aggressiveness is taken out of the game. The refs dictate the game too much. I'm not blaming the refs — I'm not blaming anybody — I'm just saying that the league is making the refs decide the game when the players should decide the game. I liked it better eight or nine years ago. I remember going into New York or Washington or Pittsburgh when they had tough teams. We used to have a tough team and the fans were into it and there wasn't much scoring. It was like a 4-3 hockey game and there was the odd fight here or there and a lot of tough hockey. I'd like to see that, but obviously it's changed and I've changed with the times. I have to make some money and I want to win another Cup. I'll do whatever it takes, and if that means I have to walk away if somebody punches me in the face, I'll walk away. Nine years ago, I wouldn't have. I'd collapse the guy because it was more of an intimidation factor. It's hard to intimidate guys nowadays.

SF: What's the difference between Pittsburgh and Philly fans?

RT: In Pitt the fans like fighting, but they're used to skilled hockey. I'm not saying they're spoiled, but they come to games now expecting us to win and they expect us to beat a team pretty bad. If we squeek out a win, they're quiet. In Philly it was different. I'll give you an example: when the Rangers would come to town, the fans at the Spectrum didn't care if we scored a lot of goals. They liked it if we won and they really liked it if we beat the hell outa them. The fans are different because of the different styles of the teams. In Philly, I might score two goals in a game and afterwards would go into a night club or restaurant. People would come up to me and want to talk about my fight, not about the two goals I scored. It was unbelievable. In Pitt they talk more about your offense than the aggressive part.

SF: What's the major obstacle to Pitt winning another Cup?

RT: Complacency — in thinking we're so great. We have to have confidence that we're good, but we can't think we're too great. Don't become complacent; that's the key. We have to realize that other teams are going to step it up a notch, and we definitely have another notch. We also have to remember that when we won in 1992, we had a lot of things going our way. We're going to have to work even harder this year. It's going to take guys like myself, Mario, Francis. It's going to take us rebounding from the 1993 playoff loss. It's going to take Kevin Stevens rapping a few of the young guys in the head once in a while and saying, "You're not as great as you think you are!" It's going to take a team effort.

SF: You make it seem as if Bowman didn't get involved. What did he do?

RT: He was a good bench coach. He's a good tactician behind the bench. He gets all the right match-ups. It's amazing. He'll want to play Mario against guys like Pierre Turgeon and Joe Sakic.

SF: Was the team happy when he returned as Penguins' coach in 1992-93?

RT: Most of the guys were happy. I'm sure there were some guys who weren't happy about it all, but you can't please everybody.

SF: Can you precisely describe the feeling you got winning the Stanley Cup in 1992?

RT: I'll go one step better. I'll tell you what the feeling was like *before* we won it. We took the cab to Chicago Stadium about four-thirty on the afternoon of Game Four. In my head I was thinking that I was just 60 minutes of playing time away from my first Cup. I can assure you that the time before winning was as exciting as actually taking the whole shebang. When we did win it, it was the greatest thing that ever happened to me. I was on top of the world for a few days, not just one. We became the focal point of the whole city, especially when they had the parade. I'll always look at my Stanley Cup ring and remember those three or four days as something to cherish. I'll also remember that scene at Chicago Stadium after all the skating around with the Cup. The guys started going downstairs to the dressing room and, suddenly, I remember the baseball scene when the Mets won the World Series and Ron Darling just sat on the mound, all alone, drinking a beer and taking in all the great feelings. If I could gave pulled up a chair and sat out there on the ice with the Cup, I would have done it.

SF: Was there a team party?

RT: We had one at Mario Lemieux's place, right down at poolside. Guys were diving into the water with the Cup, and did it ever take a beating. I went off the diving board with it a couple of times.

SF: It sounds like the Penguins are a fun team.

RT: There's no club in the league that jokes as much as this team. I might have the worst night of my life and the next night I'll get torn apart. This much I can tell you; if you can't take it, you can't play for the Penguins. If you can't take a joke, you will not be able to survive on this team. Ulf Samuelsson, Kevin Stevens and myself are the worst for jabbing. Nothing's safe. For instance, there was an ongoing joke a while back that Stevens didn't even know about because he was hurt at the time. After practice, me and Ulf would take the plugs out of the head of his car. When he tried to start the buggy, it wouldn't start. The car was only a month old and he thought there was something wrong with it. It was an ongoing joke that the whole team knew about except Kevin. Every day someone would say, "How's the car running?"

SF: How do you guys jab?

RT: Here's how: I remember when I was in Philly how little Keith Acton once punched Ulf Samuelsson in the head. So after I came to Pitt, Ulf started needling me, saying Mark Recchi was scoring for the Flyers and that Pittsburgh never should have traded him for me. I turned to him and said, "At least I don't get beat up by five-foot midgets!"

SF: Ulf has the reputation of being dirty. Does he deserve it?

RT: The media's built up about him being dirty. He's given me a few charliehorses and I know I've gone after him a few times. Then there was that business with Cam Neely. I don't think Ulf was the problem with Neely; I just think he worsened the problem. I like his attitude. I don't think he's as dirty as people think he is. He just plays the game very hard and everybody takes cheap shots. No question, though, if you had to pick a team, he'd be on your defense.

SF: Are you ever going to get married?

RT: I'm looking. I always wanted to be married after hockey, but I don't want to be married when I'm playing hockey. I would be very difficult to live with because I don't take losing very well. Sometimes I like to be by myself after a game or if things aren't going well. I don't want a distraction.

Chapter 22

TOUGH GUYS WITH SKILL

MANHATTAN MESSIAH: MARK MESSIER

"The game isn't nearly as violent as it was when I broke into the league. In those days, if you were going to do something out there, you had to be able to back it up. Now if you want to play dirty, you can get away with it."

Among all the NHL superstars of the past decade, the most intimidating physical presence has been Mark Messier, first as an Edmonton Oiler and more recently as a New York Ranger.

In 1984 Messier's physical presence was a pivotal factor in the Oilers' first Stanley Cup championship. His arrival in New York in the fall of 1991 rejuvenated the Rangers so dramatically that the Broadway Blueshirts won the President's Trophy for the first time in club history.

Ever controversial, Messier emerged as New York's number-one athlete in 1991-92, although his star plummeted a year later.

In an interview with Stan Fischler held at a restaurant near his mid-town Manhattan luxury apartment, Messier spoke in depth about his background and his NHL career.

SF: You are notorious for your ability to tame the opposition. Your mother tells a story about when you were a kid and were given an ornery horse named Billy. Nobody could tame him but you.

MM: (Laughs) I don't know if I actually tamed him, but I learned early to show who was the boss.

SF: When you were eight and your father, Doug, was playing pro hockey, you once stood in the driveway, blocking your father's car when he refused to take you to a practice. Your father finally relented and took you. Remember that?

MM: I do, and I also remember that I had the luxury of my father being a professional hockey player and him knowing that I liked the game. I recall having to get up early for practice when it was real cold and me being lazy and not wanting to go. That's when my father would kick me in the ass to go, and I went. But I'll say this — both my parents had a sound feel when enough hockey was enough for me.

SF: Are you sorry you dropped out of school before reaching college?

MM: I actually was offered a scholarship when I was in grades 11 and 12, but that's when I decided to turn pro with Cincinnati in the World Hockey Association at 17. Now I don't miss not having gone to college. I've traveled enough and have been surrounded by intelligent people. In my own way, I've learned a lot.

SF: In the opening 1992 playoff series with the Devils, you were given a particularly hard time by Claude Lemieux, who shadowed you all over the place. How much of a competitive situation was that?

MM: I've been in ugly series before, so I know how to separate the personalities from the actual game. I'm out on a 200-by-85-foot surface and there's only so much room and both people are trying to get the same spot. A lot of things are going to happen. I don't harbor any ill feelings toward him. I enjoyed that competition because you find out a lot about yourself and your team and who you want to be with. But it would have been a lot more fun if I hadn't been hurt.

SF: How long do you push yourself before you finally get scratched from the lineup?

MM: There's a very fine line there, because if you want to be successful, you have to play through injuries, play through pain. If you're the leader, it's a calculated decision whether you're going to help the team or hurt the team by playing or not playing.

SF: The furor over Adam Graves's slash that took Mario Lemieux out of the 1992 playoffs seemed to distract the Rangers more than the Penguins. How do you cope with distractions like that?

MM: One lesson we learned from that was that you have to be able to handle the media circus, block it out and concentrate solely on the task at hand. There was a helluva lot said and written after Lemieux went down but there's no point in getting distracted by all the fuss. I always say you have three months during the summer to worry about why you won or why you didn't win. Apart from all the media distractions, in the end we really missed not having Adam in the lineup for the last three games. He's a huge player — a real leader.

SF: Are you saying that Graves shouldn't have gotten a four-game suspension for what he did to Lemieux?

MM: I've seen as bad or worse infractions committed in this league with less punishment, like Ron Hextall chopping Kent Nilsson in Game Four of the 1987 finals. The NHL let Hextall continue playing for the rest of the finals, and he nearly beat us single-handedly. We had to take the Flyers to seven games. If Hextall had been suspended the way Adam was, maybe we would have taken Philly in five games instead of having to come from behind in the seventh game at home to beat them.

SF: How do you feel about the fuss over fighting in the NHL?

MM: I don't think we have to worry about the violence, because that's not what's wrong with hockey. The game isn't nearly as violent as it was when I broke into the league. In those days, if you were going to do something out there, you had to be able to back it up. Now if you want to play dirty, you can get away with it. The rules today protect players from having to back it up, and that's wrong.

SF: If violence isn't a league problem, what is?

MM: We need to better utilize the players' talents. The new crop is getting so big, fast and strong. Until the league changed the rule you didn't get to see the true talents of the Lemieuxs, Gretzkys, Coffeys and Leetches. The game was much more exciting when the league allowed three-on-threes and four-on-fours. Those were the times you had your best players on the ice from both sides and now it's back to that again. Rather than concentrating on violence, we should stop players on the ice from clutching and grabbing the Lemieuxs and shadowing the Gretzkys.

SF: One goal stands out among all you scored at Northlands. It was against the Islanders in the 1984 Stanley Cup finals. It was perhaps the biggest goal in Oilers' history, and in your life.

MM: The series was tied one apiece after the first two games at Nassau Coliseum and now we were back in Edmonton. The Islanders had gone ahead 1-0, and Billy Smith looked good in goal for them. A bit later I got the puck on left wing, picked up speed and went one-on-one with [Islanders defenseman] Gord Dineen. I deked around him and in almost the same motion put a wrist shot past Smith. At that time we needed to believe that we could beat the Islanders, because it was a real tug-of-war between two teams going in different directions. They were hanging on and we weren't quite sure if we could do it or not. We beat them, 7-2, and finally believed that we could do it — and we did. When I look back, so many great things happened off that one particular play. But who knows what would have happened if I didn't come through, and Denis Potvin or Mike Bossy came down and scored to put them ahead. It could have turned out a lot differently for us.

SF: You are a believer in what you call "self-talk" being an important part of an athlete.

MM: I believe you make your own dream come true. You have to have a determination to achieve your goals. Too many times, things don't go well and athletes beat themselves up until they finally just talk themselves into depression. You have to instil a positive feeling. A player may try to cheat his way during a season, but you can't cheat your way to the Stanley Cup. You have to know what you want — you have to set goals for yourself and for the team.

SF: The John Kordic tragedy has produced a number of ideas re-garding league policy over drugs and steroids. What are your thoughts?

MM: It's easy to say drugs shouldn't be in sports, but athletes are no bloody different from people in any other walk of life. I don't know if random drug-testing is a bad idea. With the policy now, if you're caught doing drugs, you're out of the league. There's too much opportunity for players to do drugs, and not everybody has the capacity to say no. It's important not to scare good people who have problems from getting help. By not having a drug policy, the league scares people away from getting help when they do need it. The team should be responsible and help its players. The players shouldn't be hung out to dry. There should be a warning and then a suspension. If a player knows there's random drug-testing and still does it, he has a problem. We players are a fraternity and we should help each other. We showed that with the strike in 1992.

SF: Despite the accolades you've received, there's still a feeling that your total game is not appreciated. You never get points for body checks and your other intangibles like dressing-room leadership.

MM: I've got two Hart Trophies. To me, the ultimate prize is the Lester B. Pearson Award [presented annually to the NHL's outstanding player as selected by the Players' Association]. Twice I was voted best player by my peers, and I can tell you there's nothing like having the respect of your peers, because there's no cheating over what happens in front of them on the ice. I don't feel that I've been short on recognition. I'm the luckiest guy in the world.

SF: It seems that you outgrew Edmonton.

MM: What I needed was a change, a challenge. Not that I ever lost any spirit, but I had to have something to rekindle the fires, and the best way was to change cities. A number of times before I ever came here, I envisioned what it would be like playing in New York. I wanted to live downtown. I wanted to experience the whole thing — playing in a major media market and feeling the pulse of the city. I wanted the whole adrenalin rush of doing it all and now I've got it. When I'm in my apartment, looking out the window, I sometimes feel like I'm in a movie. I needed to get in the middle of things. Hockey-wise and life-wise, there was the need for an energy-booster and I came to the right place to get that.

SF: You're among the top marquee players in your sport, but you earn relatively little compared with a Bobby Bonilla or a Michael Jordan. How much does that bother you?

MM: It doesn't bother me that much. It's like matching apples and oranges — you really can't compare the two. The top paid players are starting to get closer to those in other sports. Way back when Wayne Gretzky was getting $160,000 a year, some of the best athletes in other sports were making millions, so we've finally begun to catch up. I certainly can't complain about the way the game has treated me. I'm sitting in New York, enjoying a pretty nice lifestyle because of hockey.

SF: Gordie Howe played until he was a grandfather. How long do you want to play?

MM: I'd like to play forever, if I could. It's amazing that Howe played to the age of 50 goddamned years with great strength and mental capacity. You pay a price to do what he did. First, I'd like to focus on the next three years and play at a high level. I'll be 35 then, so I'll see what happens and then make a decision. Funny thing is that it seems like yesterday that I broke in. I mean I can't believe I've played 16 years already.

SF: You Won the Hart Trophy [for MVP] first as an Oiler and then, in 1992, as a Ranger. Compare the two.

MM: When I won the Hart in 1990, it was the last time Edmonton won the Stanley Cup and everything went right for me. I stayed away from injuries, we played well as a team and the other parts fell into place. To be truthful, I never thought I'd win the Hart a second time. Yet, it happened again in 1992 in much the same way. We had a great bunch of guys — Leetch, Amonte, Graves and the rest — and good things happened.

Chapter 23

I WILL SURVIVE: WARREN RYCHEL

Marty McSorley on Warren Rychel:

> *"His desire to play is his biggest strength. He's willing to do things that other guys aren't willing to do. He's willing to finish his checks every time he's out on the ice. He's willing to go out. He's willing to fight guys even though he's not sure he might win because there's a difference in weight and everything else. But he's still willing to do that. So his desire to play is by far and away his biggest strength."*

The world of hockey agentry is filled with hyperbole and chicanery. Nevertheless, there are many player representatives who take a sincere interest in their clients and are rational in their appraisals.

One such individual is former NHL defenseman Tom Laidlaw, who implicitly believed that Warren Rychel could play in the bigs, and play well.

Laidlaw finally found a home for his client in Los Angeles and Warren, in turn, repaid both the Kings' and his agent's faith with a productive rookie season in 1992-93. Warren demonstrated early on that he could handle his dukes, fighting the Islanders' rugged Mick Vukota at Nassau Coliseum. He lost the fight by a decision, but the bout proved a catalyst for the Kings who then proceeded to beat the home club.

Playing on a team whose left-side scoring is provided by Luc Robitaille, Rychel had to accent aggressive defense and fight, if necessary.

During the regular season, Rychel played on the Kings' checking line with right wing Dave Taylor and center Pat Conacher. He ranked last among the King regulars in scoring with six goals and seven assists this season, but he led the NHL with 30 major penalties and was second on the team with 314 penalty minutes behind McSorley's 399.

Rychel understood his role and that of his fellow Kings' checkers. "Normally, our reward during the regular season is just knowing that we contributed by checking, blocking a shot, killing a penalty or getting into a fight to lift the guys up," Rychel said. "As long as the coach and the guys in the locker room know that we're helping this team, that's all we care about. Sometimes people don't realize it because we don't show up in the score sheet. But we know we're helping the team win."

The incident with Vukota also symbolized the fire that Rychel brought to the Los Angeles lineup. Warren played a significant part in the Kings' march to the playoffs and their victory in the Campbell Conference championship round. Rychel even played on a top line with Wayne Gretzky and Tomas Sandstrom in the post-season and provided goals, assists and penalty minutes. He scored the Kings' game-winning goal in Game Four of the opening round against the Calgary Flames.

"Warren Rychel has contributed to our team all year physically," Luc Robitaille said. "It's certainly was nice to see him get the big goal. He's going to remember that all his life."

Now an NHL regular, the vibrant forward detailed his feelings about life in the big tent to a pair of reporters, David Margalit, after a practice at Madison Square Garden, and Andre Palai at the Great Western Forum.

DM: What sports did you play when you were growing up?

WR: I played all sports — baseball, hockey, basketball, everything. I was active. I played Junior C hockey when I was 16 and I got drafted by the Sudbury Wolves late in the 13th round.

DM: What teams did you follow when you were a kid?

WR: I followed the Detroit Red Wings and the Toronto Maple Leafs. We saw the Leafs on TV all the time, but Detroit was right across the river. So it was a little bit of both. It was a kick to see a good hockey game. It was part of growing up. There's excitement when you go to the rink. In Canada, everyone's into it.

DM:Who were your favorite players?

WR:I liked Terry O'Reilly of Boston. He was a good player and he also fought. He could do everything. He was the type of player I wanted to mold myself after. I play a regular shift, I penalty kill and I also can scrap.

DM:Were you a tough kid off the ice?

WR:I was a normal kid — happy-go-lucky. I wasn't a bully or anything like that. I did well in school.

DM:Where did you play in the minors?

WR:I played Junior hockey but I wasn't drafted so I signed on as a free agent. I played in Saginaw for two years. Then I played in Indianapolis of the International League for a couple of years. I played the last couple of years in Kalamazoo.

DM:When did you get into fighting?

WR:That came about in Junior hockey some seven or eight years ago. It was pretty tough. They needed players like that and it was the same situation when I came to L.A. If you check hard and get in people's faces, you're liable to get in fights. That just happens, and that's how I got into scrapping.

DM:Was fighting a very large part of Junior hockey?

WR:Yes, it was, although it's not as much now as it was back then. A lot of very tough guys came out of the OHL, and it was the same in the Western League. That's the way hockey is and will be for a long time to come.

DM:How do the physical aspects of the minor leagues differ from the NHL's?

WR:There are a lot of tough guys down there and they scrap. They want to get up to the NHL. They're quick to drop their gloves down there because they're fighting to get to the NHL.

DM:How would you compare fighters in the minors to those in the National Hockey League?

WR:In the NHL they are a little smarter and more experienced. The fights are a little tougher up here. I've been in a lot of fights as a member of the Kings. I've fought some good ones and I've lost a few. Nick Kypreos pounded me pretty good. Gary Roberts and I had a great fight. We went at it for a long time. Roberts is the type of player who I would want to be like. He's a great player. He and Rick Tocchet are two of the best. They can play well and they play a lot. They do a lot of things for their teams and they're both as tough as nails. They have great offensive abilities. I had 30 goals and over 300 penalty minutes playing minor league hockey. I'd like to have numbers like that up here.

AP: Did all those fights in the minors get you ready for the NHL?

WR:You figure pro hockey is pro hockey. A grown man is a grown man. There are big guys everywhere. Two of the toughest guys I've faced are Tony Twist and Link Gaetz. Here [in the NHL] everyone's a little bit smarter and faster. That's their job. They don't want to get beat. They know how to prepare and they're very, very, strong and big.

DM:You came to the Kings in an unusual manner. Explain how you made the team as a walk-on.

WR:I was very fortunate that [coach] Barry Melrose gave me a chance. I was in the minors for five years. I did a lot of work down there. I worked on my entire game. I had 30 goals and 300 penalty minutes the last two years. I was in a tough situation when I was with Chicago. They had a good team and I wasn't getting an opportunity. Finally, I got to the Kings as a free agent. I knew it was probably my last kick at the bucket. They had so many skilled players and they needed a couple of grinders and muckers. So the opportunity arose and here I am.

DM:In October 1992, when the Kings played the Islanders, you fought Mick Vukota. Although it wasn't your best fight, Barry Melrose praised you for your effort in standing up against him. Why?

WR:Sometimes during the game, you're in a situation where the team's not up and you need a lift, whether it be a big hit, a goal, or a fight. That was the circumstance right there. It got the guys going and I think we scored three goals in the next two minutes. Any way I can help is why I'm up here. If I'm not going to do it, they're just going to get somebody else to do my job.

DM:In what type of situations do you usually decide to fight?

WR:You have to watch things now with the new rules and stuff, but you just know when the time is right; that is, when anybody takes advantage of me or my teammates. There are different situations but I think most of the guys know when the scraps are going to take place.

AP: Do you enjoy fighting?

WR:I don't think anybody enjoys fighting, but it's a reality of hockey and probably the scariest thing in pro sports. Two men fighting bare knuckled — that's pretty much down to it. Nobody likes to fight but that's an ingredient you have to have on your team to be successful in the game of hockey so things don't get out of hand in other departments — like sticks. Anyone could walk over anyone if they knew they're not going to be dealt with and that keeps everything on an even keel. It's not the prettiest job in the world.

DM:How have the new rules affected the game?

WR:They are good because they limit the guys who just play one shift every period from coming out and fighting. There are some guys like that and it's fine, but they can't come out and get in a scrap because it's going to cost their team two minutes and they're going to get thrown out of the game. As you know, you're only allowed three. If you fight a willing partner, that's great, but you can't just go out and jump somebody like you could before.

DM:There's been a lot of talk about eliminating fighting.

WR:This new rule does a lot. It eliminates nonsense like guys coming around and jumping each other. You've got to really think about it because it puts your team in jeopardy. Players have to use their heads and so do the coaches. You just can't go out there and start a mêlée — it will cost everyone in the long run.

DM:How do you respond to a teammate like Wayne Gretzky who is anti-fighting and wants to eliminate it from the game? Do you ever talk to him about it?

WR:He understands. Fighting is part of hockey and he knows it's part of it. Some of Wayne's favorite players are scrappers. He understands that there's a time and a place for it. He wouldn't want one of us to just go out and jump guys, but if someone takes advantage of your team or teammates, you have to step in. You can't let that happen.

DM:Do you have a specific style that you like to use in your fighting?

WR:I like to know what the opponent does before I fight him because I'm not the biggest guy compared to some of the other guys. I'm six feet tall and some of these other guys are real big. You have to know what you're getting into — whether they're left-handed or what their style is or what they like to do so you can counter them successfully. I like to think that I'm a smart fighter.

AP: How do you adjust your style when you fight a bigger player?

WR:A lot of guys have size on me, so I have to rely on my strength. If I keep in close, as the fight goes on I get stronger and wait for the prime opportunity to make the play. You can't stand back and go toe-to-toe when you're six feet tall. If the other guy is 6-feet-4, you have to use your head. Preparation is important; knowing how the other guy fights is a big part of it. You can't go into a gunfight not knowing what to expect from the other gunfighter. Rumors go around the league on certain guys — how they fight, what they tend to do. Sometimes I talk to our guys before the game. I might talk to Marty McSorley.

AP: Do you rate Marty McSorley with the NHL's top fighters?

WR:Marty is right up there, one or two in the league. He's so strong and big. His punches are real hard. I've seen him swing with the biggest guys from Stu Grimson to Craig Berube and I haven't seen him take a licking. Barry believed in him and he believes in me. The good thing about it is that we didn't get tapped on the shoulder one shift a period. We played a regular shift and Marty also played the power play.

DM:Did McSorley teach you anything?

WR:I've learned a lot from Marty. I've talked to a lot of guys and picked up some things. Marty has been a great help. I roomed with Marty on the road. He's been around the league and he knows a lot. He's a strong person, a very smart fighter. He punches very strong. He doesn't like to talk about his fighting that much. He helped me out and showed me pointers when I asked him. He was good to be with. He's someone who I have been able to talk to and he's taught me a lot.

AP: How well do you handle yourself in a fight? What's the usual outcome?

WR:I don't like to talk about that although I've done fairly well. I haven't really got hurt badly in a fight. Nick Kypreos hit me pretty hard and that was the hardest I was hit all '92-'93. I've done well. I've fought all the big guys and I'm not afraid of anybody. I can hold my own, as I've proven against people like Gary Roberts who is a good fighter. It was a long fight. I got some good licks in there and he was fortunate to get the good lick in at the end and I hit the ice. I respect him; he's a great player and there's no hard feelings.

DM:If you have lost any, how do you respond to a fight that you lose?

WR:I don't think there's a player in the NHL who has won every fight he's been in. When you lose one, you just pick up your things and keep your head up and go back on to the ice again later. You always have to keep it in the back of your mind and remember it for the next time.

AP: What kind of a toll does fighting take on the body?

WR:It really drains you, especially when you go up against a bigger guy. You're using your strength, you're on skates, you're doing everything. You're trying to punch and you wear yourself silly. But it's just like anything else — your cardiovascular and your strength conditioning comes into a big part of it. People don't realize it but it does drain you a lot.

AP: Would you say that you are an intimidator or more of a complete player?

WR:When I first broke into pro I was a hard worker but didn't have a lot of skill. My skill level wasn't developed so in order for me to make the team and play regularly, that's the role I had to play — a tough role. Sometimes I wouldn't play a lot — maybe one shift a period. You have to go in there and muck it up and fights happen. There's tough guys on every team. Pro hockey is pro hockey. In order to survive and play that's what I had to do. I just wanted to play so badly. My skill level at that time wasn't up to par and that's what I did. Then things started to change. I learned a lot in the minors in Saginaw and Indianapolis. Darryl Sutter told me that in order for me to make the NHL I had to be a complete player defensive-wise — not just the fighting — and be able to play a regular shift. I developed under him. We won the Turner Cup Championship that year. There were a lot of fine players on the team — Brian Noonan, Bobby Bassen, Jimmy Waite, Mike Eagles, Darren Pang, Cam Russell, Mike Stapleton — we had a really good team.

DM: How would you characterize yourself as a player?

WR: I think of myself as a hard-working, honest player who pays the price to help his team win. I'll do whatever the team needs me to do. I always have to put the team first. If they need me to fight, I'll fight. I go out there and work as hard as I can. Whatever is most important to help us win. We work hard and play hard together.

DM: When two heavyweights are out on the ice at the same time, do they look to square off or know that they're going to wind up fighting eventually?

WR: If you get in each other's faces, it's bound to happen. If you keep bothering each other, there will most likely be a fight.

DM: You're also one of the better hitters in the league. Do you ever go on the ice specifically looking to make the hit or the check?

WR: When you go out on the ice, you have to make the big hits. You look for them. It helps open up the ice and gives the really skilled players on the team a chance to operate with the puck more. If the opportunity arises to make a good hit, you have to take advantage of it.

DM: What are your thoughts about coach Barry Melrose?

WR: Barry has been great. He gave me the chance to play. That's the most important thing to me. He's given me the opportunity to play with some good players and he's given me some ice time. He's a great coach.

DM: Is there any one aspect of your game that you've been trying to improve or that you feel you need to improve?

WR: I'd like to work on my scoring touch around the net. I'm looking to get some good chances to score. I had two or three a game in the minors. It's important for me to bear down on my chances around the net. I don't play around with the puck that much. I'm out there to give the skilled players room to operate. When a good opportunity to get a shot or a scoring chance arises, I take advantage of it.

Chapter 24

THE WILD THING:
BIG AL IAFRATE

*"He [Ed Beers] was pounding on me
pretty good, and then he had me down
and gave me the old face gouge. All
the guys on the Calgary bench were
saying, 'Welcome to the NHL!'"*

*An iconoclast with a capital I, Al Iafrate skates to a
drummer different from anyone else in the National
Hockey League.*

*He also shoots the puck harder than anyone else,
moves faster than any other defenseman and rides
better-looking motorcycles. One would be hard-pressed
to find another player in the league who smokes more
cigarettes or cares less how others view his modus
operandi.*

*Al Iafrate is his own man and also one of the finest
performers in the league. He is tough in a funny kind of
way. The Michigan native does not run all over the ice in
attempts at intimidation, nor does he engage in fights just
for the sake of fisticuffs.*

*Yet there is a quiet toughness about the man. His huge
physique signals that the Italian-American is not one to
trifle with, particularly when the chips are down.*

*At Capital Centre he is known as "The Wild Thing."
The Capitals promoted the image by circulating color
posters of Iafrate astride a Harley-Davidson chopper with
ethereal smoke enveloping man and bike.*

*Al, himself, downplays his Wild Thing motif, suggesting
to friends that it's all overblown and he really isn't as
off-the-wall as people suggest. Perhaps, but there's no*

arguing the fact that Big Al is different. Call him a bad
boy with charm, affability and, most of all, talent.
   To obtain an all-inclusive view of Iafrate, reporter Eric
Servetah and Stan Fischler huddled with Al over dinner
at a New Jersey restaurant as well as at Nassau Coliseum
prior to a Washington-Islanders game.

SF: Let's start off with a funny Al Iafrate story.

AI: One time, me and Jeff Greenlaw and a bunch of the boys on the team chartered a flight after our game in Montreal, since we were off on Tuesday. We took the flight to Manhattan and went to hang out at the legendary China Club. A bunch of the Pittsburgh Penguins were there. They had just played the Rangers on that Monday night. It was me and Greeny, a bunch of the Penguins and a bunch of the Rangers were there, hanging out and partying heavy. We were in the China Club till the wee hours of the morning and then we went outside to hail a cab. So we got in a cab and we were driving and our cab driver had to be smoking something when a truck came head-on at us. We yell, "Look out!" So the cabbie swerves and hits the median, which flips the cab right over. Me and Jeff are left on the roof of the turned-over cab and are laughing our asses off. We crawl out and just then some bums come running up saying, "Do you guys have any money?" Anyway, next morning at breakfast we hear that our teammates were at a deli across the street from the accident. They're saying, "You should have seen this cab that tipped over last night." We started laughing and said it was me and Jeff in the cab they were looking at.

SF: What about your passion for heavy metal?

AI: I can remember catching one concert a couple of summers ago. It was at an a outdoor amphitheater called High Knob in Clarkson, Michigan. Half of the seating is seats and the other part is lawn — general admission. When Ministry came on, we were down in the third row and all of the people in the lawn, started tearing up the sod and started throwing it at us. So it was a big sod-throwing war going on and then when it got dark and the Red Hot Chili Peppers came on, the sod war stopped and people started putting their clothes in big piles and they started dancing around as they lit about 10 fires all around the concert area. People were dancing around pretty wild. Then there was a freak show in-between Ice Cube and Pearl Jam, and this guy took a shishkebab skewer and stuck it through his esophagus. It went right through the esophagus and I thought that was pretty cool and one of the wierdest things that I have ever seen at a concert. He had pierced nipples, that were pierced with big thick industrial bobby-pins. He had chains hooked through them attached to cinder-blocks and he was lifting them up with his nipples. It was seriously wierd. He was bent over and would scream and lift them up as his nipples hung down almost to the floor. It was pretty sick.

SF: What about your Wild Thing image?

AI: I try to enjoy my life to its fullest every day because you never know what may happen. It is easy to get down about things but I think that I am pretty lucky, being gifted by God and all that. I'm living out a dream and with the way the world is today, a lot of people may never get a chance to do the same. So I feel pretty lucky. Too often no one cares about anyone and there's not a lot of respect in the world. A lot of people try to put on a facade that they got it all together, when they are just as crazy as you. Like the nickname I have, the "Wild Thing," which the fans call me in Washington. That is because of what they think of me. Yet, I don't even really let loose. I think that people put on too much of a facade and don't want to let anyone know who they really are or what they are all about. I think most people in the world today are pretty phony. There are people who may not be normal, but they act normal in front of other people, so people think that they are not crazy. I grew up in a big city [Detroit] so I'm into places where there is a lot to do and a lot going on. I'm not a real homebody at all. I try to keep myself busy and run around in order to make the most out of every day. I'm not a big sleeper and I like to stay up late at night. If there is no curfew and I'm alone at night, I would go out to a bar by myself, rather than stay at home. I don't go from Maryland to Washington, D.C. much because it is too far from where we are. I like to chill in Baltimore and Annapolis. I like it there, but it is kind of small and you could run out of things to do there. But as for the hockey, I like it there, because it is not a real hockey town at all. No one really knows who you are, so you could be just a regular Joe. That's why I like it.

SF: When you played for the Maple Leafs, you had instant recognition in Toronto. This was both good and bad for you. Can you recall any incidents that back up this point?

AI: Once, I was pumping gas near Maple Leaf Gardens and there was a high school nearby. A car with six kids pulled up and one said to me, "Hey, you f . . . ing bum, that's what you should be doing for a living!" I started laughing my ass off. I thought that was very funny. They were just fans fooling around with me. Then there was the incident during a game at the Gardens, where they don't have glass partititions behind our benches, some hot blonde chick and her friend gave me her phone number right in the middle of the game. I thought that was pretty funny. I just gave the number to one of our trainers. I'm not really into picking up chicks; I don't go to a bar to pick up chicks, I go to the bars to party. You could quote me on that, too.

SF: How do your teammates react to the heavy music you play in the locker room?

IA: The way it was with the Capitals in 1992-93, I was not allowed to listen to the death music that some of my friends listen to, like Goraphobia or Over Kill. I listen to those groups a little bit, but mostly Pantera or Metallica. The guys on our team other than Greeny think that groups that aren't even hard any more, are considered heavy metal. I mean Guns and Roses old stuff is much harder than their new stuff. For example, if I put Guns and Roses on or something like that in the locker room, most of the guys are like "oh," or they pretend like they are smoking a joint or something. They think it is death music, when it really isn't. They watch too much MTV and they think groups like Poison are real hard.

SF: How do you feel about the Russians on your team?

IA: It sounds like every word these guys are saying when they get into the corners or something, start talking to each other is like "Yaba dabba doo." It's really wierd to listen to them and especially when every other word sounds like "Yabba dabba doo."

SF: What was it like winning the shooting contest at the All-Star Game?

AI: It was fun. Winning the shot thing was a career highlight. I had been thought to have a hard shot and being fast and just to be there on TV and decisively beat everyone, was really neat. It was no question that I won.

SF: Did the other players treat you with respect?

AI: I don't know and I don't really care. It was like, "Hey, you thought you were fast but I guess you really weren't that fast." Anyone who thought they had a harder shot, I guess they were proven wrong. I showed I could skate, too, although [Rangers forward] Mike Gartner beat me in 1993 at Montreal. Being that I am a defenseman and being quite tall, and considering the size of the rink, if I'm pretty even with a guy, I don't think that he will outskate me. If I have my stick, I always feel that I will be close enough to get a stick on a guy.

SF: How much of hockey is mental and controllable?

AI: Some things you can't control. You are out there with five other guys and no matter how badly you want to do something, sometimes it doesn't matter. Because you could be doing whatever you want or work as hard as you want, but circumstances may happen where a goal is scored when you are on the ice and there is nothing you can do about it. Yet somehow you end up getting blamed for it.

SF: How much of a spontaneous person are you? Give an example.

AI: Once Scott Pearson and I were at Rock 'n Roll Heaven in Toronto and the band was playing some Metallica cover tunes. This was about eight or so years ago; the first time I was an All-Star. The dude announces, "We have Al Iafrate here from the Maple Leafs and he's a big heavy metal fan." The crowd starts clapping and stuff. Then, he says to me, "Come on up here and sing a song." I wasn't expecting it and I said, "Nah, Nah," and stuff like that. Well, the place was packed and everyone started booing and shit like that. So I said to myself, "I'm going to have to get up there and sing." So I went up there and sang Metallica's "Seek and Destroy." That's a killer tune. So I sang backup to "Seek and Destroy" with this band and it was cool. I once had a bachelor party for my buddy and we had three dancers over at my house. So the girls come walking into the garage and they see my Harleys sitting there. One of the girls says, "You have Harleys. I would love to dance on one of those." So about five of us picked it up and carried it into the house and placed it in the center of the living room. Later on she started dancing on it and it was pretty cool. It was the best bachelor party I ever had.

SF: Do you consider yourself a carefree spirit?

IA: I'm carefree about things that I don't think are important. When I'm serious about something, then I'm serious. It's not like I don't give a damn about anything. I think it is right that you have to live life and do things that make you happy. Yet when there is something that you have to be serious about and committed to, then I am. It's just my code of honor and what I believe in. I live and walk on that line of what I think is important and what I don't think is important. If I don't care about something, then it isn't going to be important. If it's something important to somebody else, then it isn't important to me. As long as I follow my code and if I cross it, then I only have myself to blame and if I don't, fine. That's the way it should be. Don't get me wrong, I'll always help a friend. But let's say someone thinks buying a Harley is a waste of money, or buying three of them and spending a lot of money on them is cool. Someone else might think that's stupid, but if they think that's stupid, then I'd say too bad.

SF: Tell me about your first NHL fight.

IA: It was against Ed Beers of the Calgary Flames. He was pounding on me pretty good, and then he had me down and gave me the old face gouge. All the guys on the Calgary bench were saying, "Welcome to the NHL!" I was scratched up and beat up and stuff and all the guys were yelling, "Welcome, you punk, pussy, homo" . . . hard shit like that. It was really funny. When I fought

Bob Probert, he knocked my tooth out in the back and pushed several others in the wrong direction.

SF: What do you think about fighting?

AI: Nobody minds a good, fair fight. It's when guys start cross-checking you in the face, it gets scary. One great fight I remember was Bob Probert and Kevin Maguire in Joe Louis Arena. It was rock'em-sock'em robots. It was unreal and they went toe-to-toe. They were going at it at center ice and it was unbelievable. I was also at the bench-clearing brawl between Detroit and Toronto, when Bob head-butted McGill unconscious to the ice. I was paired off with Randy Ladouceur and I was 18 at the time. We didn't fight and I didn't see it happen because it was a bench-clearing brawl, but I saw it on the tape after the game. Our GM Gerry McNamara came down and it was pretty scary.

SF: When do you lose your temper?

AI: A couple of summers ago I was out golfing with a buddy of mine and he had a seven iron and I was walking up toward him. Then a very strange thing happened. He cranked it and hit me with the ball. He hit me although he didn't try to shoot it at me. He hit me in the shoulder and then it carommed into my temple. It instantly started getting red and stuff, and it hurt. That scared me, and I looked at him and he started laughing and I walked over and said, "What's so funny?" He kept on laughing and I said, "Don't you have something to say?" and I was waiting for him to say, "I'm sorry," and he just kept laughing. So I took his clubs; he had nice clubs. One by one, I started throwing them in the lake, one by one, and after about five clubs were in there, he grabbed mine and started whipping them at my head. Meanwhile, there were people waiting on the par three, and there are people waiting on the tee, watching us do this. They thought this was pretty funny and so did I. As I was running to pick up my clubs, he was trying to run me down with his golf cart.

SF: What do you enjoy doing most?

AI: Playing hockey and looking into my daughter's eyes.

VI

THE HISTORIC BATTLE AND THE BATTLERS: TIE DOMI VS. BOB PROBERT

Chapter 25

INTRODUCTION: PROBERT vs. DOMI

Normally fights in the NHL are spontaneous — the result of a collision or the felt need of an enforcer to exact retribution for an indignity committed against a skilled teammate.

That's why the bout on December 2, 1992 at Madison Square Garden between Tie Domi, then a Ranger, and Bob Probert of the Detroit Red Wings, was an anomaly; principally because the ebullient Domi went out of his way — with considerable media help — to trumpet the bout with Probert.

As was his custom, Probert maintained a low-profile attitude ever since an earlier fight with Domi on February 9, 1992, during which Domi left Probert black-and-blue and with a bloody nose. Probert didn't lose that fight, but the pugnacious Ranger at that time emerged from the fisticuffs pretending he was the NHL's heavyweight champion. Domi's histrionics tickled the fancy of bloodthirsty New York Ranger fans, but did not sit well with League officials or many of Tie's peers, who believed he was denegrating the ways of a true enforcer.

Domi was suitably abetted by a hypocritical media which, on the one hand, criticized hockey's violence, but on the other wasted no time playing up the Domi-Probert rivalry for all it was worth.

No single piece of journalism did more to magnify the December 2, 1992 Domi-Probert bout than a column by *Toronto Sun* sports editor Scott Morrison. In the piece, Morrison liberally quoted a pumped-up Domi who orated, "You know how much I've been looking forward to this one? I knew before the start of the season what day the game was."

Significantly, Morrison pointed out that Domi-Probert was as much of a news story as Mario Lemieux's scoring exploits. "The hockey world and Don Cherry have been waiting for this championship bout since early last February when Domi and Red Wings' thumper Bob Probert engaged in a memorable Sunday night punch-up at the Garden," wrote Morrison. "That night, Domi declared himself champion, strapping on an imaginary belt, urging cheers from the crowd. He looked more boor than [Riddick] Bowe, but still packed a mean wallop."

Domi's "mistake," if it can be called that, was his natural candor. He couldn't help speaking his mind, and what was on his mind was another encounter with Probert. "I knew before the season that our first meeting was December 2," said Domi "I know one thing — there'll be no instigator in this fight."

Domi uttered a few other gems that created a mountainous amount of publicity. The *Detroit News*, for example carried a "Tale of the Tape," with oversized caricatures of the two warriors. Finally, NHL president Gil Stein was questioned about the propriety of Domi's pop-offs. "I believe people have the right to defy the law if they wish, as long as they understand that they will pay a penalty for doing it," Stein said.

Throughout the furor Probert characteristically ducked comment, but on the eve of the meeting, he exploded at reporters. "You media people blew the whole thing out of proportion," said Probert. Whether they did or not, there is no arguing that a fight of major proportions was going to erupt. Less than a minute into the game the fight was on.

It started this way: at the 30-second mark, Probert stepped on the ice, whereupon Ranger coach Roger Neilson sent out Domi, who skated right up to his foe for the face-off. A split-second after the puck was dropped, Probert twice cross-checked Domi, and the fists were flying faster than an out-of-control windmill. Probert went on the offensive, throwing the first eight punches out of a total of 47. In orderly retreat, Domi tossed 23 blows, but clearly lost the bout on points.

Hockey Night in Canada commentator Don Cherry, the ubiquitous critic of hockey fights, considered the 48-second tussle a world-class event. "It was a definite decision for Probert," said Cherry. "But I think it was a strong showing by Tie. It was no pushover, which is what made it even better. It was a good battle and the officials let it go. I knew they were going to let it go."

Many observers believe that the most devastating blow of all was one that never landed, a round-house Probert punch that just missed his foe. "If he had connected, Probie might have ended up in jail or Tie would be in the hospital," said Cherry, who watched the game on TV at his home. "It looked like Probert wanted this one, he was psyched. I didn't think he could ever match the [Troy] Crowder ones, but he did."

As for the principals, they had varying comments.

Domi: "A fight's a fight. You win some, you lose some. I'm just very, very, very happy that we won the game."

Probert: "It's just another day at the office. I just don't have anything to say."

Many claim that Tie ("The Albanian Assassin") Domi's shenanigans can only hurt the ever-fragile image of the sport. *Detroit Free Press* columnist Keith Gave, commenting on Domi's pre-game hype, accused Tie of "Harboring no concern about reducing a major-league sport clamoring for respectability to the level of big-time wrestling."

Whether the media misquoted Domi and fabricated the spectacle or not, this whole episode clearly reduced an important game between two skilled teams down to the level of a circus. If anyone had previously felt that Domi was any more than just a goon, such suspicions were probably silenced by that Wednesday night's "Main Event."

And what came of it? Domi was pummelled. The massive attention focused on the match-up left the NHL with a public relations black eye. It was clear that the league never again would tolerate a premeditated fight. Many critics blamed Rangers' coach Roger Neilson as much as Domi since the home-team Rangers had the right to match any line Detroit put on the ice. Neilson ensured that Domi faced Probert.

Interestingly, Domi saw little ice in the weeks after the fight and eventually was traded to Winnipeg. Neilson was soon fired as Rangers' coach.

In retrospect it was an incredible fight, but one not likely to brew up (and be blown up) again.

Chapter 26

THE ALBANIAN AGGRESSOR: TIE DOMI

"Everyone knows that I'm here.
I'm doing my job and I'll stick up for
my teammates. I don't predict fighting.
I don't think about fighting. When
it happens, it happens."

No player in recent memory has obtained more publicity for fewer points than Tie Domi. There are several reasons for this phenomenon, not the least of which has been Domi's innate ability for self-promotion, followed closely by his natural charisma.

A better-than-fair Junior hockey player, Domi became notorious for his fistic ability and showmanship after reaching the NHL. The 5-foot-10, 195-pound Albanian-Canadian appeared destined for a long career on Broadway as a member of the New York Rangers. However, the much-discussed bout with Bob Probert on December 2, 1992 at Madison Square Garden detoured Domi's New York express. Tie immersed himself in league hot water after an interview with Scott Morrison of the Toronto Sun. Domi made it clear that he planned to fight Detroit's Bob Probert during their next encounter. While the bout covered Domi with headlines, it also brought the wrath of NHL president Gil Stein down on him. It also precipitated a rift between Domi's former pal, then Rangers' assistant coach Colin Campbell (a close friend of Probert) and himself. Tie soon was traded to the Winnipeg Jets along with Kris King in exchange for Ed Olczyk.

The deal had a stunning effect on all the personalities as well as the respective teams. The Jets, who had

*previously seemed destined to miss the playoffs, were
galvanized by Domi and King. Winnipeg went on a
tear that eventually took the Jets to a playoff berth. By
contrast, the Rangers lost spirit and fibre without Domi
and King in the lineup and eventually finished last in the
Patrick Division after a first place finish the previous year.*

*After being traded to Winnipeg, Domi met with reporter
John Ploszay and spilled out his feelings about many
subjects.*

JP: Why do you think the Rangers traded you?

TD: I did not want to leave New York, but how could I sit 12 games
out in a row? Management was trying to get a message across to
me. I got a little too popular for my own good there. They
wanted me to ask for a trade so it would make it look easier on
them. But my loyalties were there, and I put my heart and soul
into the Rangers every year I was there, but I got pushed away.
Then I heard a lot of things said behind my back. It was very
disappointing to hear things like that. I got lots of support from
my teammates, but I don't think I got support from management,
and that hurt a lot.

JP: When you first joined the Rangers, how did your role begin and
how did it change? You saw this change right before your eyes.

TD: I never really got one shift just to prove that I could play a
regular shift. In three years there I never got one game to really
prove myself, although in training camp I had four goals and
three assists in six games. I thought I'd get a chance, but in the
first five games of the season I sat out and that was real disappointing. I've always said ice time is confidence and confidence
is the whole game. And the confidence wasn't there. I knew the
writing was on the wall when they called up other forwards.
Those guys stepped right in and I got pushed out. I knew they
didn't have confidence in my ability, but John Paddock did. I
played for him in the minors for a while, and I was leading the
league in scoring when I was playing for him. He played me a
lot. I was penalty-killing, working the power play, I was on the
number-one line. I was leading the league in scoring. I even had
a four-goal game. And the next day I was in the NHL. Then
nothing.

JP: After you were traded to Winnipeg, did you think about the past
experience you had with Paddock?

TD: It's a great feeling to know you're wanted. Somebody, in this
case John Paddock, wanted my talent, not just for the one thing
for which I have a reputation. I'm trying to shake that role and
just show that I can play, but on the other hand that I'll be there
for my teammates. I'll always be there for my teammates. I'll

never change my role because that's what got me here. I can skate. I can shoot. I can handle the puck. People get that one thing on their mind, that I'm just a fighter. That's the most disappointing part. I was 27th overall, a second-round pick and I wasn't chosen that high just to be a fighter. I was a goal scorer in Junior. I played the last two years in Junior with Mike Ricci. We complemented each other and I can play the game. I think I helped Mike in his career and I think he helped me a lot.

JP: What happened between you and Colin Campbell, the Rangers' assistant coach, who seemed to turn against you?

TD: Well, Colin and I once were really close, but it got to the point where he was losing confidence in me. After I left, he was the guy who said they had to make me work hard, and that was really disappointing. I heard from a lot of people things he was saying behind my back. Not just teammates, either; it was other people bigger than he thinks. It wasn't just my teammates and it got to the point where he told people that I wasn't working hard, that I had a bad attitude, which was totally wrong. It hurt my feelings because I'm not like that and I'd never bring my team down. I'm a professional hockey player. I get paid to play hockey. I don't get paid to practice and watch games. I've been a contender all my life and this really hurt my pride so I had to start standing up for myself. Campbell and I once had a meeting and I told him how I felt. Maybe I shouldn't have said anything, but again I got everything off my shoulders that I wanted to say.

JP: Was it a meeting of an assistant coach to player or was it friend-to-friend?

TD: It was a little of both. I told him how I felt. I had heard a lot of things that he had said about me. That's the frustrating part. I heard a lot, not just from my teammates, but from other people. It got to the point where people in the organization — and I'm not going to say any names because they were pretty big names — heard that I wanted to be moved and that I was doing that, which was totally wrong. There was a lot of jealousy going on and I became too popular for my own good.

JP: Was somebody else pressuring Campbell or influencing do you think?

TD: I don't think so. He had his mind made up after the meeting we had that he no longer was my friend or in my corner. It's tough. At the Christmas party I made sure I went around saying Merry Christmas to each and every guy and they all said Merry Christmas to me. Same thing when I was traded. Everybody said good-bye to me and hugged me. It was very emotional. [Assistant Coach] Dan Maloney was waiting right there at the door with his skates on to say good-bye to me. But Colin Campbell was the one guy who never said good-bye to me. It seemed like he was the happiest guy in New York that day. He was laughing on the ice, during practice and everything. That really hurt my feelings. I was always in his corner.

JP: What was the significance of Colin Campbell being an old friend of your opponent, Bob Probert?

TD: He and Probert are good friends, and after my fight with Probert some things happened that a lot of my teammates didn't like. I didn't really notice, but they brought it to my attention, and that hurt my feelings. I'm not going to say what Campbell did or what he didn't do, but my teammates — not just one or two of them, but seven or eight of them — are telling me everything that he was doing and I didn't really notice, even during a game, and before a game, and after a game. Always talking to him before a game, talking right after the game, during the game, I guess. He said something to the bench. This was the biggest hyped fight in the whole league and here I am all nervous about it and all my teammates are pulling for me and everything. I don't care if Campbell coached him for seven years or not — he should be with the team that he is coaching.

JP: How do you think the Ranger fans felt about your being traded?

TD: A lot of people in New York were disappointed that I got traded and I think Campbell was the guy who got me out of there. I had a lot of things going for me in New York out of hockey. The most frustrating part is that I could have been there for life. Now, I have to start all over.

JP: Did somebody tell you when you were negotiating as a free agent in the summer of 1992 that other teams wanted you?

TD: I had other teams bidding on me. We used that for negotiating power, of course. My agent, Donnie Meehan, told me that I could be going anywhere. Donnie told me that it's strictly a business. Somewhere I learned this is a real business.

JP: What went wrong with the New York Rangers, going from first in 1991-92 to last in 1992-93?

TD: We had team chemistry in 1991-92. But a year later there was a big difference. A lot that had to do with it was that Eric Lindros trade. Some of the Rangers knew that they were supposed to be traded in the Lindros deal but it was a toss-up between Philly and the Rangers. Believe it or not that took a lot out of them. A lot of the Rangers talked about it and the guys who were involved knew. It was a disappointing thing, not just for them, but for the whole team, because where does your loyalty stand?

JP: Some people say that you got Colin Campbell fired. Did you?

TD: I had no intentions of ever getting anybody fired or anything. I heard that, you know, Roger got fired because of Messier and Colin Campbell got fired because of me. That is a crock of shit. We don't make the decisions on who gets fired. That's Neil

Smith's decision and Neil Smith's decision only. People should talk to Neil Smith because that's his job. When all that stuff was coming out about me, Neil wasn't coming out and sticking up for me. He has to start sticking up for his players. Management, the coaches, the players all have to be together. You can't be against each other. That's very important.

JP: What should Neil Smith have done?

TD: He should have put his foot down and said, "Mark Messier didn't get Roger Neilson fired. I fired him. It's my job." It was very unfortunate for Mark Messier, because he was like a big brother to me. Everybody hears what they want to hear from management's side of the fence. I'm on the players' side. I know what's going on on that side and so does every other guy in that dressing room. People in the media know the coaches' and managements' side. They don't hear the players' side because the players aren't like that. It's not classy for the players to do that. We're professional athletes. We're paid to play hockey.

JP: Explain your relationships with Mark Messier, Joe Kocur, Paul Broten and Kris King.

TD: Joe Kocur and I have a really close relationship. We're like brothers. My leaving New York was very unfortunate because we loved playing together with Randy Gilhen in the middle. In the 1992 playoffs against New Jersey, he scored one in a game and I scored in another game. We beat New Jersey and the next series we went to Pittsburgh and I didn't play at all. That was very unfortunate. Joe and I really loved playing together. He's been in the game a long time. He's been doing the job I have for a long time. I learned a lot from him. Paul Broten, on the other hand, is a checking right winger. In the summer of 1992 I asked Roger Neilson if I signed as a Ranger would I get a chance to beat out Broten and Kris King. He said yes, I would. I did in training camp, but as soon as the season started I didn't. That was unfortunate. I never got an opportunity to beat out one of those guys. I got traded and Paul Broten was still there.

JP: What effects did the fight with Probert have? The media hype?

TD: I did an interview with Scott Morrison of the *Toronto Sun* that was pretty much on fighting and the rule changes. He threw the odd question in about Probert. He asked me if I was aware of the game coming up. I said well, of course. I'd be there and fight the guy. I know that later it was brought up to me as a premeditated fight, which is very unfortunate.

JP: What do you think of some of the tough guys in the Smythe Division?

TD: Every team has tough guys. Every team has bumpers and grinders. I've got a reputation for being a tough guy. I'm now a Winnipeg Jet. Everyone knows that I'm here. I'm doing my job and I'll stick up for my teammates. I don't predict fighting. I don't think about fighting. When it happens, it happens. Once you start thinking about it, that's when you get in trouble. I don't care if I win or lose, as long as I'm there.

JP: Other players, such as Rob Ray of the Sabres, have called you a "joke." Ray added, "He can't play and he can't play any other way. He builds shit up like the Probert fight just so he can get publicity, 'cause that's all he can do."

TD: Guys are entitled to their own opinions. He can say what he wants. That goes to show you what jealousy does. A lot of guys are jealous. What am I supposed to do? I've got a personality . . . I mean, who cares? I don't think those guys care what I'll be doing after my career. I'm getting paid. I'm getting paid pretty well to do something I love doing. I'm not complaining. I really don't care what Rob Ray or anybody says. That's coming from a tough guy and I'm trying to stick up for us tough guys. I got the balls to blow it clean. I don't see these tough guys say they got balls and say what they want to say. I'm just trying to stick up for my job and my peers. Part of my job is obviously fighting. If those guys want to back off me then they're entitled to their opinions. I can back up whatever . . .

JP: Does Tie Domi have a fighting style?

TD: No. When I'm fighting I just go. Whatever happens happens. Anybody can beat anybody in any given minute. It doesn't matter who it is. Fighting isn't always the solution to trying to get even with somebody. Sometimes it can be a big check. I can throw a hit and knock the wind out of an opponent, which proves that fighting is not always the solution.

JP: Who are some of your heroes?

TD: By far Tiger Williams. Tiger Williams is my idol. Bobby Clarke and Paul Holmgren are right behind them. But Tiger Williams gave me the inspiration for riding the stick. Tiger Williams by far. Outside of hockey, John McEnroe.

JP: Have you ever met Tiger Williams or Holmgren?

TD: I got to meet Tiger a couple of years ago at a Special Olympic golf tournament. It was a great honor. The best thing about it was that he knew who I was. That made me feel really good. Holmgren, I see all the time. He's always real nice and so is Bob Clarke. When he says hi, I get a big feeling because I still idolize him.

JP: Do you have any regrets about your career?

TD: Oh no. As a kid, I was always athletic. I had scholarship offers in three different sports: football, soccer and hockey. Believe it or not, hockey was my third-best sport. I chose hockey because I like the rough stuff. I love what I'm doing and it's a dream to be in the NHL. I don't take any of it for granted.

Chapter 27

THE HEAVYWEIGHT CHAMP: BOB PROBERT

"Reporters would rather talk about my fights and penalty minutes, but I broke Gordie Howe's playoff record for points."

"I've gotten to know Bob fairly well over the last few years," said Detroit-based hockey analyst Jim Ramsey. "He's a really nice, gentle and caring person. Even after a loss, he still talks to me before he leaves the arena. I really like the guy."

Like so many of hockey's rough-and-tumble heavy hitters, Probert offers a double image. For nearly a decade he has come across on the ice as a menacing, two-fisted slugger who would just as soon kayo an opponent as fire the puck into the net. Off the ice, his image is multi-faceted.

In January 1990, he received a deportation order limiting his travel to the United States as a result of a March 1989 arrest on the U.S. side of the Detroit-Windsor tunnel that led to a federal drug conviction. It wasn't until December 7, 1992 that Probert received a waiver from immigration authorities that allowed him to travel to and from Canada.

Despite the problems, Probert also has become known as a dedicated worker for charitable causes and one — as Jim Ramsey points out — who is a warm friend to those he trusts.

To teammates and opponents alike, Probert connotes toughness to the nth degree. The majority of NHL hitters interviewed for this book singled out Probert as the single most feared fighter in the league. Conversely, Bob has gone out of his way to minimize his macho image. Time after time he has rejected interview requests to discuss fighting, preferring to focus on other aspects of the game.

Nevertheless, a series of episodes — not to mention the media's craving for hockey fight stories — pushed fighting to the forefront in any Probert discussion.

Furthermore, Probert confrontations seemed to take on a life of their own. When players such as New Jersey Devils' forward Troy Crowder actually victimized the Red Wing, an aura of heroism above and beyond the call of duty seemed to surround the challenger. In that regard Tie Domi earned notoriety as a result of a pair of fights with Probert. Typically, Bob himself downplayed them while the other protagonist went to enormous lengths to glorify the fights.

Probert's value far exceeded his powers of intimidation and his fistic ability. He has, over the years, demonstrated offensive prowess and the ability to put the puck into the net. But as long as journalists choose also to annually pick an NHL heavyweight champion, Probert will be as much discussed as a slugger as he is a scorer.

To provide insights into Probert, we are utilizing material from a pair of separate interviews conducted by Jim Ramsey of Detroit. The first was held in February 1992 at Joe Louis Arena, and the second was held there a year later.

"The thing that impresses me the most about Bob is that he thought about the answers before he answered them," said Ramsey. "My only hope is that more people get to know the wonderful person the off-ice Probert really is."

I grew up in Windsor, Ontario, right across the river from Detroit, so it was kind of neat that I was able to come and watch the Red Wings when I was a little guy. Back then they played at the old Olympia Stadium, which was located at Grand River and McGraw.

As a youth, I was very active and into every type of sports, from baseball to football, lacrosse and hockey. The biggest influences on me were my parents who helped me get involved in hockey. My brother, who is a year older than me, and I were encouraged by my parents who would travel with us to our games. It meant a lot to have our parents behind us.

My feeling then — as it is now — is that you have to keep working hard to succeed. Basically, if you have the talent and keep working hard, you can make it. The trick is to work on your skills and never give up — that's what makes the difference.

The more I got interested in hockey, the more I developed favorites. The Red Wings were my top club, but my individual hero was Bobby Orr of the Bruins.

My career developed the more I played and eventually I moved up to the Ontario Junior Hockey League playing for Brantford for two years [1992-83 and 1983-84] before moving over to Hamilton and Sault Ste. Marie [1984-85]. While playing for the Soo, I had the good fortune of going to the Memorial Cup finals and, even though we lost, it was a great experience and I could tell that my skills were developing.

In 15 playoff games that year, I had six goals and 11 assists for 17 points. I also had my fair share of fights, so I learned about every aspect of hockey. I knew that I had to participate in every area of the game if I expected to get to the NHL.

I considered it my job to stick up for my teammates and I was fortunate to have the size. I was one of the bigger players on the team and I liked the rough style of play. I took it upon myself that I had to stick up for them.

Some people made a big thing about me and Joey Kocur once spending time at a boxing gym with Tommy [Hit Man] Hearns' trainer, but that was blown out of proportion. We flew out to Arizona and met with him and talked to him for about 20 minutes. Then, we spent the rest of the afternoon lying in the sun. Everyone thinks we went through his boxing program, but that's not true. We met with him and he gave us a few pointers and that was it.

I don't like to make a big deal out of the fights. I've been in so many they run together and I don't really think about them. Really, none of them stands out in my mind. I just take it one game at a time and forget it when it's over.

I made it to the NHL in 1985-86 and played on a fourth line. At first I sat out a lot but, when I got to play, I played hard and eventually won a spot on the first two lines. I always had the skills and just needed the chance to play more so that I could show them.

After a while I proved that I could score. In 1987-88 I got 29 goals and 33 assists — 62 points in 74 games. I averaged more than a point a game in the playoffs [16 games, 8-13-21] that season.

When I first started in the league I felt that I had to fight in order to stay in the NHL. I felt that it was necessary to play physical and, if called upon, to drop the gloves and fight. That's what I did and I stayed in the NHL.

Over the years I gained a reputation and I'm sure that that can work to your advantage — or against you. There always will be guys who want to test me, but the advantage I've gained is that I get more room on the ice.

There are times when the opposition takes shots at me but I try not to retaliate, so I try to stay on the ice and help my team win. I can't help my team when I'm sitting in the penalty box. I try to keep my composure but it can only last that long out there before I blow up and take a stupid penalty. That's an area where I've tried to improve.

It's very hard to turn the other cheek, but I've found that in a playoff situation I can't be taking stupid penalties or the extra two minutes for being the aggressor because that can hurt the team, and that's one thing I don't want to do.

When I'm in a fight, I just want to win-win-win as much as I want to win the hockey game. That's programmed into us as far as that goes. It takes a bit to get me mad, but after a fight really gets going then I am going to get mad. What I like to do is get the sweater over my head. To me that's a bonus because then the other guy doesn't have anything to hold onto, so if I can get it off, that's great.

Intimidation is a factor you hear plenty about in hockey. Intimidation is a big part of the game and if I can help in that area it's a bonus. I've gained a reputation over the past years and if I can still intimidate the other players, that's great. But the game has changed over the years. In the past, known heavyweights on each team would go at it for the sake of going at it — just by looking at each other the wrong way. Lately, guys are less prone to fight than they were back then.

I'm a hockey player, not a fighter. I fight when I have to, but I'd rather play hockey. An incident usually happens because you're a little upset. Once it's over, it's over, unless the press makes a big deal out of it. That happened with the Troy Crowder incident. It was almost like I was expected to go out there and fight with him again, which was a joke. It was unbelievable the big deal the press made out of that.

I've never been told to fight but it's obvious that other players on other teams have been told. They're sent out there by the coach and I don't think that's right. In situations like that the player should stick up for himself; he shouldn't have to be told.

I don't think fighting will ever be eliminated from hockey because it's always been a part of the game and it always will be. But if it is eliminated, you'll see a lot more cheap shots and high sticks. A lot of people come just to watch the fights and there would still be people who would come to watch the hockey game.

It's like reporters would rather talk about my fights and penalty minutes, but I broke Gordie Howe's playoff record for points. I've always had goals and assists and my penalty minutes have been high, but that's the type of game I play. People like to focus on my fighting rather than on my hockey ability.

VII

ERIC SERVETAH'S DETAILED SCORECARD OF THE BEST FIGHTERS IN THE NHL

Chapter 28

Who is the best fighter in the National Hockey League?

It is a question often debated by hockey fans who enjoy an occasional bout with their body checks, goals and artistry on ice.

Reporter Eric Servetah, who has studied hockey fighters with scientific precision for the past decade, offers the following detailed analysis.

His evaluations are based on a number of critical criteria. A primary purpose of these ratings is to delineate individual strengths of each player. The ratings do not necessarily suggest who would be the winner in a fight.

For example, Dave Brown has twice fought Tie Domi and beaten him both times. However, Brown received only a 114 in his rating and Domi had a 117. In a fight during the 1992-93 playoffs, Marty McSorley was decisioned by Wendel Clark, yet McSorley is way ahead of Clark with a 118 rating as compared to Clark's 108.

If there's one given that should be understood about hockey fighting, it is that anyone can beat anyone else on any given night. This is the most predominant thought expressed by the ice cops.

Many elements decide whether a player wins or loses a fight. For example, a player could be at the end of a shift when he fights — and lose due to fatigue. Vitality provides an advantage to the fresh player who might normally have lost that fight under different circumstances. On another occasion, a player's jersey might get caught over his head and hands during a fight. If this happens to the *so-called better fighter, he might take a beating because of the sweater situation. Sometimes linesmen jump in too soon and cause the fight to stop with only a few blows being landed. They may come in and tie up only one combatant while the other fellow lands cheap shots. A player may be trying to tire his opponent — while taking some shots — but when he's about to return some of his own, the fight is broken up.*

Thus, while the numerical rating is meaningful in one sense, it does not suggest overall superiority in any single fight. In hockey, more than in boxing, diverse elements determine the winner of a fight. The purpose of these ratings are to detail the specific strengths of each fighter.

WILLINGNESS (W)
STAMINA (ST)
KNOCKOUT PUNCH (KP)
STRENGTH (STR)
QUICKNESS (Q)
SWITCHING HANDS (SH)
TYING UP (T)
BALANCE (B)
FAIRNESS (F)
INTIMIDATION (I)
SMARTNESS (SM)
TAKING A PUNCH (TP)
FUTURE POTENTIAL (FP)

NAME	W	ST	KP	STR	Q	SH	T	B	F	I	SM	TP	FP	TOTAL
Bob Probert	10 *	10 *	9 *	10 *	9 *	10 *	8 *	10 *	10 *	10 *	9 *	10 *	9	124
Craig Berube	10 *	10 *	8 *	10 *	10 *	8 *	10 *	9 *	10 *	9 *	10 *	10 *	9	123
Link Gaetz	10 *	10 *	9 *	10 *	9 *	9 *	9 *	9 *	9 *	10 *	9 *	10 *	6	119
Tony Twist	10 *	10 *	10 *	10 *	8 *	7 *	7 *	9 *	10 *	10 *	9 *	9 *	10	119
Marty McSorley	10 *	10 *	9 *	10 *	7 *	8 *	10 *	10 *	7 *	10 *	10 *	9 *	8	118
Randy McKay	10 *	9 *	8 *	9 *	9 *	8 *	8 *	10 *	9 *	9 *	9 *	10 *	9	117
Tie Domi	10 *	10 *	8 *	8 *	9 *	10 *	8 *	10 *	8 *	7 *	9 *	10 *	10	117
Louie DeBrusk	10 *	8 *	8 *	10 *	8 *	8 *	9 *	9 *	10 *	9 *	9 *	8 *	10	116
Rick Tocchet	8 *	10 *	7 *	10 *	10 *	10 *	9 *	9 *	8 *	9 *	10 *	9 *	7	116
Shane Churla	10 *	10 *	8 *	9 *	9 *	9 *	9 *	8 *	8 *	8 *	10 *	9 *	8	115
Ken Daneyko	8 *	9 *	7 *	10 *	8 *	9 *	10 *	9 *	10 *	9 *	9 *	9 *	8	115
Dave Brown	7 *	9 *	10 *	10 *	8 *	6 *	9 *	9 *	10 *	10 *	9 *	10 *	7	114
Joe Kocur	7 *	9 *	10 *	10 *	8 *	7 *	10 *	10 *	9 *	10 *	9 *	9 *	6	114
Jim McKenzie	7 *	9 *	9 *	10 *	8 *	8 *	8 *	9 *	9 *	9 *	9 *	9 *	9	113
Stu Grimson	8 *	9 *	9 *	10 *	8 *	8 *	8 *	9 *	9 *	9 *	9 *	9 *	7	112
Todd Ewen	9 *	9 *	9 *	10 *	8 *	8 *	10 *	8 *	9 *	8 *	8 *	8 *	8	112

NAME	W	ST	KP	STR	Q	SH	T	B	F	I	SM	TP	FP	TOTAL
Owen Nolan	8 *	8 *	8 *	9 *	9 *	8 *	10 *	9 *	8 *	8 *	9 *	8 *	9	111
Adam Graves	7 *	9 *	7 *	9 *	10 *	8 *	9 *	9 *	8 *	8 *	10 *	8 *	9	111
Gino Odjick	10 *	9 *	8 *	9 *	8 *	8 *	10 *	9 *	6 *	9 *	7 *	9 *	9	111
Dave Manson	7 *	9 *	9 *	9 *	8 *	8 *	9 *	8 *	9 *	9 *	9 *	9 *	7	110
Darin Kimble	9 *	9 *	9 *	9 *	9 *	9 *	8 *	8 *	8 *	8 *	8 *	9 *	7	110
Mike Peluso	10 *	8 *	9 *	10 *	8 *	7 *	8 *	7 *	7 *	9 *	8 *	9 *	9	109
Wendel Clark	6 *	9 *	7 *	8 *	9 *	8 *	9 *	9 *	8 *	8 *	10 *	10 *	7	108
Kelly Chase	9 *	9 *	6 *	7 *	10 *	10 *	10 *	8 *	7 *	6 *	10 *	8 *	8	108
Mario Roberge	8 *	9 *	7 *	7 *	10 *	7 *	10 *	10 *	9 *	7 *	10 *	7 *	7	108
Brendan Shanahan	8 *	8 *	8 *	9 *	8 *	7 *	8 *	9 *	7 *	9 *	9 *	9 *	8	107
Mick Vukota	8 *	7 *	9 *	10 *	8 *	9 *	8 *	8 *	6 *	9 *	9 *	8 *	7	106
Alan May	7 *	9 *	8 *	8 *	8 *	9 *	10 *	9 *	7 *	7 *	10 *	8 *	6	106
Nick Kypreos	10 *	8 *	7 *	8 *	9 *	7 *	9 *	8 *	7 *	7 *	9 *	8 *	8	105
Kris King	7 *	9 *	8 *	9 *	8 *	8 *	9 *	8 *	7 *	7 *	9 *	8 *	8	105
Enrico Ciccone	9 *	8 *	9 *	8 *	8 *	7 *	7 *	7 *	7 *	9 *	7 *	8 *	10	104
Jay Caufield	9 *	7 *	9 *	10 *	7 *	7 *	7 *	6 *	8 *	9 *	7 *	8 *	7	101
Greg Smyth	10 *	8 *	8 *	8 *	7 *	6 *	7 *	7 *	9 *	7 *	7 *	8 *	7	100
Rob Ray	7 *	10 *	7 *	8 *	9 *	7 *	7 *	7 *	5 *	8 *	8 *	8 *	8	99
Warren Rychel	7 *	7 *	6 *	7 *	9 *	8 *	9 *	8 *	8 *	6 *	9 *	7 *	8	99
Glen Featherstone	8 *	7 *	8 *	8 *	7 *	6 *	9 *	7 *	7 *	9 *	8 *	8 *	6	98

Willingness

1. TONY TWIST — The Twister has not come close to leading the NHL in fighting majors, but the man loves to fight. It all comes out in conversations with him. Tony seems to believe that fighting should be taken seriously. When he fights, he does it full tilt. There is no holding on, turtling or hiding behind the linesmen. And nobody in the NHL throws bombs in the manner of the Twister.
2. Craig Berube — Doesn't drop them as often, but still loves to throw 'em.
3. Tie Domi — If Tie didn't fight, we wouldn't get to see him smile.
4. Bob Probert — Bob's always willing, but not many others want him!
5. Mike Peluso — Mike's 1,161 penalty minutes in 199 games says it all.
6. Randy McKay — Randy doesn't mess around with yapping. He drops 'em and goes.
7. Marty McSorley — Always willing to throw, but his play makes him too valuable.
8. Gino Odjick — He gets mucho penalty minutes, but is not as good as the others.

9. Shane Churla — He threw them hard and often in Juniors and still does.
10. Greg Smyth — The "Bird Dog" may not win many, but he hasn't lost the passion.

Stamina

1. MARTY McSORLEY — The longer the fight, the better for Marty. A typical McSorley fight goes like this: Gloves are dropped, Marty dances around for a while, if possible. Then he grabs his foe and pushes-twirls-tugs-and-stretches him, in no particular order. A punch or two is thrown in the process and if the opponent fails to fall or simply stays away from Marty's grasp, he will continue to throw punches and grapple. Only a linesman's intervention or the kayo of an enemy stops his bout. Marty has been involved in some long fights with Craig Berube, Wendel Clark and Tie Domi.
2. Bob Probert — As long as he's standing, Bob throws and throws with no remorse.
3. Tie Domi — He's ususally smiling and the last guy throwing as the fight ends.
4. Shane Churla — Gets stronger as the fight goes on and as his opponent weakens.
5. Craig Berube — "The Chief" boxes during the off-season to better his stamina.
6. Rick Tocchet — Toc turns to overdrive as the going gets tougher.
7. Link Gaetz — The "Missing Link" doesn't know what it means to stop.
8. Tony Twist — Tony doesn't throw many, so he's not expending much energy.
9. Rob Ray — Rob always has his jersey off late in the fight, still throwing.
10. Randy McKay — His disdain for defeat keeps him firing.

Knockout Punch

1. TONY TWIST — Tony has a right-hand resembling a rock. The Twister is the only ice cop who conditions his knuckles by banging them on the floor in his spare time. His infrequent blows appear to come from the next state and have put the fear of god in many a man. The Twister dented Kirk Tomlinson's helmet with a punch and has had countless knockouts in his

Junior and IHL days. When Tony fights, he's not looking to wrestle, he's looking to hurt you. The bottom line is many guys look to avoid Tony's right, most notably Gino Odjick.

2. Joe Kocur — His right hand is the scariest in hockey.
3. Dave Brown — When the Big Left hits you flush on the face, it's lights out!
4. Bob Probert — Bob's not known for the bomb, but he can apply a quick kayo.
5. Jim McKenzie — Jim is big and strong with a steel punch.
6. Marty McSorley — Marty's raw power and intensity equal rare ferocity.
7. Link Gaetz — Here's a fighting machine with weight behind him to boot.
8. Todd Ewen — Ask Bob Probert if Todd can throw them hard.
9. Stu Grimson — Stu is 6-foot-5, 220 pounds, and throws them crisply. He will hurt you.
10. Mick Vukota — At one point all Mick could do was bench press. 'Nuff said.

Strength

1. LINK GAETZ — At 6-foot-2, 225 pounds, the man is a veritable bull on skates. Link loves to lift weights and has that farm strength to go along with it. Combine the Linkster's physical strength with his exuberance and look of intimidation and we're talking about a devastating challenger. Link routinely manhandles his foes and is one of the few to have tossed Tony Twist around in their first fight back in Juniors.
2. Jay Caufield — One of the biggest men in the league and works on it daily.
3. Mick Vukota — Whether Mick is fair or not, he easily body-slams the enemy.
4. Marty McSorley — You just don't outmuscle Marty in a fight or for the puck.
5. Todd Ewen — Another one of the big fellows with a lot of weight behind him.
6. Stu Grimson — Stu is always in top shape for a battle and often tosses guys.
7. Craig Berube — His peers say, "Chief is a big, strong man."
8. Tony Twist — There is a reason for his killer knockouts!
9. Mike Peluso — His three older brothers provided basic training. Works out hard.
10. Ken Daneyko — Dano is a strong man and has a throwback mentality to an earlier era.

Quickness

1. CRAIG BERUBE — When an enemy squares off with "The Chief" and is about to grab on, he'd better be ready for a speedy barrage of punches. Craig easily throws the quickest flurry of right hands in the league. Whether it's an overhand, uppercut or straight punch, they come often and fast. Routinely in Berube's fights his speed overwhelms his opponent, who has no choice but to duck and hold on until it's over. Strong evidence of this was shown in his fights with Tie Domi, Darin Kimble, Phil Bourque and Rudy Poeschek.
2. Adam Graves — Throws them real fast and is underrated as a fighter.
3. Rick Tocchet — In a fight with Toc, the foe will get hit first and often.
4. Mario Roberge — He doesn't lose many fights. His quickness is a good reason.
5. Kelly Chase — He's the best at taking advantage of bigger slower opponents.
6. Shane Churla — Exchange punches with Shane and chances are you're going to lose.
7. Bob Probert — Bob's the best of the big guys at providing no reprieve.
8. Tie Domi — He's quick but doesn't get to let them fly against the big men.
9. Darin Kimble — Darin has one speed — fast.
10. Wendel Clark — Wendel usually gets the jump and gets his punches going.

Switching Hands

1. BOB PROBERT — It's rare when a big man is able to switch hands without losing steam in his punches. Watching how easily Bob switches hands in a fight shows you how dangerous a man he truly is. With his long reach, Bob is able to surprise his opponents with both hands. Without hesitation Probie is able to switch to the left when his right is tied up and be no worse for wear. This dimension is what makes Bob so dangerous and separates him from fellow heavyweights such as Dave Brown, Craig Berube and Tony Twist.
2. Kelly Chase — Right hand, cross-grab, left hand, cross-grab, right hand etc.
3. Rick Tocchet — Toc's able to land with either hand and still hurt the other guy.

4. Tie Domi — Typical little guy — adept and dangerous with both hands.
5. Link Gaetz — Equally sharp and dangerous with either hand.
6. Shane Churla — Shane's too small to stand back and just throw rights.
7. Alan May — A crafty man who uses this ability to compete with the big boys.
8. Mick Vukota — A righty, yet he broke his left hand throwing them in 1991-92.
9. Ken Daneyko — A lefty who easily switches to the right. Very dangerous!
10. Darin Kimble — With a mangled right, Darin switches hands more often.

Tying Up

1. CRAIG BERUBE — "The Chief" knows where he wants to grab and has made it an art form. Craig attaches his left a bit above the sleeve of his opponent's power hand and starts throwing from that point. Berube has strong hands and forearms that cling to the jersey. Rare is the night when "The Chief" takes a lot of punches. Even when he loses his grip, he's fast at recovering and getting a hold again. The only enemies to have launched many shots at Craig were Lyndon Byers and Bob Probert.
2. Kelly Chase — He's been beaten so many times, he's now good at the tie-up.
3. Mario Roberge — The art of tying up best serves his quick and strong hands.
4. Ken Daneyko — Dano rarely gets hit. His strength and speed help.
5. Alan May — Will smother your arms until he sees an opening.
6. Owen Nolan — Ties up well vs. heavyweights and surprises them with a return.
7. Joe Kocur — Uses his powerful grip to keep away from shots until he unloads the bomb.
8. Gino Odjick — Throws fast at little guys, but against a heavyweight he ties up.
9. Todd Ewen — An abused right hand forces "Bam Bam" to tie up more than he'd like.
10. Marty McSorley — Loves to get his big arms around you and hold the jersey.

Balance

1. BOB PROBERT — Top fighters cite balance as one of the most important aspects of being successful. In that regard Probie is one of the strongest fighters on skates. Rarely does Bob get tossed around, knocked off balance or dumped to the ice during a fight. Bob's solid base enables him to receive and throw punches as he's moving backwards, a tactic he loves to employ. Bob's strong balance is the biggest element that separates him from Dave Brown, Mike Peluso and Stu Grimson.
2. Mario Roberge — Compensates for lack of size and strength with sturdiness.
3. Randy McKay — Balance is Randy's forte.
4. Tie Domi — Tie may get pushed around but rarely does he fall.
5. Joe Kocur — Once he gets the death grip, it's hard to put him to the ice.
6. Marty McSorley — He'll twirl a victim around in a circle and enjoy it.
7. Craig Berube — "The Chief" keeps his feet solidly under him and just throws.
8. Louie DeBrusk — Has a lot of weight and leg strength in a 6-foot-1 package.
9. Nick Kypreos — For his size he takes on the big boys and hangs in tough.
10. Adam Graves — A well-built kid with plenty of strength to keep upright.

Fairness

1. BOB PROBERT and CRAIG BERUBE — Best evidence of fair fighting came in a battle between the two during the 1992-93 season. When Berube had Bob's jersey over his head and a chance to pound him, he simply held off until Bob became loose. At the end of the fight, when Craig went to the ice, Bob did not throw any punches. They display enormous respect for each other. Both love nothing more than to square off. They never throw sucker-punches before and, more importantly, when the fight is over.
2. Tony Twist — Wants to square off and believes that sucker-punching proves zero.
3. Dave Brown — His peers say he's one of the most respected fighters around.

4. Ken Daneyko — Goes about the fighting business with class, honor and honesty.
5. Louie DeBrusk — For a young fellow, he's done nothing to diminish his respect.
6. Link Gaetz — The man has no fear and only wants to fight 'til the end.
7. Randy McKay — When the fight ends, McKay always skates away, good or bad.
8. Jim McKenzie — Doesn't fight too often, but is always willing to square off.
9. Todd Ewen — Still has the WHL mentality of squaring off to decides who wins.
10. Dave Manson — Loves to stand back and exchange punches until it's over.

Intimidation

1. BOB PROBERT — When the big guy puts his game face on, nobody dares to mess with Probie. This usually comes with a menacing glare and a evil smirk which signify that Bob means business. At this point, Probie runs every opponent in view goes right to the net, nails the goalie and forces the defensemen to take feeble swipes at clearing him out before he puts in a junk goal. Not many opponents care to get near him at this point, let alone fight the big fellow. The problem, however, is that Bob appeared to mellow during the 1992-93 season. Nevertheless, challengers understand when Probie gets going, he still gets his room.
2. Dave Brown — Sure he's over 30, but he's still a mean 6-5, 215-pound lefty.
3. Joe Kocur — His right is a wreck, but nobody looks forward to fighting Joey.
4. Link Gaetz — When Gaetz is in shape, he's a terror.
5. Marty McSorley — With or without the goatee, Marty's a loose cannon on the ice.
6. Tony Twist — The word is out, loud and clear — "WATCH THE RIGHT!"
7. Jim McKenzie — Here's a sleeping giant, not to be awakened.
8. Craig Berube — Utterly fearless, Berube likes to fight, so prepare to be hit.
9. Ken Daneyko — Tireless competitor who will grunt and check an enemy into hiding.
10. Stu Grimson — They don't call him "The Grim Reaper" for nothing!

Smartness

1. KELLY CHASE — Smaller players must be smarter fighters, which explains why Kelly has a varied bag of tricks in his arsenal. Chase realizes that his reach is limited and therefore he cannot stand back and throw with the bigger sluggers. His modus operandi is to get inside tight and throw short uppercuts while constantly switching hands. Kelly masterfully manuevers his opponent's jersey and is especially adept at cross-grabbing — freeing his hands for jabs — while tying up the foe's power hand. Kelly has defeated many oversized guys simply by beating them to the punch.
2. Mario Roberge — Avoids punches and waits for his opportunity to counterattack.
3. Alan May — Has fought many bigger men and survived. A great technical fighter.
4. Craig Berube — Decisive grip on the jersey and an arsenal of shots is the key.
5. Rick Tocchet — Toc will tie up, switch hands, knee, gouge and even head-butt to win.
6. Shane Churla — Knows that he's overmatched because of his size and adjusts.
7. Adam Graves — A smaller version of Berube with a strong grip and quick blows.
8. Wendel Clark — Surprises with quick jabs and then gets inside.
9. Marty McSorley — Oversized jersey keeps his arms free and away from punches.
10. Bob Probert — His top technique: moving backward while keeping the right free.

Taking a Punch

1. TIE DOMI — Win or lose, he always emerges with a smile. Tie never gets hurt when he tussles thanks to a pain-resistant cranium. Hit him and hit him, yet Tie will wait, take the shots, and then fire back with roundhouse punches. Even in beatings he absorbed from Bob Probert, Dave Brown, Craig Berube and Rob Ray, Tie emerged with a minor reddening of the face, a smile and his inimitable mock boxing signal.
2. Bob Probert — Only Todd Ewen decked him. His strategy is to take a punch.
3. Randy McKay — Took strong shots from McKenzie and Brad May yet came back strong.

4. Craig Berube — Hung in like granite even in his worst beating by Lyndon Byers.
5. Dave Brown — This icon has been in many fights, but few have floored Brownie.
6. Link Gaetz — With all of his battles, you would think Link can take a punch.
7. Wendel Clark — Hung in there with the toughest from Behn Wilson to Bob Probert.
8. Ken Daneyko — The few times he gets hit, he dismisses the blows as if nothing.
9. Tony Twist — When in trouble, the Twister loses it and comes back bombing.
10. Rick Tocchet — His philosophy is that smarts make a good fighter.

Future Potential

1. LOUIE DEBRUSK — The raw elements that comprise a top fighter were visible when Lou was still a Junior. DeBrusk measures 6-foot-1, 225 pounds. He throws with either hand and is tactically smart, disciplined, intimidating and fearless. He displays patience in taking punches and tying up his opponent while picking and planning the counterblows. All that can detour Lou from being the best is his gentle, off-ice nature. If DeBrusk can stay mean on the ice, employ the traditional tricks of the trade and not think he's Wayne Gretzky, he will be a force in the Heavyweight Division.
2. Tie Domi — If he's willing to keep on throwing: Watch out!
3. Tony Twist — Make him a regular and he could be the heavyweight champ.
4. Enrico Ciccone — A huge kid with potential to become a top super-heavyweight.
5. Craig Berube — Knows his job and takes it seriously. He'll stay on the top.
6. Mike Peluso — He's constantly improving; a year or two away from contention.
7. Randy McKay — He hasn't been fighting for many years and is getting better.
8. Jim McKenzie — If he makes a commitment, he will be among the top three.
9. Owen Nolan — The man should achieve the 30-goal, 300-penalty-minute plateau.
10. Gino Odjick — With work on balance and fighting fair, he'll earn respect.